FAITH, DUTY AND THE POWER OF MIND

Hanging on to gentility in nineteenth-century England could be a precarious business. The experiences of successive generations of the Clough family demonstrate this and show what a lifeline was provided by the expansion of the professions. At the centre of the story are two women members of the family: Anne Jemima Clough and her niece, Blanche Athena Clough. Their experiences show the particular vulnerability of middle-class women to economic reverse; and as first and fourth Principals of Newnham College, Cambridge, their lives and work enact the revolution in women's education which allowed women too at last to enter professional occupations and construct their own economic lifelines. Their experiences also show the role of the women members in maintaining the networks of family and friends so vital in times of crisis.

Anne Jemima's brother and Blanche Athena's father was the poet, Arthur Hugh Clough, who lost his Christian faith painfully and publicly at the end of the 1840s. Yet loss of faith did not free these generations from a sense of duty. Rather it strengthened that sense, which fed in turn into the ethic and rhetoric of service which marked English professional life.

Attractively illustrated and engagingly written, *Faith, Duty and the Power of Mind* is a distinctive and distinguished contribution to English (and American) history, with much to say about the trajectories of middle-class lives, and about the changing place of women within English society during the Victorian period and beyond.

GILLIAN SUTHERLAND is Fellow, Gwatkin Lecturer and Director of Studies in History at Newnham College, Cambridge. Her many previous publications on British social, cultural and educational history include *Ability, Merit and Measurement. Mental Testing and English Education* 1880–1940 (1984).

FAITH, DUTY AND THE POWER OF MIND

The Cloughs and their Circle 1820–1960

GILLIAN SUTHERLAND

CAMBRIDGE
UNIVERSITY PRESS

CAMBRIDGE UNIVERSITY PRESS
Cambridge, New York, Melbourne, Madrid, Cape Town, Singapore, São Paulo

Cambridge University Press
The Edinburgh Building, Cambridge CB2 2RU, UK

Published in the United States of America by Cambridge University Press, New York

www.cambridge.org
Information on this title: www.cambridge.org/9780521861557

© Gillian Sutherland 2006

First published 2006

Printed in the United Kingdom at the University Press, Cambridge

A catalogue record for this publication is available from the British Library

ISBN-13 978-0-521-86155-7 hardback
ISBN-10 0-521-86155-1 hardback

In Memoriam

Ian Sutherland
1978–1997

Alister Sutherland
1934–2004

Contents

Illustrations

Illustrations 5 and 6 are reproduced by permission of The British Library Board; illustration 1 is reproduced by permission of Yale University Art Gallery, Mabel Brady Garvan Collection; illustration 2 is reproduced by permission of Liverpool Record Office. The remaining illustrations are reproduced by permission of the Principal and Fellows, Newnham College, Cambridge.

Acknowledgements

Many debts have been incurred in the making of this book. The Principal and Fellows of Newnham College have supported the research both financially and intellectually; and my colleagues have become used to conversations which treat Annie and Thena Clough, Henry and Nora Sidgwick, Pernel Strachey and their generations as part of the extended family.

Many friends and colleagues have read all or parts of the draft, in some cases not just once but several times, with expert and constructive comment on content, context and tone. I owe particular debts to Mary Beard, Christina de Bellaigue, Emily Clarke, Helen Fowler, Jean Gooder, Phyllis Hetzel, Julian Hoppit, Michael O'Brien, Ann Phillips, Catherine Seville and Chris Stray. The readers for Cambridge University Press performed a signal service in prodding me to spell out some of the wider implications of the story. Needless to say, I am responsible for the errors and imperfections which remain.

For permission to make use of copyright material in their charge I am indebted to the Principal and Fellows of Newnham College, Cambridge, the Master and Fellows of Trinity College, Cambridge, the Master, Fellows and Scholars of St John's College, Cambridge, the Master and Fellows of Gonville and Caius College, Cambridge, the Mistress and Fellows of Girton College, Cambridge, the Principal and Fellows of Somerville College, Oxford, the Master and Fellows of Balliol College, Oxford, the British Library Board, the Bodleian Library, the West Yorkshire Archives Service, Hampshire County Record Office, West Sussex County Record Office, the South Carolina Historical Society, The Women's Library, London Metropolitan University, the British and Foreign School Society, the University of London Library, the Harold Acton Library, British Institute, Florence and the Comptroller of Her Majesty's Stationery Office.

I am grateful for much patient and courteous help from all the archivists and staff of the institutions listed above. The Newnham Archives have been enriched by the references and transcripts deposited by Joan Stubbs, who hoped for many years to publish a biography of A. J. Clough herself; and I have benefited from all her work, so generously made available. The contribution to every aspect of the project made by Anne Thomson, Archivist to Newnham College, and latterly by her colleague, Pat Ackermann, project archivist for the Harrison and Wallas Papers, has been exceptional. Both have also read the manuscript with care and shared in the work of choosing the illustrations.

Belinda Norman-Butler and Hester Duff, both of whom knew Thena Clough, took time and trouble to share their impressions of the person with me. Sadly, Hester died before the book was finished. Tony Clough, the present head of the family, has encouraged me and helped with a complex family tree. It has been illuminating also to visit places and houses where those I have been writing about lived. I am especially grateful to Mr and Mrs Philbrook, Mrs Carolyn Brebbia and Mr and Mrs Templeton, who allowed me access to their houses and made available to me material from their own records. I owe a special debt of gratitude to Christine, Carol and John Hill, whose knowledge of Liverpool and interest in the Cloughs have been a superb and continuing resource.

Without the unfailing support, practical help and intelligent comment of my family, none of it would have been possible. Anna has transcribed texts, pursued references, and read and checked proofs. It is an enduring grief that neither Ian nor Alister will see the book in print.

Family trees

The Clough family

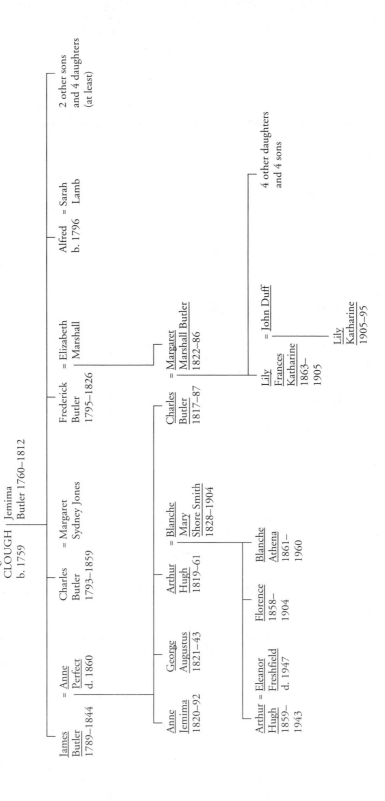

The Perfect family

Seriously incomplete, but the best that can be done with the information in the Dawson Papers and the will of William Perfect, d. 1857

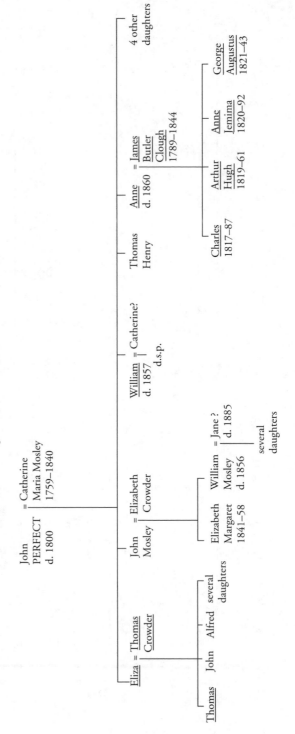

The Smith family

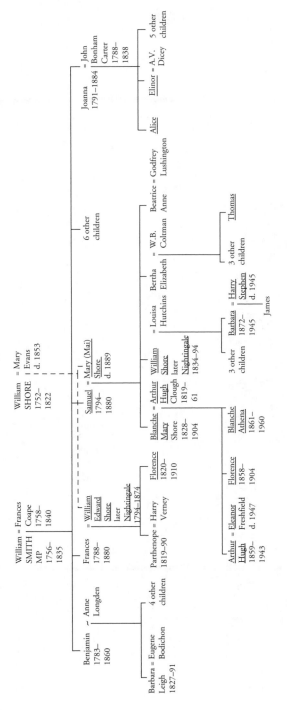

Introduction

In January 1823 a Liverpool merchant named James Butler Clough set sail with his wife and young family for Charleston, South Carolina. Based in this city, he hoped to make his fortune in the cotton trade. He failed wretchedly, going down into bankruptcy not once but twice, and finally retreating back to Liverpool in straitened circumstances, saved from total collapse only by the support of his and his wife's extended family networks. His youngest son, George, fell victim to yellow fever and lies buried in the churchyard of St Michael's Church in Charleston. Yet two of his other children, Arthur, his second son, and Anne Jemima, his only daughter, would make the name Clough celebrated in the England of their day and subsequently. Arthur became a poet, whose verse strikingly divided his contemporaries. The best of it, especially his great poem *Amours de Voyage*, has worn extraordinarily well: his ear for the cadences and rhythms of conversational exchange, his delicate scepticism about grand postures of belief, whether emotional, moral or political, have a startlingly contemporary ring. He also lost his Christian faith, painfully and publicly, paying a high price materially and emotionally.

For Annie, Arthur's sister, the collapse of the family fortunes proved to be an opportunity. She wanted to open a school, one of the few things 'ladies' could do without losing caste. She began in a room of their house; and gradually began to address questions of the education and training needed to pursue this work properly. Eventually this led her to play an important role in the transformation of schooling for middle-class women in nineteenth-century England, from an essentially informal, domestic enterprise, sometimes exciting and creative, sometimes a sham parade of 'accomplishments', into something altogether more structured and systematic, and ultimately more stable and enduring. Part and parcel of this process of transformation was the development of institutions for the higher education of women; and in 1871 Annie became the first Principal of Newnham College, Cambridge. Annie's beloved niece, Arthur's youngest child Blanche

Athena, always known to her family as Thena, came to share in this work. Thena, an administrator of rare talent, became a key member of the second generation of women in higher education, who had to build on the foundations laid by the pioneers, often a less glamorous task, but no less vital in consolidating the transformation and preparing for new phases of growth.

Studies of Arthur's life and poetry have become a minor academic industry. Fresh light can be shed on these by a fuller consideration of his family and their context. Moreover to put his sister and his daughter at the centre of the study is to grasp a thread which leads us deep into the moral, mental and material world of a key stratum of the English middle class, those who sustained gentility through the practice of a profession. In his novel *The Bertrams* in 1859, Anthony Trollope somewhat cynically defined a profession as 'a calling by which a gentleman not born to the inheritance of a gentleman's allowance of good things might ingeniously obtain the same by some exercise of his abilities'. Much grander claims had been made two years earlier by Henry Byerley Thomson, in his 1857 guide, *The Choice of Profession*: 'The importance of the professions and the professional classes can hardly be over-rated, they form the head of the great English middle class, maintain its tone of independence, keep up to the mark its standard of morality, and direct its intelligence.' Temperamentally not disposed to follow his own father into the Church, James Clough had attempted to make his own way and sustain the lifestyle of a gentleman by trading in cotton. When this definitively failed, his son and daughter had to turn elsewhere. Arthur became first a university teacher and then a civil servant. His sister became a teacher who metamorphosed into an educational reformer. His son followed him into government service, while his daughter followed her aunt, eventually becoming a powerful university administrator. And the fluctuating fortunes of other family members and friends show again and again the economic and status lifelines which 'some exercise of their abilities' could provide. This study is more than a biography and a family history: it is a case-study so situated as to help us follow the evolution and expansion of professional opportunities and roles for the English middle class over almost a century and a half – a crucial period. In their classic study, *The Professions*, published in 1933, Carr-Saunders and Wilson wrote, 'within the ranks of the professions are to be found most of those upon whose special skill the functioning of modern society depends'.

To put the women members of the family at the centre of the story is also to make the point that the rise of professional occupations in England was not a purely male affair. 'Some exercise of their abilities' proved eventually to be able to sustain ladies as well as gentlemen. The women members of the Victorian middle class were peculiarly vulnerable to, and often victims of, its fluctuations in prosperity and status. For much of the nineteenth century they were able to do so much less than their menfolk to shape their own destinies and control their own lives. The need first to transform the provision of secondary education and create institutions of higher education for women meant that their entry into the professions came at least a generation or more behind that of the men, and the occupations on offer at first were a much more restricted group. But by the beginning of the 1920s there were systematic opportunities in teaching both in secondary schools and in universities where none had existed before; and Thena's experience showed too that the new institutions offered scope for those who were administrators as well as those who were teachers and scholars. Slowly, other opportunities and career patterns would take shape. Putting the women centre stage reveals also their crucial roles within the family networks which are so marked a feature of the Victorian and Edwardian middle class. The public rhetoric of middle-class achievement might be individualist; but the wider family mobilised loans, cash, contacts, possibilities, time and again; and the women were often the correspondents, those who kept the networks alive and in good order, the exchanges of information flowing. When, at the beginning of the 1930s, the affairs of Thena and her brother collapsed into bankruptcy, a melancholy echo of the bankruptcy of their grandfather almost a century before, they, and the young cousin Thena had brought up, were sustained by networks of family, friendship and profession, expressed in and intertwined with the institution she and her aunt had done so much to create.

In drawing on such networks the Clough family was typical. In two other respects it was distinctive and especially illuminating. Few families produced outstanding educational innovators in two successive generations, two women who played key roles in the creation and development of an institution, Newnham, which was both symbol and agent of the transformation of educational opportunities for women. Few families and their friends acted out so vividly and publicly the crisis of Christian faith faced by the mid-nineteenth-century generation and demonstrated the continuing power of a Christian sense of duty, even when belief had faded. Arthur's honesty about his loss of faith cost him dear. For the generation who followed him, epitomised by Henry Sidgwick, the Cambridge philosopher and educational reformer, the material costs were less high; but the analogies between his intellectual and emotional journey and that travelled by Arthur formed the bedrock of his relationship with the

Clough family. Newnham was the first institution in either Cambridge or Oxford to be without denominational affiliation; and among Thena and her Bloomsbury friends and contemporaries absence of faith was taken for granted.

To be part of the movement for the secularisation of intellectual life was to align oneself on the left, to be among those whom Arthur's friend Matt Arnold was to call 'the lights of liberalism'. In this company the creation of educational opportunities and structures for women took its place with other schemes for enlarging access to education, a concern with class as well as with gender, a concern that Cambridge and Oxford should behave less like corrupt little oligarchies and more like responsible elites. Among Annie's schemes of the 1860s was the germ of what would become the University Extension Movement; and at the beginning of the 1920s Thena would fight to get the Asquith Commission, considering the affairs of the two universities, to take an appropriately broad and truly national view of their roles and duties.

Although secular, this reforming liberal agenda did not lack a moral dimension. Although Christian belief had faded, much of the moral and ethical matrix within which it had been embedded remained. The point had been made forcefully by the novelist George Eliot, one of the earliest supporters of women's education and of Newnham. Shortly after her death in 1880, Sidgwick's friend F. W. H. Myers recalled a conversation in which, 'taking as her text the three words which have been used so often as the inspiring trumpet-calls of men, – the words, *God, Immortality, Duty*, – [she] pronounced, with terrible earnestness, how inconceivable was the *first*, how unbelievable the *second*, and yet how peremptory and absolute the *third*'. Successive generations of the Clough family and the liberal intelligentsia in which they came to be embedded all acknowledged this imperative. Annie, sanguine by temperament, and with a generosity of spirit which made life endlessly interesting to her, pursued her duty most cheerfully. The depressive strain, which Arthur and Thena shared, made it harder for them; and one strand of Arthur's great poem, *Amours de Voyage*, is a reflection on the power of what he called 'our terrible notions of duty'. Thena, having done without God from adolescence, was nevertheless in no doubt that there were good and bad courses of action and selfish and unselfish ways to conduct oneself. The demands of duty are an important root of the rhetoric of service which has been so marked a feature of English professional life. Such rhetoric could be deployed bombastically, as in the remarks of Henry Byerley Thomson, quoted above, or cynically – or sincerely. The Cloughs and their friends and colleagues were strenuous in pursuing what they perceived to be their duty, sometimes at no small cost to themselves. Professional life and occupations provided them with lifelines in terms of status and material survival; but seizing the opportunities these offered was not incompatible with a genuine belief that, in ingeniously exercising their abilities, they were also serving the wider society.

CHAPTER I

Childhood and Charleston

In the first two decades of the nineteenth century Charleston, South Carolina, appeared an inviting and prosperous city of some 25,000 people. In 1817 exports from Charleston were outstripped only by those from New York. Its economy was dominated by cotton, demand for which soared with the ending of war in Europe in 1815, and in 1818 the price of short-staple cotton reached an all-time high of 35 cents per pound. Throughout the eighteenth century the city had looked naturally to Europe for cultural exchange and models; and some of the profits from cotton and rice, the other principal crop, supported both domestic and institutional building in a graceful neo-classical style. [1] At the beginning of 1823 it must have appeared simultaneously civilised and exotic to the tiny Anne Jemima Clough, just three years old, disembarking from the sailing ship which had brought her and her family from Liverpool. Forty years later the image of Charleston in the 1820s remained clear and sharp in her mind's eye. [2]

The first sight of it showed a long line of wharves made of palmetto logs fastened together into a sort of wall, stretching perhaps half a mile along the bay, and lined with the ships and smaller craft that frequented the port. As you approached from the water you heard the songs of the negroes at work on the vessels. At the end of the wharves was a battery or public walk, supported against the sea by a substantial very white wall formed of oyster shells beaten fine and hard. This species of pier extended nearly a mile along the sea, and was a favourite resort both for walking and driving in the summer. It was all roughly done, as most things were in the South, but the sunshine and clear skies made it bright and cheerful. The city was not regularly built like the Northern towns. In the lower part indeed the houses were mostly built close together in rows; but in the upper part, where the wealthier people lived, it was full of villas with gardens, all built with verandahs, and many with two, an upper and a lower one. In the gardens grew many flowering trees, such as the almond, occasionally the orange, the fringe tree, a gay shrub with a very abundant white flower, and the fig; and these hung over the garden walls into the streets. The streets, too, which were for the most part unpaved, were often planted with trees for the sake of shade. Here and there one came on a large old-fashioned mansion, that at once showed it belonged to the times before the Revolution.

Anne – or Annie as she became known, perhaps to distinguish her from her mother, also Anne – was the third child of James Butler Clough and his wife, Anne Perfect. The Cloughs traced their ancestry back to the sixteenth century, to Sir Richard Clough who acted as Sir Thomas Gresham's agent in Antwerp and was a man of substance in his own county, Denbighshire. Successive generations of Clough gentry and clergy remained based in North Wales until James, born on 22 April 1784, moved to Liverpool early in the new century, to launch a career as a merchant. Perhaps the move was linked to his father's business dealings. For the Rev. Roger Clough, Vicar of Corwyn, Rector of Llansannen and ultimately Canon of St Asaph, had married Ann Jemima Butler, a Sussex heiress; and the land she brought helped underpin his partnership in Clough, Mason & Co., private bankers in Denbigh and Llanrwst from about 1794.[3]

The assets of Clough, Mason & Co. included not only land but also a paper factory and a woollen mill. James, however, from his Liverpool base, had begun to follow a newer star in the economic firmament, cotton, whose manufacture has been described as 'the most dynamic industry of Britain between 1760 and 1800'. [4] But this very dynamism brought intense competition, with large numbers of business formations driving down profit margins. The pressures were intensified by the rapid technological development of the industry; while dependence on an imported raw material rendered the trade prey to variations in harvests and the depredations of warfare. All of these factors made dealing in raw cotton, cotton yarns and the finished goods highly speculative and risky activities: what soared high could also tumble down to earth; and the fluctuations of James Clough's fortunes illustrate this vividly. His first period of dealing in cotton came to an end in 1810. A brief relaxation in the Napoleonic blockade of Britain brought a fall in cotton prices and the failure of several houses, including that of Wilkes and Clough. For the next six years James traded in corn.

Clough, Mason & Co., his father's bank, survived the crisis of 1810, only to fall prey, like so many other country banks, to the crisis of confidence in paper money which accompanied the end of war in Europe: they went down to bankruptcy in 1816.[5] Their assets were sufficient to enable them eventually to pay twenty shillings in the pound; but realising these proved a prolonged process, which found James in January 1819 seeking a large short-term loan, writing, 'I am so circumstanced in my engagements and arrangements for my poor Father that I want the assistance of about a <u>Thousand Pounds</u>[6]

until I can convert some of his personal property into money, which I hope to do in a few months.'[7] Roger Clough made no more forays into business, but James was not at all deterrred by these early reversals. In 1816, the very year of his father's bankruptcy, he returned to cotton, this time in partnership with Thomas Crowder. This partnership was underpinned by a complex web of family connections. That same year, James married Anne Perfect, one of the daughters of John and Catherine Maria Perfect of Pontefract. Thomas Crowder was married to another Perfect daughter, Eliza; and Anne and Eliza's eldest brother, John Perfect, was married to another Crowder, also Eliza. The Perfects were Yorkshire lawyers whose success in land deals had drawn them too into banking, an involvement which was to prove more enduring and robust than that of Clough, Mason & Co. The Perfect family network and its resources were to provide a sheet anchor for both James Clough's and Thomas Crowder's families in the years to come; it was a pattern not uncommon in this period of economic transformation and upheaval.[8]

Four children were born to James and Anne Clough in rapid succession. First came Charles Butler in 1817, then Arthur Hugh on 1 January 1819, Anne Jemima on 20 January 1820 and George Augustus on 26 July 1821. In the meantime James travelled back and forth from Liverpool to the United States, spending about eight months there in 1821.[9] Then at the end of 1822 came the great bold step: the whole family removed to Charleston, South Carolina. Pressed forty years later to set down her earliest memories, this was the very first thing which Annie could remember: 'Leaving England at the end of 1822 with my Father & Mother 3 brothers & 2 nurses – We sailed on the Ship Perfect & went to Charleston.'[10]

The Cloughs settled in Charleston at 188 East Bay, a large three-storey house, the ground floor of which was office and store-rooms. Annie described it as 'a large ugly red brick house near the sea'.[11] It still stands, renumbered 184, and its proportions are graceful. Perhaps the ugliness lay in the fact that the red brick was not concealed by stucco, unlike the brick of neighbouring houses. From their back windows the children could watch the wooden wharves on the Cooper river and the house was likewise admirably close to the market and commercial areas. The first two years in Charleston were happy. The members of the family were all together and there seemed enough financial margin to allow them to travel within the United States, going north each summer to escape the worst of the heat and humidity.[12] No more is heard of one of the two nursemaids who travelled with them from Liverpool; but the other, Ann Marshall, remained with the

Cloughs throughout their years in Charleston, a devoted although sometimes temperamental family retainer. With her help and that of the black
slaves they hired as servants, Anne Clough ran the household and cared for
the children: she took pleasure in spending time with her children, teaching
them to read and then reading with them.

Yet cotton remained no less volatile a commodity and Crowder, Clough
& Co. were brought down in the general financial crisis of 1825–6, which
damaged many areas and trades, well beyond cotton. Crowder, Clough &
Co. failed on 8 August 1825: as Anne was to put it much later, 'the grand stop
to our *apparent greatness* took place'.[13] In the winter James left for England,
to try to salvage what he could. He was away this time for eleven months
and in August 1826 was formally declared bankrupt in London. The Perfect
family seem to have done what they could. Anne's younger brother, Henry
Thomas Perfect, was named in the certificate of bankruptcy, along with
Clough and Crowder, although there is no evidence that he was other than
a sleeping partner. In July 1826 Thomas Crowder had written to remind
their brother-in-law John Perfect 'of your kind promise to become security
for me'. He asked him to guarantee 'about £1500 worth of Goods for my
American friends payable in 6 Months', by which time the sale of property
would ensure that Crowder himself could meet the liability. The up-beat
tone of this letter suggests that Crowder and Clough had already decided
to use the provisions of the 1825 Bankruptcy Act, 6 Geo IV c.16; this, for
the first time, allowed traders to declare themselves bankrupt and avail
themselves of the protection of the law in limiting their liabilities and
clearing the way eventually for a resumption of trading.[14]

For the household left behind in Charleston, however, it was a lonely
and an anxious time. Years later Arthur was to remember what a great
event was the arrival of a letter.[15] The children worked at their lessons and
everyone waited. Their father's eventual return in November 1826 was a
joyous occasion: 'And then the door opened and our father was in the
room, catching up our mother in his arms, for she was nearly fainting,
while we skipped about for joy.'[16]

James Clough, ever optimistic, set about building up his business once
again. 'My father', wrote Annie much later, 'was very lively, and fond
of society and amusement. He liked life and change, and did not care
much for reading. He had a high sense of honour, but was venturesome
and over sanguine, and when once his mind was set on anything, he was
not to be turned from it, nor was he given to counting consequences.'[17]
In the short run, this robust approach paid off. The Federal Census of
1830 records a substantial establishment which included five hired slaves.[18]

Annie's mother's reaction to crisis was very different. Anne Clough was a more private person, reacting to adversity by withdrawal within the family circle. She read a great deal, nourishing her imagination and that of her children with myth, history and poetry. Underlying all this was a powerful sense of Christian duty. 'Our Mother taught us about great men & their noble deeds & with her we read the Bible & learnt to look up to our Heavenly Father.'[19]

The spring and summer of 1827 were good times for the younger Clough children. They played and tumbled on the cotton heaps in the store-rooms: 'One of our games was playing at the Swiss Family Robinson, in which I remember Arthur was always Ernest, because Ernest liked reading and knew so much.'[20] In the high summer the whole family escaped the worst of the heat by taking a house across the bay, on Sullivan's Island, a long narrow sandy strip, on which Edgar Allan Poe was to set his 1843 story *The Gold-Bug*. From Sullivan's Island, James Clough could go in to his office by boat, while the children were free to explore the fine white sand of the beach and the low myrtle woods, where the curlews wheeled and called. Annie and George went happily barefoot and paddled, although Arthur was too fastidious to do so.

The Cloughs were, however, as Annie wrote wistfully, 'too English to let us go to school'[21] in Charleston. Whether or not he succeeded in making his fortune, James was determined to follow the conventions of his family and of the day in educating his sons as English gentlemen. Formal schooling was coming increasingly into vogue for middle- and upper-class English boys: endowed grammar schools were being reformed and some, taking boarders, were turning themselves into public schools; new proprietary boarding schools were being founded; and preparatory schools were springing up. In sending his sons to boarding school, James was part of the trend.[22] Charles, aged eight, had already been taken to prep school in England by his father at the end of 1825. At the end of 1828 it would be Arthur's turn. In June 1828 the whole family set off for England, to see Charles, pay a round of family visits and sort out the first stage of Arthur's schooling. The initial encounter with a large household of cousins was something of a shock: 'Arthur could not enter into the boys' rough games and amusements, and missed the constant companionship with his father. We travelled however for some months from one relation's house to another, and by degrees Arthur became more sociable.'[23] The children paid a long visit to their maternal grandmother, near Pontefract, while their parents travelled in Europe.[24] In November Arthur joined Charles at Mr Pepper's preparatory school in Chester and the rest of the family prepared to return to Charleston. 'This was practically the end of Arthur's childhood', wrote Annie.[25]

Annie and George still had some childhood left. Observing the life around them keenly, they 'played games about people with our bricks and reels of cotton that represented people'.[26] With their mother they learnt French and read history and story books. Long afterwards Annie dated to this time too the employment of a visiting master to help with the French and her first friendships with girls her own age: but these were really only to flourish later. Most important, Annie and George shared two more long hot summers in the freedom of Sullivan's Island. The family rented the same house overlooking the bay for the summers of 1829 and 1830, from which they must have been able to watch the beginning of the works to create the artificial island to bear Fort Sumter, further out in the bay. In 1861 the first shots of the American Civil War would be fired against this Fort. The house the Cloughs rented was built on piles, creating underneath it a cool, shady space in which the children played safely during the day. The Cloughs' black servants lived in the separate slave quarters at the end of the garden, surrounded by fruit trees and a vegetable plot. Close by were abundant fig trees, which George used to climb, to provision his parents' breakfast table.

Drama was added to their stay in 1829 by the 'painful episode' of James Butler Clough's steamboat.

He got it for a debt & in his sanguine way began to run with a Captain Engineer in the summer to the Island & in the winter to carry cotton. Mother did not approve of the scheme with her usual wisdom – The engineer got drunk & one day just as the steamer reached the Island the boiler burst – very few people were hurt but the engineer was severely burnt & was brought to our house & put to bed in one of the kitchen rooms. It was very terrible to see his suffering as we passed his window. He died in a day or 2.[27]

The excitements of the following summer threatened the family altogether more closely. First there was a great storm, when the waves threatened to overwhelm the island and its houses. Only the changing of the wind saved them. The next day the children walked on the shore 'and saw all kinds of wrecks. Vessels had been driven about, some had lost masts and spars. Vessels in distress came in and a large boat full of people from a ship-wrecked vessel.'[28] Annie and George very much hoped to meet the family of little girls who, with their mother, had survived the wreck but in the end they were disappointed. Then at the beginning of September 1830 James Clough went down with yellow or 'stranger's' fever, as it was known, which, with malaria, was endemic in Charleston in these years.[29] His wife and Ann Marshall shared the nursing; although the children 'were always about the room in the day'.[30] In two to three weeks the worst was over; but his health remained precarious through the autumn. The anxiety of this combined with the Cloughs' preoccupation with their boys' schooling. It would soon be time for George to start at prep school. Charles and Arthur, watched over by James Clough's brothers, Alfred and Charles, both Anglican clergymen, had by now moved on from Mr Pepper's to Rugby School, where Arthur was beginning to flourish intellectually but Charles was not. At the end of the winter it was decided that they should all go to England again the next summer.

The visit of 1831 largely followed the pattern set in 1828. They went first to Aunt and Uncle Crowder's house, Finch House, West Derby, on the edge of Liverpool. There they were reunited joyfully with Arthur and Charles. After visits to the various Clough relations in North Wales, they went on to the Perfects in Yorkshire. Annie and George remained with their grandmother when Arthur returned to Rugby alone on 30 August, and Charles was taken off by his parents and Aunt Harriet to a new school near Neuchâtel in Switzerland. It was both a happy and a sad time. At Finch House, 'Arthur and I walked about the garden, cut all our names on a fir tree – We were inseparable. He was sad, he did not very much like school and the separation, oh the separation. But we cheered up – There were the long holidays.'[31] They all had ten perfect and long-remembered days at the seaside in North Wales, a coast very different from the one they knew in Charleston. George had to begin school in Chester in the autumn; but both he and Arthur joined Annie and their parents again in December, at the beginning of the school holidays. On Christmas Eve, however, Annie, her parents and Ann Marshall set sail for Charleston in the brig *William*.

The voyage back was terrifyingly storm-ridden: 'great waves which were tossing us up to the heavens and then letting us down into the deep . . . The waves sometimes even came into the cabin and reached us in bed.' They spent most of the journey penned below in their cabins, without hot food, praying and even singing hymns. The *William* finally limped into Charleston harbour in February, having been at sea for fifty-four days. 'Only the old House was dull & lonely now the boys were all gone.'[32] Annie and her mother had to begin to adjust to life without them.

Annie coped better than her mother. Probably she knew less about the precarious state of the family economy and she had the resilience and freedom of youth. In temperament moreover she resembled her father more closely than her mother. She had inherited James Clough's cheerful

1 Samuel Barnard, *View along the East Battery, Charleston*, 1831, oil on canvas

temper and general determination to make the best of things, and these would sustain her through many vicissitudes. Childhood, nevertheless, was ending and young ladyhood beckoned. There were to be no more stays on Sullivan's Island: perhaps Annie, at twelve, was considered too old to run about without shoes and stockings and paddle. In the summer of 1832 instead, the Cloughs removed temporarily to a more shaded house on Legaré Street. From the verandah and balcony Annie watched the neighbouring households, the way in which social life spilled outdoors as the heat of the day receded, and longed to join in more. She was a keen observer of the society around her, perceptive, often entertained but never malicious in her humour. The French lessons resumed and she was allowed to join a dancing class: gradually her circle of friends was enlarged, extending beyond other expatriate merchant families like that of the Calders and Richardsons to longer-established Charleston families like the Kings, Campbells and Wagners.

The friendship which flowered in these years, and which came to matter most to Annie, was that with Maria Lance, daughter of a Charleston attorney and only five months her senior. It 'gave much brightness to my life. We talked to each other, we read books together & enjoyed our lives & told each one our daydreams.'[33] Maria was close enough to the family to share in the rejoicing when Arthur's poem 'The Close of the Eighteenth Century' won a prize at Rugby and to tease him for neglecting the United States in it.[34] The Lances were comfortable but not rich and had a large and somewhat exotic family circle. Maria's aunt, Caroline Fraser, married the Bonapartist Prince Lucien Murat and they came to stay in Charleston. Annie recalled that he was a 'fine looking man, dark & florid, very big & stout. He was good natured & kindly – I don't fancy that he was clever – His wife was a clever woman & when she lost her money and became poor she kept a school & kept the family principally.'[35] There was no shortage of books for Maria and Annie to share and exchange. Charleston had had a Circulating Library since the beginning of the 1770s and this was a great resource. Annie remembered reading 'Rollin's Ancient History, Washington Irvine's [*sic*] Life of Columbus, The Life of Agrippina . . . Robertson's Life of Charles the 5, The Life of Philip the 2 & 3 of Spain, Russell's Modern Europe, The History of the Crusades, The Waverley Novels, Some of Bulwer's Rienzi & The Last Days of Pompeii, Histories of Rome & of Greece'.[36] At home there were Bradley's *Sermons*, a *Life of St Paul* and Bunyan's *Pilgrim's Progress* and *Grace Abounding*; and at the end of 1833 Uncle Alfred Clough, Fellow of Jesus College, Oxford, sent 'a magnificent present of books', about which Arthur enquired enviously.[37]

Annie's particular enthusiasm, as Arthur acknowledged, was for history. The theological works in the house reflected the tastes of an Episcopalian but Low Church family, with moderate Evangelical leanings, as did the pattern of Anne Clough's teaching of her children and the choice of Rugby, then being reshaped by Dr Thomas Arnold, as the public school for Charles and Arthur. Annie remembered the intense religious as well as political discussions which animated all her English relations during the summer of 1831, midway through the Reform Bill agitation: 'much very Low Church doctrine was preached to me'.[38] In Charleston the Cloughs regularly rented a pew at St Michael's Episcopalian Church, the oldest church in the city, where James Clough was good friends with old Bishop Bowen – for, as Annie noted, 'was not my father the son of an English Clergyman'.[39] She observed the social, gendered and racial dimensions of the event that was family worship at St Michael's on Sundays:

There was [a] large porch – the whole width of the front – Here the men gathered about church time & talked together. The women & children went in. The men followed at intervals during the service. There was a gallery round 3 sides of the church – Negroes sat in the aisles. The pews were many of them large, some square, some long. Young children came with their Mothers & sat on stools at the corners of the seats with books to amuse them – & the Mothers & Grandmothers often laid the little ones down to sleep. It was a pretty sight. The devout Mothers with their little ones. The rather rugged sailors & fine looking men, the handsome young boys and girls.[40]

Charleston, like most United States cities, was not untouched by the revivalism of the Second Great Awakening. Bishop Bowen had to give way to 'a more vehement preacher'[41] and Annie, with her friends, went often to hear him. Like many another girl in early adolescence, 'This was a time when religion took a deep hold on my mind.'[42] Yet she did not surrender entirely to revivalist enthusiasm. Ann Marshall, her old nurse, had distracted her during the dreadful journey back from England in January 1832 not only with prayers and hymns but also with tales of various relations who had been led to disaster by 'a great want of self control and sense'. Religious excitement had, she said, been a factor in some of these cases. These stories made a great impression on Annie and 'the first seeds were sown that led to my great desire to learn to rule myself & study to manage my mind & get some thing to occupy me'.[43]

Religious enthusiasm did, however, enhance Annie's growing unhappiness about the institution of slavery. The tiny girl had been very frightened by her first sight of blacks, but this terror soon wore off. The Cloughs chose not to own slaves themselves but to hire them from other owners to work as servants. Annie subsequently recognised that this entailed an evasion of moral responsibility: 'As we never owned any negroes they could be sent away if they did not suit, but this was bad for their Masters.' One boy who stole, was sold away from Charleston by his owner in punishment. Lizzy, however, worked for them the whole time they were in Charleston and they became very fond of her. When she was caught and imprisoned for harbouring a runaway slave, James Clough 'with great difficulty saved her from being flogged. She had however [to] spend a fortnight at the treadmill instead.'[44] James' kindness may have been misplaced: many contemporaries thought the treadmill the more dreadful punishment.[45] This episode alone might have led to questioning of the system; but Annie added to her recognition of the sufferings of the slaves an awareness of 'the immorality of the men' that is, the white slaveowners, and 'a growing religious state of mind that made everything more impressive and fearful'.[46] Nor in retrospect was the irony lost on her of a situation in which young white enthusiasts held revival meetings in the woods, very like the camp meetings of the blacks, meetings which led some of the young men to conversion and ordination, while vehemently maintaining the moral rectitude of slavery.

It was a period when attitudes to slavery were hardening and the lines of division which would lead eventually to civil war were beginning to be drawn. In 1833 legislation to end slavery in British dominions was finally carried; it was also the year which exposed the developing intransigence over the issue in South Carolina, when violence over an unpopular tariff was only averted at the eleventh hour. Ostensibly the 'nullification' conflict between the South Carolina legislature and the Federal legislature was over the issue of states' rights: could a state convention reject a federal law inimical to its interests? It was not difficult to see, however, that in South Carolina, although the immediate issue was the level of the tariff, the ultimate touchstone of states' rights and the utility of the theory of nullification was the maintenance of slavery.[47] Two years later, in July 1835, pro-slavery activists in Charleston made a bonfire of a US Mail sack stuffed with abolitionist pamphlets and led the postmaster to determine that this 'incendiary' material was too dangerous to be distributed.[48] The Cloughs were away in the North when this happened; but they returned to an increasingly embattled society. 'The young boys made little regiments often among themselves & travelled about the streets proclaiming States Rights. The question of Slavery might not be discussed.'[49] Annie noted the severity of the South Carolina legislation: blacks might no longer be taught to read or write; if freed, they had to leave the state, either to go north or to emigrate to Africa.[50]

If Anne Clough shared the revulsion to slavery which was developing in her daughter, this must have complicated social relations in Charleston: as Annie remarked, 'It was fearfully painful especially as near & dear friends of my Mother were the victims of this horrible state of things.'[51] Did she mean that some of her mother's female friends suffered from their husbands' sexual exploitation of their slaves: or was she making a more general point about the moral corruption of a slave-owning society? Perhaps she meant both. The point remains that Anne Clough's efforts to make a social life for herself in Charleston were constrained by race as well as by class and gender. Following their return from England at the beginning of 1832, Anne, like her daughter, had worked hard to combat the loneliness which followed the departure of all the boys: 'About this time Mother got more friends & very nice ones too.' She was almost as close to Maria Lance's mother, confusingly also Maria, as Annie was to Maria the daughter: and she enjoyed discussing books with William Ogilby, the British consul, who originated from the North of Ireland. But altogether, Annie concluded, 'the life did not suit her – She wanted more excitement, more Society. There were men's dinner parties so she did not go – but when Father had a dinner party she always got in her place & talked & She was very bright & original & was a favourite & then she was very handsome.'[52]

The heat of the Charleston summers made Anne Clough intermittently ill; but she suffered even more from sea sickness and after the terrible eight-week journey back from Liverpool in 1831–2 she declared that she would not travel the Atlantic again except to go home to England for good. Steamships were beginning to make the transatlantic crossing, but only to New York: the Liverpool–Charleston route remained the preserve of sailing ships.[53] Perhaps, too, Anne Clough did not care for the nomadic existence the family were forced to lead when in England. The consequence was that when James travelled to England on business and to take the boys to Europe in 1833, Annie and her mother stayed in Charleston, Anne being 'very low and sad for she could not bear My Father to leave her. She hardly went out at all except to church.'[54] Many families, including the Lances, had gone north to escape the worst of the heat: but Anne Clough could not – or would not – contemplate a journey out of Charleston without her husband. Annie would sit up in the nursery, watching the wharves and reading the Waverley Novels, then walk out on her own to visit the friends who remained.

There was great rejoicing when James at last returned, bringing Charles with him. Charles had now finished with schooling and was preparing to join his father in business. James, however, had recognised that he would

have to make plans to move the family base back to England. He wrote to
Annie from Liverpool in September 1833:

I have got the books you wished me to procure and shall not forget the pencils,
Crayens [*sic*] etc. etc. For I am happy to say that the Cotton trade this year will
afford a liberal supply. If I co'd. only have had a little more foresight than my
neighbours I might have made an independent fortune this year in Cotton. It has
been more from good luck than any peculiar degree of wisdom that those engaged
in it have made what they have done so that no one can boast much excepting
as to the quantity of profits he may have made by having been more daring &
speculative than his neighbour.

I am contented & thankful for what I have got, though I certainly sho'd. have
rejoiced greatly if I co'd. have brought you all to old England to live once more,
instead of leaving you to be stewed & broiled in that wearisome climate. We must
be patient, however, & still live in hopes.[55]

A year later, Arthur was writing consolingly to Annie that there were only
two more years to wait before they would see each other again.[56]

In compensation for the dreariness of 1833 Annie hoped for a trip to the
North with her father.[57] Finally in the summer of 1835 this came about:
Annie, Charles, both her parents and the old nurse, Ann Marshall, all set
off together. Leaving Charleston by steamer early in July, they went first
to Norfolk, Virginia. Travelling onwards by a combination of steamer, carriage and train, they proceeded to Richmond, Fredericksburg, Washington,
Baltimore, Philadelphia and New York. After two weeks in New York at
the beginning of August, they travelled north up the Hudson to the Great
Lakes and Canada, visiting both Montreal and Quebec. Returning down
the Hudson Valley in late September, they stayed first at West Point and
then in New York again before sailing back to Charleston again at the end
of October.

The journey up the Hudson Valley, north from New York, was by now an
established route, followed by many cultivated Americans as they began to
explore and engage with their own magnificent landscapes.[58] Nevertheless,
to travel first from Charleston to New York, and then onwards, made
the journey a considerable odyssey for the Cloughs. Although at the time
Annie kept a careful record of each stage for Arthur,[59] the vivid detail with
which she still recalled people, landscapes and her own reactions nearly
thirty years later offers an indication of the profound impressions made
and the eagerness with which she soaked up new sights and encounters.
She had a deep and unashamed interest in the world about her, both in
its physical complexion and in the doings of people, which she was never
to lose and which, even in her old age, would disarm and engage those

who met her. In Virginia she was chilled by the sight of gangs of slaves being taken to be sold, yet not convinced by the nervous lady who feared a slave uprising every Fourth of July. At Mrs Percy's Boarding House on Broadway in New York, she observed 'a young newly married lady whose husband was engrossed in business & she seemed much occupied with dress & amusing herself'. The company in the hotel at Saratoga Springs, on the other hand, included a merchant from Charleston who 'tried to amuse himself but did not seem to know how'.[60] At Cauldwell, on the shores of Lake George, she and Charles encountered the first numbers of *Pickwick Papers*.

The landscapes which left the deepest impression – perhaps because they were so different from those Annie knew best – were those of the Great Lakes. Steaming up the St Lawrence River,

We passed a multitude [of] picturesque towns and villages built close to the water. The roofs were steep & covered with tin, the houses had gables. The tin roofs glittered in the sunshine like silver and the little properties along the banks went far back but each had a water lot – the cultivation was indifferent for the French Canadians were not hard workers.

At the Falls of Montmorency she was entranced by the 'long foaming fall, the bay filled with rainbow spray'.[61] These images are the ones she cherished and rehearsed again thirty years later. But also on the return journey down the St Lawrence she fell overboard and nearly drowned, and for nearly a decade afterwards she marked the anniversary of her deliverance – 17 September.[62]

Returning to Charleston, Annie felt a different person, the effect of the 'excitement of so much travelling & change & getting acquainted with so many new people; the feeling grown up. Girls of 15 married in Charleston & I was nearly 15.'[63] Writing at the beginning of the 1860s this was the only cryptic reference she allowed herself to the appearance of possible suitors. Yet there seem to have been at least two, an entirely mysterious R.D., who had paid her flattering attentions in New York, and Atkinson, James Clough's assistant and subsequently partner in Charleston. Although Atkinson's first initial was C., he is always referred to by his surname. Perhaps he was considered not quite a gentleman?[64]

Instead the immediate test to which this new maturity was put was a break with all the friends and familiar scenes of Charleston. James Clough had fixed on 1836 as the year in which the family base would be moved back to Liverpool. His wife's views were clearly of central importance to this decision. Yet perhaps Charleston no longer looked as inviting as it once had, even to one of his incorrigibly optimistic temperament. The hardening political attitudes and violence have already been mentioned: and in the 1830s cholera joined malaria and yellow fever to ravage the population.[65] Although James still cherished hopes of making 'an independent fortune', the local economy of Charleston was looking less buoyant. There had been no repeat of the catastrophic collapse of the market in 1824–5, but neither was there any sign of the re-emergence of a long boom, on the scale of that of 1801–19. The development of steamship routes between Europe and New York was gradually eroding Charleston's status as a primary port. In 1835 at last a Liverpool–Charleston steam packet company was chartered, with five vessels: and work on the railroad designed to link Charleston to the Mississipi Valley ground slowly on. Yet although exports of cotton and rice from Charleston continued to rise in absolute terms during the 1830s, the port's share of national production of short-staple cotton continued to fall. In 1824 it had been 28%, in 1830 18% and by 1837–8 it would be 16%. The only advantage came from Charleston's continuing monopoly of long-staple cotton.[66]

As the time to depart approached, Annie found herself desperately torn. On the one hand, England was still 'home' and they would at last be reunited with Arthur and George; on the other hand, she would leave behind the surroundings of a childhood which had been emotionally secure and often happy, the life she had made and all her friends. May was a month of farewells, many of them tearful: 'I see my young friend Maria Lance going out of our gate & I have still [the] handkerchief that was her last token of affection.'[67] On 1 June 1836 Annie set sail from Charleston for the last time. On this voyage it was she who was 'very ill', her distress deepened by her sense that the break with the past was irrevocable and the contours of the life to come entirely unknown. As they at last approached the English coast, however, characteristically, she rallied and began to focus her energies and emotions on the reunion with the two brothers whom she had not seen for five years.[68]

CHAPTER 2

'A land . . . with strong foes beset'

Reunion with the boys in Liverpool was this time a hugger-mugger rather than a joyous affair. They did not meet at Finch House, for one of their Crowder cousins was dying. Instead they gathered first in the house of an old friend, Thomas Corrie, in Bedford Street and then went to lodgings which Arthur had found for them, near Shaw Street. He guessed correctly that Annie would miss Charleston badly and ever after she remembered a 'dreary return to England'. A semblance of normality gradually returned over the summer, with visits to Clough relatives in North Wales and Perfect relatives in Yorkshire. Then in September the family broke up again: Arthur went back to Rugby, Charles sailed for Charleston and the remaining members settled in a furnished house in Liverpool, at 24 Hope Street. [1]

Now Annie had to set to work to establish a new pattern of life for herself in a very different environment. Liverpool, like Charleston, was a commercial rather than a manufacturing city but one not dependent on a single product. In the early eighteenth century Daniel Defoe had described Liverpudlians as 'universal merchants', trading in Irish wool, linen and beef, American cotton, colonial tobacco and sugar, Midlands metals and pottery, Cheshire salt and Lancashire coal and textiles.[2] The tonnage of vessels using the port doubled every fifteen years between 1749 and 1857. The writer Nathaniel Hawthorne, who was to become American consul in Liverpool in 1853, described

the immense multitude of ships . . . ensconced in the docks; where their masts make an intricate forest for miles up and down the Liverpool shore. The small black steamers, whizzing industriously along, and many of them crowded with passengers, make up the chief life of the scene. The Mersey has the color of a mud-puddle; and no atmospheric effect, so far as I have seen, ever gives it a more agreeable tinge.

Liverpool had grown dramatically during the eighteenth century and continued to do so during the nineteenth: the Census of 1841 recorded the

2 *Liverpool from Toxteth Park, 1834*, drawn by G. Pickering, engraved by J. Sands

population as not far short of 300,000; and ten years later, in 1851, it had grown by almost another 100,000. It was far larger than any American city and Hawthorne would remark, 'I think I have never seen a populace before coming to England.'³ Some fine building was done: but with the dominance of commerce and mushroom growth came a continual pulling down, rebuilding and extension. Those very first lodgings which Arthur had found for the Cloughs seemed to Annie to be in the middle of a building site.

No single issue resonated through the life of Liverpool as slavery had through that of Charleston. Nevertheless there were powerful ethnic and sectarian tensions in the city, adding to and feeding on the instability inherent in expansion and the constant demand for casual labour. Liverpool was invariably the first destination of migrant Irish – Roman Catholics from the South and Protestant Ulstermen from the North – and both groups engaged with vigour and often violence in the politics of the city, the Ulstermen contributing a powerful populism to the rhetoric and organisation of local Toryism. In the aftermath of Catholic Emancipation, at the end of the 1820s, the Corporation had attempted to encourage toleration, supporting two non-sectarian elementary schools; but by the end of 1841 the experiment had collapsed and denominational segregation remained the order of the day, not only in the schools but in most other areas of life.

This turbulent, sprawling city provided the base from which the male members of the Clough family moved outwards, into their various public activities. Arthur, in his last year at Rugby, Head of School House and already garlanded with honours and prizes, was preparing to sit for scholarships to Oxford in November. James intended in due course to follow Charles back to Charleston, for he still believed that bases both sides of the Atlantic gave him a trading advantage. He retained his links with his long-time associate, Atkinson, who was beginning to cast a critical eye over Charles' first forays into dealing in cotton.⁴ George had been taken away from King William's College in the Isle of Man and now attended school in Liverpool as a day boy.⁵

No such opportunities or mobility beckoned for the female members of the family. For women of their social position in the early nineteenth century, the accepted sphere was the private, domestic one; and financial insecurity reinforced this. Wealth and rank might allow some women to challenge conventions: the Cloughs were sustained by neither of these. Annie and her mother were expected to remain at home, to provide a tranquil, private, morally uplifting environment, serving both as refuge and as secure base for their menfolk.⁶ For the private person who was

Anne Clough, it was probably enough to be back on the 'right' side of the Atlantic, in closer touch with both her immediate and her extended family. For her daughter Annie, on the verge of adulthood, it must have seemed as if horizons were contracting rather than expanding. Afterwards, with heroic restraint and euphemism, she looked back at those first few months in Liverpool as 'rather dull' and certainly not helped by the climate. Hawthorne, coming from the dry bright cold of New England, would grumble about Liverpool's cold dampness and the near-perpetual cloud of fog and coal-smoke which enveloped the city.[7] The first winter of Annie's return, the winter of 1836–7, was so cold that the water in the bedroom ewers froze.[8] The contrast with the warmth, the whiteness, the lush vegetation, the clean beaches and water of South Carolina was extreme. Annie wrote copiously to Maria Lance in Charleston; but inevitably their paths began to diverge, a divergence which would increase following Maria's marriage to Wainwright Bacot in 1838.[9] A young woman of Annie's energy and social curiosity badly needed more to occupy her time.

She began with a programme of self-education, of both reading and writing. At Christmas 1836 Arthur had come home with great armfuls of books: Wordsworth, Coleridge, Scott, and Boswell's *Life of Johnson*.[10] He encouraged her to read her way through the plays of Shakespeare and she was regularly translating from German, which he thought would help her English style. She was also learning Greek. Often she got up early, to work while the house was quiet. By the beginning of 1841 Annie was continuing with German, reading and translating Schiller, Goethe and Kant, attempting to work regularly through problems in Euclidean geometry and to persevere with the Greek and, as always, reading extensively in English prose and poetry. She had reached *Othello* in her reading of Shakespeare and added Byron and Cowper to Wordsworth and Coleridge, although she continued to find Milton difficult. As for prose, she had worked conscientiously through Milman's *History of the Jews* and was beginning on Hallam's *Constitutional History of England*.

It was an ambitious programme by any standards, comparing favourably with that offered in boys' public schools and in the handful of exceptional girls' schools which did exist, such as the Misses Franklin's school in Coventry, where the young Marian Evans – to become the novelist George Eliot – had been a pupil.[11] Nor did it command universal approval: Annie's North Wales cousin, Margaret Clough, remained wholly unconvinced of the need for women to learn Latin and Greek. Annie, however, persevered. Her general objectives were self-improvement and self-discipline: she wrote earnestly in January 1841, 'I desire knowledge

I do not think so much for its own sake but for the sake of exerting my faculties in acquiring it. There is an uneasy restlessness about my mind & it is only by constant exertion & constant employment it can be in any measure appeased & kept quiet.'[12] Moreover both Annie and Arthur recognised that self-education might turn out to have an economic dimension. Given the precariousness of the family finances, school-keeping might one day enable her to earn her living; although Arthur wondered whether there was a mismatch between the ambition of her programme and the demands of the market. 'I have thought occasionally', he wrote in November 1840,

about the possibility of your being in the situation you speak of as having occurred to you – of having to earn your livelihood – and have regarded it in what I have advised you to do (as for example in attending to your writing). I don't think you can do any better in this way than attend to the writing of English, which you do by translating from German; as for Murray's Grammar, I really know little or indeed nothing of it, but I dare say it will do you no harm. As for keeping a school, you know how necessary Music, etc., etc. are even to those of a humble kind; but I do not doubt that as things go on, in a few years there will be more demand for such things as you have been learning. So long then as you have anything to occupy you in the same way as before, I think you might as well go on with it. Have you read King John and King Richard II?[13]

A sense of the possibilities of school-keeping had surely also been nourished by the charitable work upon which Annie had embarked. Work with children, whether in running a small school for children of one's own class or helping as a volunteer in elementary schools, schools for the labouring poor, was one of the few things a young woman of the middle class – a 'lady' – could engage in without compromising her own status.[14] Annie began tentatively, helping out on a voluntary basis in the Welsh Sunday School, in February 1837. From this she was soon drawn into the work of the associated Welsh Girls' Day School, going first in the afternoons and then also one morning a week.[15]

Annie enjoyed the work with the girls. In April 1839 she compiled a careful record of their names and addresses, adding comments about character and subsequently notes about their destinations.[16] She gave parties for them in the school holidays and grew very close to some of her pupils, especially Jane Doyle. What she found much harder was the expectation that the lady helpers would also visit the pupils in their own homes – 'Dislike it very much', she wrote. She was daunted by the maze of back streets and shocked by some of the poverty and degradation she saw. Some fifteen years later Hawthorne would be simultaneously fascinated and repelled by Liverpool's 'darker and dingier streets, inhabited by the poorer classes', observing people

filthy in clothes and person, ragged, pale, often afflicted with humors; women, nursing their babies at dirty bosoms; men haggard, drunken, care-worn, hopeless, but with a kind of patience, as if all this were the rule of their life; groups stand or sit talking together, around the door-steps, or in the descent of a cellar; often a quarrel is going on in one group, for which the next group cares little or nothing. Sometimes, a decent woman may be seen sewing or knitting at the entrance of her poor dwelling, a glance at which shows dismal poverty. I never walk through these streets without feeling as if I should catch some disease; but yet there is a strong interest in such walks; and moreover there is a bustle, a sense of being in the midst of life, and of having got hold of something real, which I do not find in the better streets of the city. Doubtless, this noon-day and open life of theirs is entirely the best aspect of their existence; and if I were to see them within doors, at their meals, or in bed, it would be unspeakably worse. They appear to wash their clothes occasionally; for I have seen them hanging out to dry in the street.[17]

It is startling that a well-brought-up young woman, who was not yet twenty, might be expected to walk in such streets and visit such homes on her own. At the beginning, both her mother and Arthur supported Annie, often accompanying her. At Christmas 1837 and again in the summer of 1838, in his vacations from Oxford, Arthur made visits with her. Eventually she felt able to sum up the work of the year 1838: 'Get more interested in the children and not so afraid of visiting the Parents.' By 1839 she was fully into the swing of things: 'Now get completely into the school. Begin to lend books & visit generally.' To her teaching she was beginning to add 'district visiting', involvement in visiting all the poor in a particular area. In January 1841 Annie and her mother took charge of the distribution of the St David's Church Collection of coal, potatoes and cash to seventy-one poor households. She did not become blasé about the conditions she saw, writing in February 1841, 'I get wearied & worn out with the sight of so much misery & worst of all degradation – sometimes baseness and wickedness – This is the worst to bear.' She was affronted, however, when the aunt who was her cousin Margaret's guardian decreed that Margaret, on a visit to Liverpool, was 'not to go with me to any of the poor places'.[18]

Such charitable work followed a classic Evangelical pattern; and Annie also conformed to this pattern in one other respect at least: in May 1840 she began to keep a journal. What helped trigger this action is unclear. Was it the urging of a particular preacher? Did she know that Arthur too kept a journal? She consciously modelled herself on William Wilberforce, writing, 'I think I must keep an exact account of how my time goes, it certainly often keeps me from wasting it. I learnt this plan for [*sic*] reading Wilberforce's Life, it has been of great service to me. The more we can do the better. If we are in the habit of giving an account to ourselves we shall be better prepared to give an account to our Judge at the last day.'[19] It was also a way of combating loneliness and a periodic sense of isolation: there are times when she seems to be talking to herself.

Annie did not write up her journal every day; often she summarised several days or a week at a time. She recorded the hours spent in study, her reading, her school work and visits, and her social encounters. When she thought she could give a good account of the way she had spent her time, the adjective she always used was 'tolerable'. But frequently she reproached herself for laziness, roughness, rudeness and impatience. She was anxious about time wasted in day-dreaming and fantasies and discomposed by the addiction of her North Wales relations to gossip about lovers, although she was honest enough to admit that she usually joined in. Their social life was also more elaborate and extensive than hers: it was in North Wales not in Liverpool that Annie went to balls. After one such excitement, she concluded with rueful amusement that it was just as well for her that her family was not rich. 'If I were an heiress like Margaret & in the way of so many balls & amusements I should have great difficulty to keep right. But one now & then does me good.'[20]

She wondered whether she would ever marry, continuing to cherish the memory of the attentions paid her by the mysterious R. D. in New York,[21] but worrying about her gauche behaviour and uncertainty about social signals in mixed company. Returning to Liverpool in January 1841, after a Christmas and New Year spent in North Wales, she wrote sadly,

My mind has been filled with idle vain thoughts produced by the talks we had at Rhual Issa [the home of Margaret Clough and her maiden aunts] about flirting marrying etc. I wonder whether it is good. I do not dislike such talk certainly I delight but it makes me feel light and wandering. Oh how I could speak of the past. The truth of the matter is, I am very soon touched, a little attention, a single long talk will often move me & then I am blind and fancy all sorts of things – For this reason I fear to go out much because I might get considerably wrong – And almost always feel shy before men.[22]

Although Evangelical models exerted a powerful influence on Annie's charitable work and the form in which her journal was cast, she remained her own person, honesty and directness recurrently breaking through, as when she admitted that an occasional ball did her good. She was, too, repelled by sectarian rhetoric. The Clough households in North Wales were inclining more towards the High Church end of the Anglican spectrum and becoming energetically and vociferously critical both of Low Churchmen and Dissenters. She found herself having to defend Arthur's revered Headmaster at Rugby, Dr Arnold, and his Broad Church associations and reflected, 'I don't like these Parties they create a great deal bad feeling. I will try to do what appears to be right & improve myself as much as I can without troubling my head about these Parties.'[23]

Annie also used her journal to explore her complex feelings towards Arthur. She was deeply in awe of his learning and his piety and craved his good opinion, but sometimes to the point where her sense of her own inadequacy constrained and inhibited her in talking to him. In August 1840 she wrote, 'I have been considerably bothered with vain show off thoughts with regard to Arthur. Too much desire of praise & too little love of being concealed & quiet, then again, I fancy I want to talk to him & ask him a good many questions & yet I am afraid & don't know how.' By the beginning of September she was very discontented, feeling neglected and treated as of no account by the whole family but especially by Arthur. At last they managed a long walk and private talk – and she was overwhelmed by what she learned of his own anxieties.

He seems very much out of Spirits & fearful about his examination turning out well, he says he has not been well since Easter, but all the time he has been home he has seldom if ever complained & has been most especially kind & considerate to every one & cheerful too, though some times a look of deep distress & inward pain has passed over him. How patiently he has taught me my German & how attentive he was to Mother when she was ill.

In truth he has been a bright example to us all for he has been patient & uncomplaining, ever cheerful when his secret mind was torn with secret fears & sorrow & when his spirit was wounded & burdened.[24]

Living with his iron composure remained demanding:[25] but it helped to know that when they walked and talked on their own together, he could sometimes unburden himself. She watched for such opportunities during his visits home.

Annie acknowledged ambition in herself, despite being 'only a woman'; and the long self-examination on which she dutifully embarked, immediately following her twenty-first birthday in January 1841, is a revealing mixture, combining the familiar litany of self-criticism with some shrewd insights. The journal entry begins and ends with prayer; between she writes:

I believe I am considerably changed in the last year yet I know not how exactly – I now act very much more from impulse & I think more quickly. I am much happier in my mind I seldom if ever feel puzzled what to do. When I go out to parties I am more gay & lively though sometimes I am very stupid & in a general way cannot talk well to Gentlemen. I cannot talk the common flirting slang or nonsense (not that I suppose all or very many do) then I do not like to speak about books & so I seldom find a subject. I do not regularly get acquainted either for I almost always meet new people every time I go out. I think I still [like] visiting my poor friends though sometimes [it] is a burden to me, I have so many to look after, & it gives me the horrors to go into some [of] their wretched dens. I would often fain stay at home and read my books. However duty must then come in & take the command & I trust I shall never prove rebellious or lazy. Yet I am often comforted & encouraged by many sweet scenes of kindness to each other, family affection, innocent childhood, though I sometimes meet with disappointments where I expected more – but upon the whole I think the good predominates, at least if it does not, there is a large portion of it. And we must not let wickedness [and] misery weary us from seeking to promote goodness & happiness. This is not our rest, be it always remembered. I fear I have been rather lazy in study, I do not work my mind enough & then lately . . . I have taken a great fancy to Rhyming & waste a good deal of time that way – not that I write much but I am always trying & beginning half a dozen pieces. I am still reserved until the ice is once broken & then it is almost impossible to stop the stream of my thoughts & feelings & actions being all precipitated from their bed & I think they rush down with greater violence from the former restraint. But I think I ought rather to cultivate reserve in some things. I am naturally so dotingly fond of praise & of such a boastful proud turn of mind, it is absolutely necessary for me to be reserved unless I would become one of those who seek the praise of men. I dare not even allow myself to think much of things I do in this way – at least I ought not. The heart does indeed require strict watching & we must indeed deny ourselves daily & take up our cross.[26]

This is an earnest young woman of passionate enthusiasms and interests and a wish to see the best in people. She has no small talk and can feel anxious, gauche and simultaneously shy and over-impulsive in social situations; but she can look at herself dispassionately and is beginning to trust her own judgement, instincts and values, beginning to feel at more ease with herself.

At the beginning of 1841 it must have seemed as if patterns of life for Annie and her brothers were becoming settled. She had her school and charity work. Arthur was in his last year at Balliol College, Oxford, with everyone confidently expecting him to be awarded a first class in his final examinations, going on to academic distinction and a career first as an Oxford tutor and then in the Church. George had left school and at Christmas had gone out to Charleston, to join Charles and to begin to learn the business.[27] In the course of that year, however, things began to unravel. At the beginning of June came the great disappointment of Arthur's second class degree: Annie wrote fiercely, 'I could not endure that he should be beat by anyone.'[28] Far worse was to come. James Clough and his associates had weathered the economic slump of 1837 but they did not survive the next, deeper slump, which would bottom out only at the beginning of 1842.[29] On 10 August 1841 Thomas Crowder Junior wrote to his cousin, William Mosley Perfect,

> You will have already learnt from Dicky of the pretty mess we are in here, which is fairly announced on 'Change this morning. Should the present bad times continue you will find a good many in the same Dance that we have led off. J. B. Clough goes to pot along with us. When he was told it was all up with us, he said he should stop too as if we went he should go too eventually, so he might as well pull up at once. As to the Govnr [his father] I never saw him in such a state as he was in all last week; now however that he is fairly in the thick of it, he is rather more rational, though still low enough at the prospect ahead.[30]

Annie was staying in North Wales. First came a letter from her mother, telling her of the Crowders' failure. Then 'Father's letter arrived with the news that all is up with him.'[31]

It was an anxious and difficult autumn for them all. Arthur rejoiced to make a contribution to family finances by coaching pupils throughout the summer but was correspondingly cast down when he failed to get elected to a Fellowship at Balliol at the end of November.[32] George and Charles had arrived back from Charleston in July, a month before the crash, and in late August some discussion of the whole family moving back to Charleston began. What contribution to such discussions was made by Atkinson, who also arrived in England in October, is unclear.[33] But in November Charles found a situation in an office in Liverpool[34] and in the event only George was to return to Charleston. Their father cast around in various directions, in December setting off to London in pursuit – unsuccessfully – of an insurance agency.[35] On the occasion of this crash, the Perfect family resources were primarily devoted to helping out the Crowders and there was some unhappiness in the Clough household about this.[36] Help was forthcoming to the Cloughs, however, in the form of a loan from James' brother, Charles, Vicar of Mold.[37]

Annie meanwhile was desperate to help. On 22 August she wrote, 'Wish I could do something to earn a little that I might be independent.' At the beginning of October, 'This debt to Uncle Charles haunts me. I cannot bear the thought of being idle so long as it is unpaid.' Now, if ever, was the time to put her plans to keep a school into action and she was profoundly irritated that Arthur did not seem to take them seriously.[38] She persevered, however. They had moved from Hope Street to St James' Terrace in 1838; now it was decided that they should move again, to somewhere less expensive. House-hunting with her father, Annie appraised each one with an eye to its situation as a school.[39] Friends and acquaintances were encouraging; and those already in the business offered practical help. Annie spent a day observing at Miss Parry's school, while Sara Corrie invited Annie to come to stay and observe the schemes of work followed by her French teacher, Mlle Brioland.[40] Annie gratefully accepted the invitation, spending four days there in late November and two more days in early December. It was an instructive experience, although she thought the establishment as a whole verged on the pretentious: 'there is a portion of humbug about [it]'. In the same period she was also taking drawing lessons from another friend, Augusta Wotherspoon.[41]

This hurried apprenticeship was threaded through not only with family worries but also with deep sadness: Jane Doyle, the former pupil of the Welsh Girls' School, to whom Annie had become very close, was dying. Annie visited Jane frequently, spending time with her every day in the week up to her death on 9 December.

My visits were painful she suffered so much . . . How softly how gently she used to talk to me & tell me all her heart . . . I have watched over her and she has been very dear to me . . . She has been a great anxiety to me ever since her Aunt died & now that she is gone it is a great satisfaction to think that I have never as far as I can remember neglected her. And yet so many anxieties, so many occupations have come upon me that I cannot help feeling thankful she is released for I was beginning to find it difficult to look after her so much. But I shall miss her love, it was indeed a pleasure to know that some one was pleased to see me.[42]

To the time spent with Jane, time spent in observation of other schools and practice at drawing were added also the time and worry of the search for pupils – 'Have been on some scholar hunting expeditions which I did not like at all but was always kindly received.' Annie became so despondent that she thought she might be driven to seek a post as a resident governess – if she could get her family to agree. However by 20 January 1842 she was able to report, 'Began my school. My scholars Emma Anne Mary & Jane Pilcher & Margaret McConnon manage pretty tolerably.' By the second week, the gilt was wearing off the gingerbread: 'they are not nice children – upon the whole considerably impudent – Little M the best'.[43] It is tempting to wonder whether the Pilcher parents were only too relieved to pay someone to get their four cheeky daughters out of the house for a portion of each day. How Annie arranged the day and what precisely she taught, she does not say; although we know from her later work that she preferred to make an individual programme for each child. Whatever the details, Annie was at last making a contribution of her own to the family economy.

Through 1842 and into 1843 the members of the family worked to repair their fortunes. Arthur was working as a private coach in Oxford, while preparing for the Oriel College Fellowship examinations in late March 1842. This time he did not disappoint himself, his family or his friends. When he paid Liverpool a flying visit in celebration of his triumph, Annie wrote joyfully, 'He was more like himself than he had been for a long time.'[44] He would not take up the Fellowship until the autumn; but it helped to enhance his standing, and the flow of private pupils through spring and summer enabled him not only to keep himself but also to send some money home. He kept going, despite a severe blow in June, when Dr Arnold, mentor, friend, in effect second father, died suddenly. Arthur and other friends, who had also been numbered among Arnold's favourite pupils, did their best to sustain each other and he was always close to two of Arnold's sons, Matthew – invariably Matt – and Tom.[45]

Charles was still working in Liverpool; and eventually, at the beginning of September 1842, George went back to Charleston.[46] Annie soldiered on with her pupils. Teaching as employment was proving much more demanding than teaching as charitable work, although she seems not to have abandoned the charitable work altogether. Entries in her journal become less frequent, scrappier – and much more difficult to date. She now writes only every few months, summarising the main events of the past three or four. Early in 1842 she had been frank about her anxieties in a long letter to Maria Lance Bacot in Charleston. When Maria eventually replied, in June 1842, she apologised for her delay – she had had troubles of her own – but 'you are one of the few who will rejoice with me when I do rejoice & who will weep with me when I weep'. She did her best to console and encourage Annie, in the process showing a shrewd understanding of her respondent:

Your last letter indicated a great depression of spirit & indeed I do not wonder at it. I am only astonished at the energy you evince in the sad state of your affairs. I cannot think of anything more wearying than toiling to plant the seed of knowledge in soil unpromising & perhaps after all one's efforts to find that it is perfectly unfruitful. I am sorry your scholars are so uninteresting but hope they may improve as they get more attached to you – only gain their <u>love</u> and then your task will be comparatively light. No doubt you have accomplished it ere this for you have always professed a happy knack of drawing children to you.[47]

Annie's Perfect relations also came to the rescue, inviting her for a long visit to Yorkshire towards the end of June, once the summer holidays had begun.

The detail in which she records the visits, the sights and the many energetic walks vividly conveys her pleasure at escaping from the school-room into the open countryside at last. But the economic pressures remained; and in August school began again. She had lost one of her first pupils but gained two new ones. The autumn work was, however, relieved by a deepening friendship with Augusta Wotherspoon, who had been teaching her drawing; and reviewing the year in December 1842 Annie counted among her blessings, 'Employment which is only sometimes irksome & is I trust useful.'[48]

Annie's mother is unfortunately a silent presence in the midst of all this activity. Yet her father, after the early shocks, was displaying his usual resilience. When Arthur confessed to a bout of illness at the beginning of 1842, James wrote robustly to assure him that the family could cope and he was not to undermine his constitution by over-work in the effort to help: 'nothing on earth can compensate for *loss of health*'.[49] In spite of all the previous upsets, James returned to cotton and the transatlantic trade and in October 1842 he followed George to Charleston.[50] Trade was at last beginning to look up and he was soon sending optimistic bulletins back. With breathtakingly selective recall, he wrote at the beginning of March 1843,

Indeed I cannot call to mind any period of my life, except a few months in the early part of the Memorable 1825 perhaps, when I have been so thoroughly occupied in active & positive work as I have been during the last four months here. What the result will be eventually I cannot yet pretend to say. It looms large, as they say, & on the right side so far to a greater extent certainly than we had any reason to calculate on for the first year.

It would be a little time yet before the extent of their profits could be securely calculated: however he hoped not only to discharge various old debts and pay the interest due to his brother Charles, but also to repay a portion of the principal due to him. And while joking that George, because of his inexperience, was counting chickens before they had hatched, he was not above doing the same himself and making bold plans for their new, financially secure life. Specifically, he wanted Annie to give up her school:

I sho'd. be glad if you wo'd. prepare for giving up your schoolkeeping as soon as you can with propriety, & with justice towards the Parents & children. For the occupation does not at all remunerate you for the time & care bestowed upon it, though it was at one time an object to gain even that little on almost any terms.

The necessity however in which your kind resolution to undertake the task originated, no longer happily exists. Why then sho'd. you any longer waste your time, which at any rate be employed more agreably, in pursuing one of the most trying & troublesome of occupations in life, when there is really no occasion at all for your doing so. For I think there cannot be a doubt now, but the business I have been the means of reestablishing here by coming out again will in future yield your dear Mother, yourself & I amply sufficient for all our wants & to spare by whomsoever it may be conducted in future . . .

There is no need, therefore, my dearest daughter, for you to bother yourself with teaching a parcel of little brats any longer, & I am sure it will be a great relief to your good Mother too to get rid of them all & to have the house quiet to yourselves once more, instead of making slaves of yourselves for a mere nothing. You have done your duty most nobly, my dear Girl, in our time of need, & may surely now rest upon that reflection.

So pray send all the little things away as soon as you can. We will fit the room up as a nice little sitting room, which will be a great addition to our comforts, & we shall then be snug enough until we can get into some more desireable [*sic*] residence, over the water perhaps, [Birkenhead? N. Wales?] where we may live in peace & quietness for the rest of our lives. What says dear Mamma to all this?[51]

What *did* Mamma say? She, of all people, had heard talk like this so many times. At all events, Annie's school continued to the summer holidays, which she spent in Ireland – and resumed again at the beginning of August 1843, although now only with four pupils. James had returned from Charleston on 24 June and there was yet more discussion about a general move back to Charleston in the course of July. Annie mused, 'I am half inclined to think I should be happier there. Here we have few friends. I scarcely any companions and yet I love my native land & Arthur is a strong tie to it and Margaret too. Then there is that horrible slavery.' It came to nothing: although it was now possible to travel by steamship, perhaps Mamma continued to set her face against another Atlantic crossing and James returned alone to the United States at the beginning of November 1843.[52]

His first landfall was Boston, where he was greeted with the dreadful news that George had died of yellow fever on 5 November, the day after his father had left Liverpool. All their Charleston friends had rallied round during George's illness. Dr Campbell had attended him; Lizzy, the hired slave whom they all knew well, had nursed him; and Lizzy and Atkinson had been at the bedside when George died. All their efforts had been in vain and after a well-attended funeral, George, aged twenty-two, had been buried in a Wotherspoon family plot in the churchyard of St Michael's Church. When the news reached Liverpool, Annie reproached herself for imagined unkindnesses just before George had left. Why had she not asked his forgiveness on the eve of his departure? 'The thought too that his own family were all away from him was very bitter.'[53]

This devastating blow knocked much of the stuffing out of James Clough. Laboriously and painfully he made arrangements for the disposition of all George's possessions and effects – including the lock of his hair which Atkinson had cut off and kept for Annie. Charles came out to help him with the business; and together they watched bleakly as the earlier hopes of great profits shrivelled and died. This became the harder to endure when Charles confessed that he had secretly become engaged to Jane Ross, the widowed sister of William Ogilby, the British consul in Charleston. Her mother-in-law, Lady Ross, was hostile; Jane had no money of her own – and neither had Charles. As James expostulated to Annie, 'I am, like you, averse to long engagements . . . But how it is to be managed in this instance I really cannot conceive.'

In that same letter of February 1844 James signalled a change of tune about school-keeping: 'While we live where & as we do in Liverpool I cannot object to your continuing your present occupation, for I am satisfied it suits you well, though I sho'd. be very glad to see you so circumstanced by our moving to a more desireable residence either on the same or the other side the river, the latter of which I sh'od. like best.' By late May he was telling his wife that,

We had better be content to remain where we are for another quarter or half year. By the end of the latter we shd be able to calculate how the next season's business is likely to turn out & as I have good hopes that it will be very much better than the present. I shall, if it happily proves so, be able & willing to move from our present situation . . . When we do make a move, however, I do trust there will be no more necessity for schoolkeeping, & that we may be able to enjoy ourselves a little more than we have done in peace & quietness, & in a friendly intercourse with our widening number of relatives – without incurring much more annual expence than we do now . . . I think it wd. be as well therefore for Annie not to attempt the severing of scholars on the other side the water as yet.[54]

His efforts at optimism now have a hollow ring.

In these months too James acknowledged the unrealism of all talk of a move back to Charleston and began to face the fact that Annie, now aged twenty-three, might never marry. 'Believe me, my dear daughter', he wrote at the beginning of May, 'this is not the market I wo'd. bring you to in search of a husband or a home, were I more anxious than I am to part with you in that way.' It would have been too much to expect him to acknowledge the problems presented by her lack of fortune; and he was too kind ever to allude to her shyness, and her lack of easy sociability and small talk. Somewhat clumsily, but with transparently good intentions, he went on to try to reassure and console her:

We must, however, reluctantly consent to part with you, I presume, & will not be so stubborn as old Lady Ross seems to be. But until something more desireable than is to be met with in these parts, of that character, occurs, I trust you will find yourself happy with your old Father & Mother, who, I can answer for it, will never be weary of your company, though they wo'd naturally be rejoiced to see you happily & comfortably married & settled in life. But husbands really suitable to your character & truly worthy of your affections are, I fear, <u>very rare birds</u>.

Whether you are to live single, however, or are destined to enjoy matrimonial life, you need not despair of as much earthly happiness as is good for you, for I know you have that within you, my dear Annie, which will carry you happily through this world of woe, so far as depends on yourself. And happily will it be for us if we sho'd. be blessed with your kind & charming attentions in our declining years.[55]

James eventually left Charleston in July 1844 and arrived home in Liverpool on 29 July, plainly unwell, although any diagnosis of his illness offered by the doctors was not recorded by either Annie or Arthur. He took to his bed almost immediately, tossing and turning with fever and occasionally delirium. His doctors tried successive applications of leeches, blisters and bran poultices. These seemed, if anything, to make him worse and eventually they tried simply to sedate him. In late August he appeared to rally; but this did not last and by mid-September it was plain that death was close. Arthur was away coaching pupils in Yorkshire for a short spell early in September; otherwise he remained in Liverpool, delaying his return to Oxford, and taking a full share of the nursing with Annie and their mother.[56] Charles was sent for and a few hours after he had returned from the United States, on 19 October, James died. He was buried in St James' Cemetery, to the east of the site on which Liverpool's Anglican Cathedral now stands, and the gravestone commemorates not only James but George, lying far away in Charleston.[57]

As the exhaustion of the ordeal receded, Annie tried to write an account of her father's last weeks and months, but found herself utterly unable to complete it.[58] She came to regard Arthur's poem, *Jacob*, completed in 1851, as 'a sort of remembrance of his father: of the struggles and trials of a mercantile life, the hard battle that a real gentleman and a Christian man, with an affectionate, honourable and too yielding character, had had with life'. Arthur wrote of the need

> To watch by day and calculate by night,
> To plot and think of plots, and through a land
> Ambushed with guile, and with strong foes beset,
> To win with art safe wisdom's peaceful way.

And perhaps the griefs of those last three years were recalled especially in the lines,

> Many have been the troubles of my life;
> Sins in the field and sorrows in the tent,
> In mine own household anguish and despair,
> And gall and wormwood mingled with my love.[59]

After the blow of this second bereavement, following so hard on the heels of the first, the surviving family members had to labour to re-establish a pattern of life for themselves and eventually to begin to move forward again. Arthur at least had the framework of his Oxford commitments: but they all had to deal with the tangle of James' financial affairs and establish whether there would be enough for Annie and her mother to live on. At first the outlook was encouraging; but there were still creditors with whom a settlement had to be reached.[60] Arthur remarked to his friend Burbidge, 'We are still a little under the waves of business-troubles.' They were rescued by the life insurance which James, for once prudent, had carried and which was paid over in the early spring of 1845.[61] The new-found financial stability was weakened only by Arthur's involvement in a scheme worthy of James at his most speculative: the contribution of a large capital sum to an annuity scheme for two ladies of uncertain health, with the prospect of handsome returns when their deaths occurred. He borrowed the capital from his mother, undertaking not only to pay her a proper rate of interest but also taking out life insurance in her favour. The two ladies proved unexpectedly robust and for the next fifteen years Arthur would have to continue to pay the interest and the insurance premiums.[62]

Nevertheless, the immediate situation looked secure enough to allow the arrangement of a modest summer holiday in 1845. Arthur took a house in Grasmere, with room not only for the pupils he would coach but also for Annie and his mother. He instructed Annie, 'You must be ready to start by the 10th of June, for we ought to have some few days to ourselves before the pupils arrive.'[63] This was Annie's first visit to the Lake District and Arthur took immense pains to show her as much as possible of a landscape he had come to know and love since his first visit to the Arnolds' house, Fox How, near Ambleside, in the early 1830s. They ranged far and wide, beyond Keswick in the north, to Buttermere and Crummock Water, over the Honister Pass, to Ullswater via the Kirkstone Pass, as well as exploring the countryside nearer Grasmere, Easdale Tarn, Silver How, Helm Crag and Sour Milk Ghyll. Annie revelled in the ever-changing play of light on the hillsides and over the lakes, the streams and waterfalls and the exhilaration of scrambling up steep paths. She enjoyed meeting the Arnold family and the writer Harriet Martineau. And expeditions and social life continued once the reading party had started.[64]

Business contacts with the USA had been finally severed and Charles had returned to work in Liverpool. Annie and her mother determined to remain in the city, to make a home for him; although they had moved house again in April 1845, to 22 Canterbury Street, no doubt a smaller and cheaper house.[65] How Charles had been disentangled from the secret engagement to Mrs Ross is unclear. Perhaps Lady Ross remained adamant; perhaps Mrs Ross herself took fright at the complications of the Cloughs' affairs following James' death. Whatever the reasons, no more is heard of her. Instead in June 1845 the news came to Grasmere that Charles was engaged to be married to his cousin Margaret –'the heiress' as Annie had once called her. Annie had mixed feelings: she liked Margaret greatly but thought it would be much better for Charles if he had to work to support his wife.[66]

Annie had taken her charity work and her school with her to Canterbury Street; and at the beginning of the new term in August 1845, was gratified by the return of six pupils, with a seventh due shortly.[67] In addition the shared experiences and grief of the past two years had done much to dissolve her sense of constraint in her dealings with Arthur and had given him a new awareness of her strength and her practical good sense. They were now talking and corresponding more as equals, not only about money and travel plans but also about books, ideas and beliefs. In the Lake District they had had much discussion of the recently published autobiography of Joseph Blanco White, who had been born a Roman Catholic and moved through Anglicanism to Unitarianism, dying among the Unitarian community in Liverpool. They began with prayer, and moved on to the status of baptism and then to forms of collective worship. In the course of these conversations, Arthur shared with Annie his doubts about the historical standing of the first three gospels and they then went on to debate at length the meaning of the doctrine of the Atonement. Annie thought she followed his reasoning when they were together, but afterwards could not reconstruct it to her own satisfaction and discussion continued by letter and when they met again.[68] Given how much she had learned about his thinking from these exchanges, it can hardly have come as a surprise when, in the autumn, he admitted to her his growing disinclination to take Anglican orders – 'quod tamen tu tacere debes' [which however you must keep quiet about].[69]

The new ease between Arthur and Annie was reflected in the plan hatched that winter, for them to go abroad together in the summer of 1846. Charles

and Margaret were to get married on 3 February and then set off for an
extended European tour, beginning in Italy and moving north in June.
Arthur and Annie began to plan their own expedition for June and July,
with the possibility of meeting Charles and Margaret in Switzerland.[70]
In the event they travelled through Belgium to Germany and the Rhine:
by steamer down the Rhine from Cologne to Mannheim, and thence by
diligence into Switzerland. They met Arthur's friend Cotton and his wife at
Lucerne and all four continued together in a carriage over the St Gothard
Pass into northern Italy. Then Arthur and Annie went on to Como, where
they joined forces with Charles and Margaret. Together they explored the
Italian Lakes and journeyed over the Simplon Pass to the glacier at the foot
of Monte Rosa.

This was Annie's first European journey and she enjoyed it enormously:
as their train rattled through Louvain, she 'really began to understand I
was abroad'. She soaked up sights and sounds and displayed an engaging
and wholly unmalicious curiosity about all the people they encountered.
She liked taking her meals on the deck of the Rhine steamer but both
she and Arthur found it an impossibly noisy place to sleep and ended up
themselves watching the dawn come up over the river. The Italian Lakes
offered many opportunities for sketching: but like others before her and
after her, she fell in love with the drama of the high mountains. Every
detail of the journeys over the two Alpine passes was lovingly recorded in
her journal. The expedition over the Simplon also had its comic moments.
The two men were expected to walk, but mules had been provided for
Margaret and Annie – without side-saddles. Decorum and secure comfort
were in conflict: there were times when it was a relief to get off and walk,
until, footsore and weary, they would balance precariously on mule-back
again.[71] The past eleven years had been difficult ones but they had not
extinguished Annie's capacity for enjoyment or her lively interest in the
world around her. Still recognisable in the woman of twenty-six was the
enthusiastic fifteen-year-old who had revelled in her journey to New York
and to the Great Lakes.

CHAPTER 3

Confirming a vocation

Annie returned from her European journey at the end of July 1846 to face
a blow: the ending of her school. What brought this about is unclear. The
school had been kept going even through the very difficult last weeks of her
father's illness in 1844. Although she grumbled from time to time about the
fatigue it brought and was perennially worried about keeping discipline,
she recognised the satisfactions that working with children brought her
and took pride in the social as well as the economic value of her work.
In June 1845, reflecting on her relations with her Sunday school class, she
had written in her journal, 'Oh is it not beautiful to possess the love of
children & to have the hope of leading them in the right way. To see the
mind begin to open, the rough rude girl become quiet & serious & begin to
think. My garden looks hopeful. May God water the plants with heavenly
dews.' During their travels in 1846 Arthur and Annie had had energetic
discussions with the Cottons about appropriate ways of educating girls:
and Annie and Arthur, on their own, had talked at length 'about our
future plans. The necessity, or rather the great benefit of women finding
work, and considering it a duty to do so, and also whether they are at
liberty to choose their own paths in some cases (I mean single women)
without reference to their families.'[1] When in August Arthur, now leading a
reading party in Scotland, heard the news about the school, his response was
ambivalent.

So the school is coming to its dissolution. Shall you go on for the quarter?
Or do you cease at once? I am not exactly glad of it, but certainly not sorry.
I wish you employed, but I am not quite sure that the school, such as you
had, was the best employment. I hope you will go on with the painting and
perhaps the German too may be worthwhile. There will be more to be said
about this, I suppose, sometime or other: for the present I only advise you to
set to work at some regular reading. Alison [the historian] would be no harm:
though he is somewhat heavy, he is generally correct and the events make him
interesting.[2]

In the privacy of her diary, Annie wrote freely of her distress at the ending of her school; and this, combined with Arthur's aside – 'There will be more to be said about this, I suppose, sometime or other' – and the sense of constraint which pervades his letter, makes one suspect that the decision was their mother's: now that she and Annie were established on a regular, albeit slender, income, surely there was no more need for the invasion of privacy, the labour and trouble which the school entailed.

To compensate, Annie threw herself again not only into a programme of reading but also back into her charitable work, her district, the Welsh Schools, a new class for older girls and a lending library. 'Thus I managed after a while to get busy again, and to begin to be contented and happy.'[3] She had already lightened the load of the German by arranging to have formal lessons with a young émigré called Migault. Her friendship with Augusta Wotherspoon, with whom she drew and painted, continued a close one, although in May 1847, after surmounting family opposition, Augusta became engaged to Migault.[4] Some time during the preceding winter Annie herself had also been the subject of attentions from a suitor, who had, however, been briskly despatched. 'There is no use giving the slightest encouragement when one is determined, even if one's feelings did waver for a moment, to stand out. By being too kind one runs the risk of being caught oneself and led into an unwise alliance, or else one may give a great deal of unnecessary pain.' Both Annie and her mother were especially sustained by the company of old friends, the Bulleys, who also had Charleston links, and new friends, the Claudes, who divided their time between Liverpool and their house at Ambleside, in the Lake District. Staying with the Claudes in Ambleside in September 1846, Annie had walked and talked with Jane Claude and 'Told her some of my notions about its being right in certain cases to quit even one's father and mother and family for work as well as for a husband.'[5] Staying in the Lakes once more in the summer of 1847, Annie again saw much of the Claudes and appreciated the opportunity to talk over with Jane and Mary the difficulties which had preceded Augusta's engagement and the extent to which she herself had been caught in the cross-fire.[6]

As Annie struggled to clarify her own sense of duty and the part played in it by the work to which she felt drawn, Arthur was confronting similar issues, but approaching them from a very different direction. It had long been expected that he would crown academic success with Anglican orders and either remain a bachelor fellow and tutor at his Oxford college, or, if he wished to marry, move to an appropriate college living, when it fell vacant. The pattern was close at hand in the career of his uncle, Alfred Clough, formerly Fellow of Jesus College, Oxford and now, recently married, Rector of Braunston, near Rugby. Two other Clough uncles, Roger, who had died in 1830, and Charles, now Archdeacon of St Asaph, had also taken orders. Arthur's career thus far, his personal piety and strong moral sense, his work at Rugby with Dr Arnold to improve the school's tone and conduct, his Oriel fellowship and tutorship, which had been accompanied by voluntary social work in the city of Oxford, all suggested to the external observer that he would make a committed and energetic priest. Yet he himself was coming to feel his position an increasingly false one. He had already decided that he would not take orders:[7] and he was coming to realise that he could not, in good conscience, continue to subscribe to the Thirty-Nine Articles, the formal statement of Anglican doctrine, to which all graduates of the University of Oxford were required to declare their adherence.

Behind these decisions stretched a long and tortured process of self-examination. The Oxford in which Arthur had arrived as an undergraduate in 1837 was in a state of theological turmoil. A group of High Churchmen, led by J. H. Newman, John Keble, Hurrell Froude and later E. B. Pusey, set out to combat what they saw as the increasingly interventionist management of the Established Church by the secular authorities in the wake of the Reform Act of 1832, by reasserting and elaborating its essentially 'catholic' nature and, by implication, its rights and its independence. They set out their position in powerful preaching and ministry, and in a series of 'Tracts for the Times', which brought them the label 'Tractarians'. Evangelicals, liberals and Broad Churchmen responded with equal vigour. Arthur's associations, through his mentor Dr Arnold, were all with the Broad Church group. As a schoolboy at Rugby his anxious conscientiousness had made him the perfect instrument for Arnold, as the headmaster sought to reshape the ethic of the school; and in the morally strenuous environment created by this charismatic teacher and leader, Arthur developed a sense of duty which at times threatened to overwhelm him.[8] Associations and temperament combined to make him a perfect target for one of his Balliol tutors, W. G. Ward, lecturer in mathematics and logic. Ward was an enthusiastic Tractarian who would in 1846 quit the Church of England and become a Roman Catholic; he was also a man who revelled in the intellectual gymnastics of argument and became over-close emotionally to his favourite pupils. Given his background and education, Arthur would anyway have engaged seriously with the intellectual debate; and he was moved and impressed by Newman's preaching, teaching and ministry. With Ward as his tutor, however, questions about the historical and theological legitimacy of his church and his faith were brought to his doorstep, into his college room, day after day, evening after evening. The relentless challenge fed his own depressive tendencies and the insecurity and self-doubt which he had briefly revealed to Annie in the summer of 1840.[9]

The move to Oriel in the autumn of 1844 brought Arthur a degree of distance from Ward but not from the issues. Edward Hawkins, the Provost of Oriel, was one of the key players in the University's efforts to manage and contain the Tractarian attack; and the questioning Ward had assiduously fostered was now too far advanced to be halted by anything. By mid-1847 Arthur had concluded that while he strongly approved of the ethical and moral teaching of Christianity, he had ceased to believe in the historical Jesus and thus in the special mission of Christian churches. Responding to an enquiry of Annie's about a passage of Schiller on which she had been working, he wrote in May 1847,

Schiller made the impression upon me, when I used to read him in St James' Terrace, which he does now on you. Coleridge has been to me the antidotive power: he was philosopher and a firm believer (so far as one can make out) in Christianity, not only as a doctrine, but also as a narrative of events. My own feeling certainly does not go along with Coleridge's in attributing any special virtue to the facts of the Gospel History: they have happened and have produced what we know – have transformed the civilisation of Greece and Rome, and the barbarism of Gaul and Germany into Christendom. But I cannot feel sure that a man may not have all that is important even if he does not so much as know that Jesus of Nazareth existed. And I do not think that doubts respecting the facts related in the Gospels need give us much trouble. Believing that in one way or another the thing is of God, we shall in the end know perhaps in what way and how far it was so. Trust in God's Justice and Love, and belief in his Commands as written in our Conscience stand unshaken, though Matthew, Mark, Luke and John or even St Paul, were to fall. The thing which men must work at, will not be critical questions about the scriptures, but philosophical problems of Grace and Free Will, and of Redemption as an Idea, not as an historical event.[10]

Such thinking meant that he could neither take orders nor remain much longer within the framework of an Oxford tutorship. In mid-1846 Arthur had already warned Provost Hawkins that he would not proceed to orders and enquired whether he might be allowed to become a part-time tutor – to which the answer was a firm negative. In the winter of 1847 he offered Hawkins his resignation from the tutorial post, to become effective at a point most convenient to the College. Hawkins made a sustained and honourable effort to dissuade him, without success; and wrote sadly in January 1848, 'In truth you were not born for *speculation*. I am not saying a word against full and fair enquiry. But we are sent into this world not so much to speculate as to serve God and serve man.' It was agreed that

Arthur's resignation from the tutorship would become effective in May that year, while he would continue to hold his Fellowship until the end of its normal term in October.[11]

The conversations begun in the Lake District in the summer of 1845 meant that Annie was fully aware of the evolution of Arthur's thought and belief. She continued to have the highest regard for his judgement, although she was never tempted to follow him towards his ultimate detachment from Christian belief and worship. Nevertheless, as Arthur laboured towards decision and public statement, Annie remained his staunch and sympathetic supporter, writing, 'He is the comfort and joy of my life; it is for him, and from him, that I am incited to seek after all that is lovely and of good report. Preach no sermons, give no precepts, but set before me a holy, beautiful example, and my heart will burn within me, and I shall surely long and strive to follow it.'[12] In the simplicity and clarity of her distinction between moral conduct and the labyrinth of doctrine she understood and conveyed his position more clearly than sometimes he did himself. Their mother, however, was shocked and distressed by Arthur's decision, failing to appreciate the nuances of his thought, feeling keenly the loss of face and anxious about the financial implications. Here he was, forgoing a modest but regular stipend, at a point when their investment income was being squeezed and the economic situation as a whole looked threatening. The year 1847 had been one of financial crises not only in England but also in North America and Europe, and in 1848 labour unrest and political agitation culminated in the great gathering on Kennington Common in London in support of the People's Charter. In the course of 1848 Annie and her mother moved house yet again within Liverpool, this time to 51 Vine Street, presumably smaller and more economical to run even than 22 Canterbury Street.[13]

Perhaps Annie argued the case for school-keeping again to her mother: certainly by now she was beginning to think and consider her own strengths and weaknesses in a more systematic way. In April 1847 she wrote, 'I still hanker after a more decided vocation of teaching but I still greatly doubt my abilities for such an office. I fear I could not keep order & being besides altogether too hot-tempered & overbearing when I have the full swing of power in my own hands. I have learnt to accommodate myself to others pretty much so I can work fairly as an occasional assistant.' Long after, her niece, reading through her aunt's journals of the 1840s, contrasted the controlled, steady determination of the last years of the decade with the 'eager hot girlhood' and intense and self-absorbed personal religion of the first years.[14] The plan which began to take shape was for Annie to seek training before attempting to work systematically in a school again. There is a first hint of this in an exchange with Arthur in July 1847. Whatever it was Annie had proposed, he responded, 'I will consider the subject you speak of, my dear; on the whole I should incline to study arithmetic and grammar, *perhaps*; – but you must remember that a great advantage is given by *any sort of cultivation*.' In the pursuit of cultivation Annie attempted to add music lessons to the drawing and painting, but in the process discovered an aesthetic blind spot. She persevered with the overall plan, however. Fifteen months later, it was all worked out and Annie had taken advantage of the hiatus in Arthur's life and plans to persuade him to spend the bulk of the time from mid-January to late April 1849 at home with their mother while she herself underwent training in London.[15]

In planning her training, Annie sought the guidance and support of the first Dissenter to be appointed Her Majesty's Inspector of Schools, the Rev. J. D. Morell. Her letter of application to Henry Dunn, the Secretary of the British and Foreign School Society, formally endorsed by a note from Arthur, and supported by a testimonial from her local vicar, sets out her situation very fairly.

Having heard of your school from Mr Morell, the Government Inspector, when he was here a short time since; I beg to apply through you for admittance as a resident student in the female department. I am 28 years of age, my health is & has been invariably good. I am unmarried & reside with my Mother who is a widow, & I have no employment except visiting schools & the poor.

I have had a pretty fair English Education but want improvement in Grammar, Writing and Arithmetic. I am totally ignorant of music and singing – Drawing I have practised a little.

I have been brought up to the Church – I have been accustomed to teach in a Sunday School for the last 11 years, have also visited day schools & taught at my own home. It is not for pecuniary reasons that I enter upon the business of teaching, but from a desire of engaging in a useful and congenial employment. At the same time, I should wish to study economy in my expences if I should be admitted into your establishment, where I could only, I believe, remain three months.

At the conclusion of that time I should desire to be at my own disposal as it may not be convenient to my Mother to leave this place for some time. If it could be allowed, I should like to omit attending some of the classes & to devote the spare time to singing & drawing.

I am anxious to be admitted as early next year as possible & hope to be favoured with an early answer to this communication.

In preparing to support her application, Morell had taken the trouble to get her to write some specimen answers to recent test papers set for trainee teachers and he wrote approvingly of her 'ability & competency'.[16]

The route Annie was trying to take was not an uncommon one. The model for the education of a gentlewoman was a domestic one in these years: ladies were best educated by their mothers, exactly as Annie herself had been. In the education of their daughter, as in the education of their sons, the Cloughs conformed to the prevailing convention. However, ideal and reality by no means always matched and schools for middle-class girls were beginning to proliferate, often in their rhetoric making deft use of the dominant model and presenting themselves as substitute homes. Many middle-class women who knew that, if they did not marry, they would have to support themselves – and sometimes their families – by teaching in such a school, prepared themselves through a process of apprenticeship, where possible attending a reputable school as pupil, working in one as an assistant, spending time in France or Belgium as an *assistante*: a process not dissimilar from that which Annie had tried to telescope during the autumn of 1841, before she set up her first school at home. A minority of women also took themselves to the training institutions which were growing up in London in this period. Both the two societies which organised and supported elementary schools for the working class, the Anglican National Society and the Dissenter-supported British and Foreign School Society, had opened Normal – training – Schools; and although the majority of their trainees came from the upper working class and would return to elementary schools to teach the working class, a small but significant number were boarding school mistresses and private governesses, who expected to teach middle-class girls.[17] Annie was only unusual in explaining that she didn't *have* to teach and as an Anglican applying to the British and Foreign School Society. She was promptly accepted and began her training in the second half of January 1849 at the BFSS's Normal School in Borough Road in south London.

In spite of misgivings expressed by Arthur about the adequacy and propriety of lodgings, Annie did settle in lodgings close to Borough Road, sharing them with a Miss Palmer, also attending the Normal School, and her mother: and the two trainees enjoyed comparing notes on school and other experiences. The work at Borough Road was both varied and demanding, a mixture of lectures, written work, and teaching practice and observation in the attached school. Annie did her best to improve her skills in Singing, Arithmetic and Grammar; but overall, she found the environment a stressful one:

The unruliness of the children at the Boro' Road was very painful . . . It seemed to be the rule to do everything by excessive energy and excitement, which certainly develops some good qualities, as quickness and spirit. But, at the same time, the children learn to prize these qualities too highly, and become self-conceited and vain . . . They are also on the whole very open and truthful and affectionate. But they are rude and overbearing to each other and to the teachers, are very much wanting in reverence, and are self-conceited and vain of their learning, which may partly proceed from the ignorance of many of the teachers. They are totally ignorant of any principle of obedience & very much wanting in nice ways & nice manners. At the same time their great openness and genuineness of character often makes them pleasing.

She taught at least three demonstration lessons, the first being bad and the third a success; but once more she felt that the vehemence of her own interest and enthusiasm let her down – 'my fault lies in not being sufficiently quiet and collected . . . I have great deficiency in power of expression till I get hot in my subject, and then I am not simple enough.'[18]

Through a growing friendship with Mary Twining, née Arnold, one of the sisters of Matt and Tom, Annie heard about the Home and Colonial School Society Institution. This had been founded in 1836 to train teachers, especially those of very young children, on the principles set down by Pestalozzi: in the 1850s it would work to bring the ideas of Froebel to an English audience also. She decided to continue her training with a spell there, moved her lodgings, and liked it much better. There was more overt religion; but it was a happier and less noisy place. 'I should fancy the teachers had not so much in them, nor so much mechanical knowledge as the Boro' R people, but that they understand things better, & that from their lessons they [*sic* – presumably the children] cd. acquire a greater love for information.' Much later she would sum up the contrast between the two institutions for her friend Alice Bonham Carter: 'Boro' Road was a valuable experience, but most squalid both for body & mind, none of the teachers had any aim beyond making a living. The Home & Colonial was quite different, like going into another air.'[19]

Annie would have liked to stay in London, after her three months of training, looking for a post in a school and closer to Arthur, perhaps making a home for him. She had been indefatigable in seeing as much of London as she could while she was there. In January 1849, just before she began at Borough Road, and again at the end of March and beginning of April, before her return to Liverpool, she enjoyed sharing Arthur's lodgings and meeting his friends. But the easy relationship of 1845 and 1846 had faded and already by the summer of 1847 the old gap and the sense of constraint between them had re-emerged. Returning from her visit to the Lake District, where Arthur had joined them briefly, Annie had written anxiously in July 1847, 'I hope there is nothing decidedly wrong in me that keeps him distant from me.' As always, she blamed herself, her shyness and self-consciousness when they were together, the deficiencies in her power of expression. Yet the decision to quit Oriel, the public buzz which followed – and the question of what next – had all taken their toll: and Annie's account of Arthur in the spring of 1849 conveys the burden of his depression: 'People seem very fond of Arthur & to think a good deal of him. But Arthur does not seem to mind much about people when they don't seem to suit him exactly & he gets worried & worn out with the continual talking about Religious Matters & I think too the pomp & grandeur trouble him . . . He is evidently very much out of spirits.'[20]

Arthur himself assured Annie that if he could secure a small regular income he would much prefer to live in Liverpool with them, and he argued that their mother would not be able to cope with a move to London.[21] But it is doubtful whether he actually wanted his mother and sister on his very doorstep, in London or in Liverpool. As he struggled to set a new direction for himself after leaving Oxford in the autumn of 1848, he needed to feel that his responsibilities were diminished, not increased. London networks and intelligence offered the best hope of employment and at the beginning of 1849 he was offered the post of Warden of University Hall, in London, a new residential hall for students attending University College, supported in the main by the Unitarians but also by other Dissenting groups. The post was to be taken up in the autumn. In the meantime, living in lodgings in London brought him contact with his friends, when he chose; easy access to publication for the poetry he had been writing; and freedom to travel. In the summer of 1848 he had escaped from the theological hothouse of Oxford to spend several exciting weeks in Paris during the fall of the July Monarchy and the creation of the Second Republic. That autumn his first long narrative poem, *The Bothie of Tober-Na-Vuolich*, about the experiences of a group of young men on a reading party in the Scottish Highlands, was published, to be followed in January 1849 by twenty-six shorter poems in a collection called *Ambarvalia*, published with his friend Thomas Burbidge. In April 1849, as soon as Annie was ready to return home to Liverpool, Arthur set off for Italy. There he found himself besieged in Rome by the invading French troops, who brought about the downfall of the short-lived Roman Republic.[22] Left behind, Annie could only wrestle with her fundamental anxiety: 'I have only wanted the certainty that he really does love me. How has my heart yearned for it. I feel so often I cannot be sure of it because I don't feel worthy of it.'[23]

The question of a move to London was reopened, however, by their mother, in the spring of 1850, once Arthur had taken up his post at University Hall. He did his best to combat the suggestion, stressing that his appointment might not prove permanent, arguing somewhat disingenuously that she and Annie would find it difficult to make friends, and, with greater truth, that it would be very hard to find a respectable house to rent in London for the sum they were paying in Liverpool. About Annie's hopes and plans, he was patronising:

To return to Annie – I quite agree with you that her love of schooling runs away with her – and it might possibly cure her to be here. But do you really expect it will? I can't say I do. She will be going into horrid places here as there: and she will have little or nothing else to do. Spite of fleas and noise and teetotums and all that, I think it is well enough that she confines herself on the whole to seeing the dirty children in the way she does at present. Then she has the occupation, to divert her, of this school of Augusta's. I had some hope of the removal here being sufficient to turn her into another direction. But since I came I have changed my mind. She won't form many new friendships: she is past 30 too, and I don't well see what better occupation one can expect for her than what she has at present.[24]

It is a mean-spirited view of a woman who, to the end of her life, had an absorbing interest in the social world around her and made friends in the most unlikely places. One has to remind oneself that he was responding to their mother – and hope that Annie did not see the letter.

By this time she had, characteristically, faced up to the destruction of her hopes of a life in London and had thrown herself back into her work in Liverpool.[25] She continued to see 'the dirty children': and 'this school of Augusta's' was in fact a rewarding joint venture. In an all-too-familiar scenario, Augusta Wotherspoon's father had suffered reverses in business and her marriage to Migault had been delayed. She came to live with Annie and her mother in Vine Street and together she and Annie ran a school for two years, the profits from which formed Augusta's 'dowry'. When she and Migault married, they moved to Germany, where, in future years, Annie would visit them: their daughter, Annie Gabrielle Migault, born in 1853, would be one of Annie Clough's first five students at Cambridge in 1871.[26]

Training, the school with Augusta, were all indications that at last the balance of power within the immediate family was tilting in Annie's direction. Once Augusta was settled, Annie reopened the question of a move from Liverpool. Charles and Margaret had spent a second year in Italy and, when they returned, settled in North Wales.[27] There is no indication that they took any particular view on where Annie and her mother should live. In the meantime, such authority in pronouncing on these matters as Arthur had once had was fast waning, reflecting the growing divergence between his life and that of the Liverpool household.

The months in Italy in 1849 had contributed in important ways to the process of divergence, although it is easier to claim that the experience *was* important than to explain *how* it was important. The evidence is oblique, highly coded, for it is Arthur's finest poem, *Amours de Voyage*. The sequence of letters which form the poem's five cantos records the experiences of a group of English travellers, a young man, Claude, travelling on his own, and a family, the Trevellyns, thrown together as they are caught up in the failed Roman revolution and the French invasion: and in recounting these experiences, the poem interweaves the personal and the political. Inferring an author's own thoughts and attitudes from those expressed by his actors is a perilous business, although that has not deterred successive biographers and critics from trying, and most have seen the poem as essentially autobiographical. Ascribing Claude's political stance to Arthur seems not unfair, if only because the narrative of Arthur's letters to his male friends in England during these months can be deployed beside the poem. Like many Englishmen, he was affronted that his own government, having made loud noises in support of Italian liberty, did nothing to deter the French from intervening to crush the infant republic. Like many men the world over, he was shaken by the contrast between high ideals and the squalid, often apparently disorganised business of fighting and skirmishing, especially in a setting of such magnificence. He had finally to decide whether he himself would fight – and found himself wanting: his liberal sympathies had their limits.

However the core of the poem is a personal rather than a political dilemma: almost in spite of himself, Claude begins to warm intellectually and personally to Mary, one of the Trevellyn daughters. How far should he take the relationship? Should he declare himself as a suitor? He has almost reached the point of declaration when an inept and possibly coarse intervention from another young man, the fiancé of another of the daughters, causes him to recoil and retreat. By the time he recovers his equilibrium and concludes that nevertheless he should try, the Trevellyns have left Rome; and although he follows, a series of confusions prevents him catching up with them, and his opportunity is lost for ever. How far Claude's hesitations, scruples, extreme fastidiousness in these personal relations can be seen as reflecting Arthur's own hesitations and scruples is much more difficult to determine. Charles Eliot Norton, the American critic and art historian, and the most sympathetic of Arthur's friends, wrote later after his death:

The spirit of the poem is thoroughly characteristic of its author, and the speculative, analytic turn of his mind is represented in many passages of the letters of the imaginary hero. Had he been writing in his own name, he could not have uttered his inmost conviction more distinctly, or have given the clue to his interior life more openly, than in the following verses:-

> 'I will look straight out, see things, not try to evade them:
> Fact shall be Fact for me; and the Truth the Truth as ever,
> Flexible, changeable, vague, and multiform and doubtful.'

Or, again:-

> 'Ah, the key of our life, that passes all wards, opens all locks,
> Is not *I will*, but *I must*. I must, – I must, – and I do it.'[28]

Here is the subtlety, here the sense of duty, which unflinchingly exposes the limitations of Claude's liberal political stance. But was Arthur really presenting himself as so uncertain, so hesitant, so ultimately spineless in his relations with women? If so, Claude becomes less of an 'imaginary hero' than an 'imaginary anti-hero'. It is a simplistic reading, which does less than justice to Arthur's sensibility and acute sense of self. No one knows whether Mary Trevellyn had any basis in reality – and perhaps it matters little. One might argue instead that while Arthur recognised the uncertainties and the extreme fastidiousness which tended to characterise his relationships with middle-class women, the poem is a fictional exploration of where, pushed to extremes, such traits might lead.

Arthur's world had been predominantly a homosocial one from the age of seven, a boarder at prep school, then at Rugby and subsequently an undergraduate at Oxford. The absence of his mother and sister in Charleston until 1836 dramatised its single-sex nature: but more generally, his experience in these respects was the norm. Establishing reasonable social relations with women, especially those of their own class, was therefore something many young men had to work at, in a society which was quick to magnify friendly exchanges into meaning much more. That obsessive observer of mid-Victorian womanhood, the Chancery barrister A. J. Munby, took the view that friendship was impossible between men and women of the same class, commenting that 'modesty is an affair of *class* as well as of sex'; and the novelist Anthony Trollope had one of his briefless barristers remark, 'I do not dare to think of a young woman of my own rank except as a creature that must be foreign to me. I cannot make such a one a friend as I would a man, because I should be in love with her at once. And I do not dare to be in love because I would not see a wife and children starve.'[29] Arthur had touched on such issues before, in his poem *The Bothie*, where his hero, Philip, falls in love with a peasant girl, Elspie, and eventually bears her away to what is optimistically envisaged as the classless colonial society of New Zealand. Claude's failure to declare his feelings for Mary in *Amours de Voyage* could be read not as damning self-indictment but rather as a study in the obstacles in the way of moving from liking to love within the tight conventions of mid-Victorian society.

Whatever there was of Arthur in Claude, the principal importance of the poem lies in its power and what that signals about his maturity as a poet. Its images are vivid, merciless, sometimes cruel, conveyed in a language strikingly conversational, supple, accessible, modern-sounding, moving easily over, almost veiling, the underlying structure of its hexameters. It is an entirely distinctive voice, like no other in mid-Victorian poetry. As V. S. Pritchett put it, 'in an age of professional trumpets, [Clough] engaged the dubious, the personal, the inquiring, the definite but conversational flute'.[30] The bulk of the poem was first drafted in 1849 and 1850. Predictably, the two English friends to whom he showed it, J. C. Shairp and Matt Arnold, didn't like it. It was Charles Eliot Norton who would finally persuade him to publish it, in the *Atlantic Monthly* for 1858.[31]

With the content and form of this long poem already taking shape in his head, Arthur had returned to London in September 1849, to take up his duties at University Hall. The suspicion that his Wardenship might prove short-lived, expressed to his mother, proved correct. There was friction with Council members almost from the beginning, over the disciplining of students and his refusal to market the Hall aggressively, thereby increasing its numbers and improving its finances. The sub-text was the anxiety of the Unitarian-dominated Council that Arthur's loss of faith might influence the students for whom he was responsible. When, in the autumn of 1851, he was courteous enough to inform the Council that he was a candidate for a professorship of classics in Sydney, they seized the opportunity to demand his resignation – and he was too disaffected and too polite to fight. He did not secure the Sydney chair; but he left University Hall in the spring of 1852, once more reducing his regular income almost to nothing.[32] Yet at the same time he had entered into a relationship which made the need for a good regular income more pressing than ever before. In the course of 1850 he had met Blanche Mary Shore Smith, the twenty-two-year-old eldest daughter of the well-to-do Unitarian banker and landowner Samuel Smith and his wife Mary (Mai), née Shore. Friendship ripened gradually into love.

3 Arthur Hugh Clough in the 1850s, drawing, English school

Whatever hesitations Arthur may have felt, Blanche was determined and tenacious in pursuing and sustaining the relationship – no Mary Trevellyn she. She had a little money of her own, but her father wished to protect her from fortune-hunters. Samuel would not give his consent to their marriage unless and until Arthur could show he expected a regular income of £500 a year. Arthur mobilised all his friends, especially the Balliol network, to seek out opportunities, particularly in government service. From the end of the 1840s young graduates, Balliol men to the fore, had begun to colonise government posts, contributing in the process to the emergence of a new kind of civil servant, well-educated, efficient, but often detached from the policies he was helping to formulate and operate.[33] Meanwhile, in October 1852, Arthur himself set off for New England, to see what the prospects might be there for making a better and more regular living by writing and teaching.[34]

The events of 1849–52 in Arthur's life, both interior and exterior, took him decisively away from the Liverpool household: there could no longer be any question of Annie and her mother moving house to provide a home for him or even simply to be closer to him. The emotional gap between Arthur and Annie continued to widen and Blanche's arrival on the scene inevitably accelerated the process. Annie was also increasingly conscious that she carried the primary responsibility for the care of her mother, who had recently had a minor stroke.[35] By the time Arthur set sail for Boston, Annie had already acted. In the summer of 1852 she and her mother finally moved from smoky, grimy Liverpool and the 'mud-puddle' of the Mersey, to the Lake District, to a newly built solid stone house, on the edge of Ambleside. The house still stands, high up on the side of the hill called Eller Rigg, and although Ambleside has crept upwards to its skirts, the views across Windermere towards the Langdale Pikes remain superb. Visiting in 1856, Charles Eliot Norton would contend that only the Wordsworths' house, Rydal Mount, was better situated.[36] Annie and her mother bought the house, which they christened Eller How, with the help of a mortgage from the local Building Society, which had been launched by the writer Harriet Martineau.[37] At last there was an end to the progression from one small rented house to another, even smaller, which had characterised the years in Liverpool since 1841 – and indeed, to a lesser degree, since 1836. The physical disappearance of those houses – and, indeed, of most of the streets in which they stood – is primarily a consequence of the destruction of two World Wars. But it is difficult not also to see it as a metaphor for the precariousness of much of Annie's and her mother's lives in those years.

The years in Ambleside were stable yet crowded for Annie. Stable, because at last she and her mother had a secure and beautiful environment; crowded, because she immediately engaged with the life of the community – soon there would be another school; and in the end stressful, as her mother's health deteriorated. They are also the years in which Annie's own voice is most difficult to hear. No correspondence, no journals – if she kept them – have survived. We are almost wholly dependent on the oral recollections of those who knew her in those years, gathered by her niece Thena, for a *Memoir* published in 1897. It is Thena's contention that this period was one of frustration and unhappiness for Annie, who longed for greater things and a larger stage. This interpretation owes much to hindsight, an awareness of the greater things and larger stage which *were* to come.[38] Setting this knowledge aside and simply comparing life at Eller How with the preceding decade in Liverpool, marked as that had been by the deaths of George and James, severe financial difficulty and the conflicts over school-keeping, the Ambleside years begin to look rather different. And as Thena herself recognised, the woman running the household at Eller How was the mature woman, clear about her own strengths and weaknesses, about her own priorities, maintaining and pursuing them with a controlled determination. Their servant during all of that time expressed it thus: 'Miss Clough must always have her way, but it was a good way.'[39] Anyone less likely than Annie to repine over the might-have-beens and to fail to address the opportunities at hand it would be difficult to imagine: remember how she had coped with the forced ending of her school in 1846. Ambleside may have been a small country stage – 'life on a remote hill-top', Thena disparagingly called it – but Annie acted upon it with all her considerable vigour.

Annie and her mother built immediately on existing friendships within the community. The Claudes, who witnessed the will which Anne Perfect Clough made in the summer of 1852,[40] had their house on the other side of the village and Dr Arnold's widow and her unmarried daughters still occupied their house and provided a base for their family at Fox How, to the south. Harriet Martineau, who lived at the foot of Eller Rigg, was generous in lending books and involving Annie in other ways. In 1848 she had begun what turned into a series of annual winter lectures to the 'Mechanics of Ambleside', to which 'no gentry were admitted, except two or three friends who took tea with me and went as my staff'. Annie was privileged, however, in being among those friends who went to tea and then on to the lecture, helping especially to send signals about audibility to the lecturer, whose profound deafness made it difficult for her to judge.[41]

Annie also began to look for involvement with a school and teaching. Her first thought, apparently, had been to help at the existing elementary schools: but there were unspecified difficulties.[42] She began to think once more, therefore, about running her own school. She turned her attention to children a little further up the social scale, children of friends and acquaintances, the children of substantial farmers and tradespeople, who didn't want their children to mix with the children of agricultural labourers in the elementary school but could find little else that was affordable. Eller How is large, with room for some boarders, and on the ground floor a great flagged central hall which could and did make a schoolroom.[43] Annie began with a couple of boarders and several day pupils and gradually built up to a school of between twenty and thirty pupils, mostly girls between six and sixteen, but also a handful of boys, up to the age of eleven. Almost all the pupils were day pupils, but there seem always to have been a couple of boarders. The 1861 Census recorded two sisters boarding, Eliza and Frances Bellasis, aged respectively eight and eleven.[44]

According to Thena Clough, one of the first boarders had been Mary Arnold, daughter of Arthur's friend Tom, who had been living with her grandmother at Fox How. In fact, Mary, who would become the best-selling novelist Mrs Humphry Ward, boarded from 1858 to 1860, and shared her time at Eller How with Sophie Bellasis, probably the older sister of Eliza and Frances.[45] Mary was a disturbed and lonely little girl, with a terrifying capacity for destructive tantrums, which no one seemed able to curb. Annie recognised the distress under the hysterical bouts of temper and resisted the brisk advice of Jane Claude to empty a bucket of water over the child. Mary Arnold's behaviour was so extreme that it was unfair of Jane to extrapolate from these episodes to argue to Thena that Annie could not control children. Nevertheless Jane Ratcliffe, née Wilkinson, one of the assistant teachers who came to work with Annie, agreed that in her gentle, low-voiced fashion, she was often too lenient.[46] Despite the experience at Borough Road and the Home and Colonial, it seems she never learnt to command groups of children easily; although the wide age range must always have complicated such efforts. Selina Fleming, née Healey, the other assistant, whom Annie recruited from the Home and Colonial in 1861, described the general hubbub, particularly in the afternoons, when every child prepared her lessons for the next day in any way she chose. Each child and each teacher had her own timetable, written out personally for her by Annie. Yet Annie responded graciously and gratefully to the moves which Selina proposed towards more orderly working in the afternoons and a common timetable.[47]

The obverse of these difficulties with groups was the warm personal relationships Annie developed with the majority of the children. She knew them and their families and had a marvellous capacity always to remember the details correctly: at midday dinner, 'she found time to inquire after dogs and dolls with profoundest sympathy'. Many of them came to feel that she rejoiced personally at every achievement and was correspondingly hurt and distressed by each failure or naughtiness. One former

4 Annie Clough in maturity, photographed by Eveleen Myers

pupil described to Thena her 'capture'. On first meeting Annie, she was frightened:

The dark eyes were keen and searching, and the mouth, I thought, looked severe, and her hair, too, was strange, silvery-white in front and surmounted by a coronal of heavy black plaits. But my doubts and fear were speedily laid to rest as a soft hand drew me nearer, my curls were pushed back around my face, and I saw the bright eyes soften as they met mine, and the lips parted in a smile, and the gentle caress and low-spoken welcome completed my capture and contentment. Of course I did not know then that I had fallen in love with my new preceptress, but I know that during the time I was her pupil, I would have endured any other kind of pain rather than that of incurring her displeasure, and taken any kind of trouble to win her approval.[48]

Sophie Bellasis, gathering her memories much later, remembered no smiles, but a perfect even-handedness, which commended itself to the children.

Although she was so strict we liked her, because she was so perfectly just. She never broke her word, nor even let us off any punishment, she gave us not a hair's breadth; but then she never punished us unless we deserved it. She had no favourites . . . and never called us stupid when we made blunders; neither would she jump to conclusions, though it might appear that a child had done something wrong when it had not, but she would inquire and make allowances. I never knew her to lose her temper, or bully, or even raise her voice, so that although she was so stern and precise and never smiled, we were very fond of her

The unanimity about the low voice and the perfect control are striking, given the injunctions to herself to control her over-hasty temper which run through Annie's journals of the 1840s. Sophie too recalled Annie's powerful dark eyes, dramatic hair – and always the plain black dress, except once, at a children's dance at Mrs Claude's, 'when she wore a grey silk and we looked at her with the greatest admiration all the evening'.[49]

French and music were taught by visiting masters; otherwise Annie shouldered the burden of the teaching in English, arithmetic, history and geography herself. Once the assistants arrived, she handed over English grammar and arithmetic with relief; but she continued with history and geography, making her lessons absorbing with illustrations from her own reading and travels.[50] The fees for day pupils were thirty shillings a quarter; and it was Thena's view that the school never did more than cover its costs. Financial anxieties were finally removed, however, at the end of 1857, when Anne Clough's last surviving brother, William Perfect, died, leaving all his nephews and nieces handsome legacies. Annie felt so rich that in 1860 she was able to head the subscription list for a new building for Ambleside's free boys' school:[51] and the enhanced resources made the employment of help, both in the school and in the household, much easier. These were increasingly needed. In 1855 or 1856 Anne Clough had a second stroke, and although she could still make herself understood, from that time onwards her health continued to deteriorate. A Liverpool friend, Louisa Crofton, came to live in the house to help with the nursing; but the brunt was borne by Annie, who slept in her mother's room. Arthur had by this time returned from New England to a post found by his friends in the Education Department of the Privy Council Office. It did not pay as much as £500 a year; but its regularity and security enabled the rest of Blanche's family to prevail upon her father to consent to their marriage. He came on short visits as often as work and London commitments allowed: and in 1858 he urged that they employ a nurse as well. The household continued to cope; but the last year of Mrs Clough's life was exhausting and distressing for everyone, including the poor patient. She was endlessly fretful, unable to rest or to concentrate on anything, and she used to call Annie's name for hours at a stretch. She was finally released by death on 12 June 1860.[52] Now Annie, aged forty, was alone, but financially independent and secure. For the first time in her life, it appeared that she had autonomy and choice.

CHAPTER 4

Family duty

In the immediate aftermath of her mother's death in the summer of 1860, Annie went to stay with Arthur and Blanche in London.[1] This visit brought a change of scene, some cosseting and the diversions represented by her baby niece and nephew, Florence, born in 1858, and Arthur Hugh, born in 1859. Then she returned to Ambleside, to pick up the threads and begin a new school year. Eller How, which she had inherited from her mother, was now quite a substantial establishment. Louisa Crofton remained with her in the house; there were the two little Bellasis boarders and two living-in servants; and by the beginning of 1861, there were also two assistant teachers in residence, Selina Healey and Jane Wilkinson.[2] Their help, as we have seen, freed Annie from teaching the parts of the curriculum about which she felt least secure – the old bugbears of arithmetic and English grammar – and brought a new orderliness into proceedings.

It cannot have escaped her notice, however, that all was not well with Arthur. Blanche was first cousin to the formidable Florence Nightingale, now well launched on her work to change the face of nursing in Britain. Since Florence had no brothers, under a complex entail, first Blanche's mother, then Blanche's brother, Shore, would inherit the Nightingale estate and its two houses, Embley in Hampshire and Lea Hurst in Derbyshire, when W. E. Nightingale, Florence's father, died.[3] The two families were perforce close; but the relationship was also a warm one, further strength-ened by the determined support given to Florence by Blanche's mother, Mai Shore Smith, in the pursuit of all her plans, including the taking of a party of nurses to the Crimea following the outbreak of war between Britain and Russia in the spring of 1854. Florence thought well of Arthur and hers had been one of the voices urging Samuel Smith to allow Arthur and Blanche to marry before Arthur's income reached £500 a year. Her support and her friendship were double-edged swords, however. She had an unrivalled capacity to absorb and exhaust all those who were drawn into her schemes, whoever they were; it was happening to Sidney Herbert,

Secretary of State for War, to Aunt Mai – and to Arthur. By mid-1859 Blanche had been living mostly at Combe Hurst in Surrey, her father's house, with the children, for over a year, while Arthur – and her mother – remained in London, at Florence's beck and call: Samuel Smith was driven to protest on behalf of them both.[4] Arthur had begun to suffer from recurrent colds and sore throats and, more seriously, caught scarlet fever that winter, necessitating a long period of quarantine and then of convalescence.[5] The following year, 1860, was little better; and by its end he had been granted extended leave from the Education Department and packed off to Malvern for two five-week stints of the fashionable water cure.[6]

Blanche was at her best in this sort of situation; fiercely protective, prepared to take on all comers, including Arthur's departmental superiors, and determined to get him away from London – and from Florence Nightingale. The medical advice now favoured sea air and lots of it.[7] In February 1861, as the weather got a little warmer, they set off to the Isle of Wight, where Freshwater had already become a magnet for both literary and artistic figures.[8] Close neighbours were the Tennysons. The poet fathers discussed the controversy generated by the publication in 1860 of *Essays and Reviews*, which challenged rigidly literal interpretations of the Bible and other Christian texts; while the Tennyson boys, nine and seven, 'patronised Florence to her heart's content', as her mother put it.[9] As Arthur walked, played with the children and translated Homer, he gradually regained some stamina. At first they had refused all evening invitations, even from the Tennysons; but as he felt stronger, so they began to be more sociable, dining not only with the Tennysons but also with their other neighbours, Julia Margaret Cameron and her family. Mrs Cameron was already taking an intense interest in photography but had yet to acquire a camera of her own. If the Cloughs were photographed at her behest, sadly no images have survived.[10] One of the contributors to *Essays and Reviews*, Benjamin Jowett, Arthur's Balliol contemporary, not yet Master of the College but increasingly powerful in Oxford and beyond, a nineteenth-century networker *par excellence*, also came to stay.

Encouraged and revivified, Arthur and Blanche began to plan a journey to Italy together, intending to leave the children with Blanche's parents. Then Blanche realised she was pregnant again. Contemporary medical advice was firmly against travel in these circumstances; and in Blanche's case there were particular reasons for caution. She had had two normal pregnancies, but before the births of Florence and Arthur they had lost their first child, a little boy, who was born prematurely in April 1855 and lived only a few hours.[11] So in April 1861, Arthur set off on his own, to follow a different route, crossing the Mediterranean from Marseilles to Athens and then towards Constantinople. Travelling across France, with the help of a courier, he was afflicted by severe neuralgia; but thereafter, although he was on his own, things went more smoothly and he began writing poetry again, after a long interval.

When Arthur returned in late June, Annie had joined Blanche, Blanche's sister Beatrice, and the two children at Lea Hurst, the Nightingale house in Derbyshire, for a summer break from her school. Arthur was deeply sun-burned and bearded and seemed stronger: but Blanche continued anxious, her apprehension deepening as she saw how stressful he found a return to London and discussions with 'Uncle Night' as to which member of the family should now dance attendance on Florence. Arthur hoped to be able to return to work in November and Blanche had already begun negotiations to try to move him sideways in the office, from his post as Private Secretary to the Vice-President, the minister responsible for the Education Department in the Commons, to something less demanding. She also prevailed upon him to seek an extension of his leave.[12] In the meantime, he was packed off south again, Blanche promising to join him as soon as the baby was born.

At one in the morning on 5 August 1861 Blanche gave birth safely to another daughter, reporting that 'Florence and Arthur are both much astounded and kind to it, F. tries hard to nurse it. Baby [as little Arthur was still known] seems to think it was always there.' 'What', she asked, 'is the young lady to be called?' Three days later, from Luchon in the Pyrenees, the reply was despatched, 'I think you must call her *Blanche Athena* – but if you don't like it, I won't insist.'[13] Blanche Athena she became and remained for the rest of her long life.

The Tennysons, whom Arthur had met earlier in the Auvergne, were also now in the Pyrenees, and for the remainder of August and the first weeks of September Arthur remained with them, helping to occupy their two boys while their tutor was away. He was concerned that Blanche should not begin her journey too soon and overtire herself: he suggested October as the earliest date for setting out. She, on the other hand, was in a fever of impatience to see how he really was. Learning that friends of her parents, the geologist and educational reformer Leonard Horner and his family, were travelling through France to Italy, she arranged to come as far as Paris with them, where Arthur met her on 18 September.[14] With hindsight, it is hard to understand why they then wandered as they did through Switzerland, crossing over the Simplon into northern Italy through the first snows, and finally fetching up in Florence, where the Horners were already installed, on

10 October. By that stage Arthur was extremely unwell: a cold, caught in the Italian Lakes, had gone to his chest and the neuralgia had returned. Susan Horner, Leonard's daughter, described him as 'looking very ill with his head quite on one side from a pain in the back of his neck' and he 'quite tottered in walking'.[15] Blanche found an English doctor and some help with the nursing. Lodgings proved a bigger problem as they could only stay in the apartment they had rented initially until the end of the month. Susan and her sister Joanna put a great deal of effort into finding them somewhere else: and they were a great deal less sanguine about Arthur's condition than Blanche. Unbeknownst to her, but with Dr Wilson's full approval, the Horners had written to alert her parents: on 20 October Susan suggested to her that she might send for 'a friend or sister from England', getting her head bitten off for her pains.[16] It was as if Blanche would not believe that Arthur could be that ill. Ten days later, however, on 1 November, Joanna Horner was despatched to telegraph for Annie and Blanche's maid to come out.[17]

Annie and the maid, Jane, reached Florence on 9 November. Arthur had not been told that his sister had been summoned, and at first Dr Wilson thought the shock of seeing her would be too much for him; 'but at night he told Blanch [*sic*] roughly it could do no harm now'. Arthur recognised Annie and, although shaken by the implications of her presence, was glad to see her. She immediately took her share in the nursing, and all through that night of 9–10 November she and Blanche took turns to feed Arthur the soup and wine prescribed by the doctor, to try to give him some strength.[18] On 12 November the doctor called at about eight o'clock, as he had each evening, and saw no change. At ten, Blanche went to lie down, leaving Annie at the bedside. Three-quarters of an hour later, Annie called Blanche: 'He was growing cold – After a little time there came a struggle for breath, for the lungs were paralysed, but it did not last long. Then it became quite peaceful. I gave him a glass of water and he said who is it, Blanche, and kissed me and his sister and sent his love to the children – and then breathed a few times quietly and all was over.'[19]

Arthur died in the early hours of 13 November 1861, aged forty-two. Aided and supported by the Horners, Blanche arranged for casts of his hand and face to be made for a death mask, and Susan sketched his profile in the repose of death.[20] Arrangements were made for his body to be buried in the Protestant Cemetery, following the reading of the Anglican burial service. In taking the decision to send for Annie, Blanche had faced the worst, and now it seemed as if she found a kind of release in a bustle of practical activities, from buying mourning clothes to choosing the words and the carving for the headstone. Annie was much more obviously fragile – and still in shock. It was little more than a year since her mother's death and the preceding months of illness and demanding nursing. With no prior warning, she had been summoned from Ambleside to rattle across Europe by train and diligence, arriving in Florence just in time to witness her beloved brother's last few days of life. At the funeral on 15 November, she was, wrote Susan Horner, 'dreadfully overcome, and almost fainted on our return'.[21] The depths of her distress, her turmoil, her sense that her world was collapsing around her, are conveyed by an extraordinary outpouring on paper two days later. It begins as a letter to an old friend from North Wales, who now lived in the Lake District, Lucy Cumming:

You have heard from Mary Claude of my great affliction. It is only to my sister dear Blanche it can be greater. He has been hers for 7 years & a half. I may say longer while during those long & to me many of them at least very painful years He has been only the distant star that I looked at & longed after but that ever gave me strength & consolation – The rock against which I sheltered myself & lent When the fierce winds of affliction were blowing over me but truly of late I have felt my sheltering rock shake & I have hardly ventured to touch it with the tips of my fingers. But my star has now set my sheltering rock has been swept away into the great ocean of eternity & I am left standing on the shore with the wild waves beating around me & the heavens still dark – It is very sad but I will take courage & gird myself for the struggle. Yes I will gaze on among the clouds where my star has set & it may be that some of the mysteries of the unknown world shall flash on me.

From this point it modulates into a passionate assertion of belief in a life after death: 'My eyes shall penetrate the gloomy vail [*sic*] of death & the assurance shall be mine that he is not dead but passed away – that his spirit still lives'; and then into a prayer to God for strength to continue bravely '& let us live to train up those young children, the fond wife's pledges of his love, to walk in their father's footsteps & in the light of thy countenance'. In her final sentences, Annie has ceased to address Lucy and instead is addressing Blanche:

My sister I thought to write to a friend but my heart deemed it otherwise, to you do I dedicate my words, to you alone. Be comforted . . . Does he still not love you – yes ever – Let us be calm, let us look on the duties of life – they shall not be bitter unto us, we shall find the tree that shall make them sweet – Oh dear sister I write on my knees – I pray for you in my heart. I give you my hand, my love & yet all these are little & as nothing to what you have lost. But still you'll take them – Won't you?[22]

5 Blanche Mary Shore Clough in Florence in the winter of 1861

Whatever went to Lucy Cumming, it was surely not this.[23] Did Blanche ever see this letter or some version of it? The resemblance to outpourings in the journals of the early 1840s is strong; and perhaps this draft is best understood as a journal fragment, written as Annie fought to prevent grief from overwhelming her, in the days following Arthur's death. Physical collapse inevitably followed: and while Annie tried to rest, Blanche devoured the sights and atmosphere of Florence, as if they would bring her closer to Arthur.[24]

Eventually, two days before Christmas 1861, Annie and Blanche set off to travel to England, to Blanche's parents and the children at Combe Hurst in Surrey.[25] Each, in her different way, would have to begin to shape a new course. Annie acknowledged her exhaustion: Dr Wilson, the English doctor in Florence, had already urged her to lead 'a quiet life and not over-exert myself mentally for a while' and she recognised the good sense of this; but it would probably mean giving up her school. Blanche added her voice to the doctor's and she and her parents pressed Annie to make her home with them. Blanche would not give up the London house in Campden Hill Road in Kensington but, particularly while the children were small, expected to spend a good part of the year at Combe Hurst. While feeling that she would 'always be the better for regular work', Annie acknowledged the case for a change of pace and scene; she also saw the care of Arthur's children as a sacred trust; so she accepted the Smiths' invitation.[26]

First, however, she had to wind up her affairs in Ambleside. On her return to Eller How, she greeted all her school-children individually; and despite the distress of those weeks in Florence, she had searched out and brought home some small thing for each one of them.[27] Although relinquishing personal responsibility for the school, Annie did not want to see it end: it was clearly fulfilling a need in the local community and there seemed no reason why it should not continue under the leadership of Selina Healey, shortly to become Mrs Fleming. The proprietary or limited company model, inviting parents and other interested persons to create capital by buying shares in the school, which had been used to create new boys' schools in the first half of the century and would be adopted a decade later by those wanting to create schools for girls, seemed the appropriate one: and Annie took pains to visit everyone and explain what was entailed, to ensure that it got off the ground. It would be a profound disappointment to her when, two years later, this scheme collapsed; although the school continued as a private venture in Mrs Fleming's house until 1894, when it was sold on again.[28] When the school moved, the house itself was sold to Henry and Eleanor Boyle.[29]

It took until April 1862 to make all the arrangements and there were many farewells and gifts. The children combined forces to give her a photograph album and all signed the accompanying note. Mrs Bellasis, mother of the boarders, sent a pretty clock.[30] Then just before she left Ambleside, Annie was presented with a formal Memorial, signed by over seventy of the principal residents, including Harriet Martineau, the Arnolds, the Claudes, and the Quillinans, into whose family Wordsworth's daughter had married, thanking her for her contributions to the community and acknowledging 'the high qualities which you have devoted to the education of the young persons who have been committed to your care'. 'We earnestly hope', they continued, 'that future visits to Ambleside will give you opportunity of seeing good fruit continuing to arise from the seed which you have sown.'[31] In ten years on her 'remote hill-top', Annie had made a considerable impact.

The sequence of events in those first years at Combe Hurst is difficult to establish. The journals used by Thena Clough in her *Memoir* have disappeared, and for a time Annie engaged in little public activity. However, even before she moved south, she had become caught up in Blanche's efforts to shape Arthur's posthumous reputation. The question was more complex than it might appear, because so little of his poetry had been published in his lifetime. He had eventually allowed *Amours de Voyage* to be published in sequential parts in the American periodical *Atlantic Monthly* in the course of 1858. But this, *The Bothie* and the poems of *Ambarvalia* apart, almost all the other poetry of the periods of intense composition between 1848 and 1853, and in the last year of his life, remained unpublished. His American friend Charles Eliot Norton had persuaded him to bring the two long poems, the poems of *Ambarvalia* and some other early poems together for a collected edition, to be published in the United States by Ticknor and Fields of Boston: and all of this material seems to have been in Norton's hands by the end of 1860, when Arthur's illness brought everything to a halt.[32] Blanche had therefore immediately to face a series of questions: should this edition be allowed to go ahead simply as it stood? Should more unpublished work, either from the earlier period or the *Mari Magno* tales, on which he had been working when he died, be added? Should there be an introductory essay, by whom, and what should it contain?

There was no shortage of advice from Arthur's friends: from Tennyson; from F. T. Palgrave, the critic and anthologist, who had followed him as a Balliol undergraduate and been a colleague at the Education Department; from the Positivist Richard Congreve, who had known him at Rugby; from the historian J. A. Froude, who had lost his faith at the same time, but whose break with Oxford – his novel, *The Nemesis of Faith*, was publicly burnt in the quadrangle of Exeter College in February 1849 – had been far more spectacular than Arthur's; and especially from Benjamin Jowett.[33] Blanche seems rather to have enjoyed her dealings with these eminent men of letters, while retaining strong views of her own. There was general agreement that there should be a memorial volume, of which the material agreed for the projected Boston publication would form the core. On everything else, she would make the final decisions. Writing to Annie about the choice of poems, she concluded, 'I must now go by my own feelings I think and on the value of their judgements.'[34] So soon after Arthur's death, Blanche's approach to the choice of additional poems was a conservative one. She had found *Dipsychus* coarse when she read it in manuscript in 1852 and allowed only a few short extracts, presented as individual poems, to go forward.[35] She was hesitant about the inclusion of any of *Mari Magno* because Arthur had never had time to revise it himself, but finally let about half of it be included.[36] After discussion with Jowett, she excluded *Easter Day*, feeling that the second part was not strong enough to cancel out the bleak unbelief of the first.[37] However she resisted Jowett's rather curious suggestion that she might leave out some parts of *The Bothie*, which had been in print for over a decade.[38]

Questions of introduction could not be dealt with in the same ruthless way, unless one was to be omitted altogether. Almost from the beginning, Blanche had been collecting material with a view to a memoir of some kind. In mid-January 1862 she wrote to ask Charles Eliot Norton whether he and other of Arthur's American friends might return his letters, 'not certainly although possibly with a view to doing something with them'. Norton and Ralph Waldo Emerson obliged, as did many of Clough's English friends, excepting Matt Arnold, who had not kept Clough's letters – or said he had not.[39] Blanche and Jowett were at one in considering 'that it wd be better to have something of a life *with* the poems to explain them not separate';[40] but someone was needed to make a selection from the letters and supply linking commentary. One name canvassed was that of Thomas Carlyle, from whom Arthur had carried gifts to Mazzini in Italy in 1849, and with whom he had corresponded throughout his stay in the United States. Annie wasn't sure he was 'exactly the man, but he will be far better than any of Arthur's Oxford friends'.[41]

Throughout these exchanges Blanche took it for granted that Annie would allow her unfettered access to all those of Arthur's letters which she held, and would, moreover, provide an account of Arthur's childhood and adolescence and all she knew about those years before Blanche herself arrived on the scene. Froude had also, more plausibly, been suggested as a possible editor and Blanche was anxious to have Annie's sketch of Arthur's early life before she interviewed him. 'I can't the least tell about Mr Froude till I see him', she continued:

I believe the <u>time</u> would be the difficulty. He need not put his name to it unless he likes; some people wd think he had better not. But I do think we must have some man's help. If I can't get anyone else, I thought of Mr Fisher. He probably couldn't write but he might give help in pulling together.

I think Mr Palgrave may be very useful – even about the Life. About the Poems I believe he is quite the best authority, better than Mr Froude who though very clear and [?] has a certain obliquity of vision, I think.

She was particularly exercised about the way in which Arthur's religious opinions should be treated and was emphatic that there should be 'no discussion of any particular question of doctrine, above all no sort of explanation or apology but if anything an attempt to sketch(?) out what a noble character it was & what a virtuous and useful life he led'. Annie had clearly ventured some suggestions on how these matters might be treated; and Blanche reacted strongly:

all that I object to in your letter which otherwise seems to me very good, is that when you say it will have to be done in a truthful spirit, it looks like saying we are going to publish heterodox opinions or to say his were not so. Now I would if possible try to say in a few words, what he did think, when one can but I would not in the least enter into what he did not think – in the first place his character was decidedly positive & not negative & 2ndly he never did it himself, never left his reasons on record & then I would never condescend to anything the least like an apology.[42]

In the light of such convoluted vehemence, it is little wonder that neither Froude nor Carlyle was to become the author/ editor of 'something of a life'. Moreover 'time' – a target publication date of 1862 – precluded the kind of work Blanche wanted done. What eventually emerged from this flurry was the parallel publication in 1862, in London and Boston, of virtually identical selections of Arthur's poems, those agreed between Arthur and Charles Eliot Norton, with Blanche's few additions, as outlined above. In London the poems were prefaced by a very brief personal memoir by Palgrave and in Boston by an equally brief personal memoir by Charles Eliot Norton. It is not known what Blanche thought of Norton's essay: although the warmth of his personal regard and enthusiasm for Arthur's distinctive poetic voice shine through, perhaps she felt it too far away to register. Predictably, she didn't like the cooler distance of Palgrave's essay:[43] and she continued to gather material for a more extended memoir, which she herself would have privately printed as *Letters and Remains of Arthur Hugh Clough*, in London in 1865.[44]

Material provided by Annie formed the backbone of this memoir. Not only did she hold all the letters that Arthur had written home, she also provided two lengthy sets of recollections, the first covering the years when the family home was in Charleston, the second beginning in 1837, when Arthur went up to Oxford as an undergraduate. Much use has been made of the first of these – 'AJC Recollections from 1822 till June 1836' – in the first chapter of this study; and it was clearly the source upon which Blanche based pages 3–9 of the *Letters and Remains*. Two versions of the second text exist, each headed '1837', one with extensive annotations and amendments in Blanche's hand. With the twenty/twenty vision of hindsight, Annie saw Arthur's undergraduate years as more troubled than his family at home had realised at the time; and Blanche's changes, as she prepared the material she would eventually deploy in the *Letters and Remains*, strengthened this interpretation further. Conversely, recounting Annie's life in these years, in my second chapter, I have made more use of her contemporary diaries than of the two versions of her later text. When, exactly, in the years between 1862 and 1865, the texts for Blanche were drafted, it is impossible to say. Each is lengthy: and although Annie had clearly produced something by the time Blanche interviewed Froude, it was probably a sketch or portion of the seventy-eight-page manuscript the 'Recollections' eventually became. The bulk was probably written once Annie had left Ambleside and was based at Combe Hurst and Kensington.[45] What it cost her to set it all down, so soon after her mother's and Arthur's deaths, we do not know. The 'Recollections' are as much, if not more, about the family as a whole and about life in Charleston as they are about Arthur, and they convey Annie's avid interest in and enjoyment of much of that period of her life. Perhaps it was comfort of a sort to gather the memories together and try to set them down with some system: perhaps it assuaged some of the hurt she had felt in not being able to write about her father's last months. Making sense of what happened to Arthur at Oxford and after must have been harder, the more so as it pulled against her own memories of the periods of distance and inhibition between them, recorded with such sadness in her diaries at the time. Whether she entirely accepted the interpretation gradually shaped by Blanche, that Arthur had been badly destabilised by the early separation from home and mother and that this, enhanced by the moral strenuousness of Arnold's Rugby, equipped him ill for the 'theological tempests', as Palgrave called them, which raged in the Oxford of his day, we do not know. Part of duty for Annie was a generous loyalty.

While she was preparing the *Letters and Remains*, Blanche was also preparing to release more of the unpublished poems. Palgrave's second edition in 1863 contained several new ones, as well as making minor textual changes to poems already published. In 1865 the *Letters and Remains* themselves included four further short poems, among them *Easter Day*, and the whole of *Dipsychus*, at last given its title. Eventually in 1869 she published for the world at large *The Poems and Prose Remains of Arthur Hugh Clough With a*

Selection from His Letters and a Memoir edited by His Wife, in two volumes. This made generally available the biographical material from the privately printed version of 1865, added more letters, added thirty-eight new poems, grouped all the poems in a new order and gave many of them titles for the first time.[46]

There proved to be no place for Annie in this energetic editorial activity: in Blanche's eyes her contribution was finished once she had made available the letters and contributed the recollections. And more generally in these years Blanche made less use of Annie's help and support than Annie had hoped and wanted. Certainly Annie spent a great deal of time with the children: for a spell she taught them herself and was often there with them when the Smiths and Blanche were away. She was, as Blanche's sister put it, 'a standby'. But it was an affluent upper-middle-class household, with plenty of servants and she was not indispensable.[47] Nor, in the event, did Blanche pay much attention to her views on the children, their education and their care. Looking back, Blanche's cousin, Alice Bonham Carter, put it bluntly: 'she [Annie] did not find she was the help & use to BMSC that she had hoped to be. BMSC was not guided by her as to the educ.n of the ch. & while she quite recognized her right to go her own way, she was distressed by it & felt it was better to be away a good deal. She felt she had no right to be at Combe if she was not justifying her existence there.'[48]

As Alice Bonham Carter had noticed, Annie's first use of the enforced leisure was to visit and to maintain her friendships. She spent some time in Ambleside and the Lakes each year, and when Eller How was finally sold she persuaded Louisa Crofton to move to the vicinity of Combe Hurst. She visited the Migaults in Germany, her Clough aunts, who had now removed to Bournemouth, and Charles and Margaret, still in North Wales, with an ever-growing brood of children, whose company she much enjoyed. With Blanche's sister Beatrice, and Alice Bonham Carter's sister Elinor, she travelled in Germany and the Tyrol.[49] When she was at Combe, she was a beneficent but self-effacing presence. The young writer and future historian John Addington Symonds had been sent by Jowett to assist in the preparation of the 1869 volumes: he would describe Blanche memorably as a 'thick-sighted woman'.[50] Of Annie he remarked that 'she usually seemed to slip out of the conversation' – unless the talk turned to educational matters, where 'it was at once clear she was on her own ground'.[51]

For although life at Combe Hurst and in Campden Hill Road had its disappointments, it proved also to have its compensations. Annie found herself in the midst of a group of well-connected, affluent and energetic

6 Thena Clough and her brother Arthur as children

women, to the fore amongst those campaigning to enhance the public work of women. They offered an environment in which Annie could articulate and develop her educational ideas and eventually join forces with campaigners of like mind. Although Blanche had a tendency to treat Annie as part of the furniture, her mother, Mai Shore Smith, and her Bonham Carter cousins, developed a warm appreciation of Annie's qualities. They recognised her commitment to education and to a larger role for women – and shared both: it was on such grounds that Mai Shore Smith had supported her niece, Florence Nightingale. This cousinhood took pains to bring Annie into contact with other women of like mind. Through them she began to get to know the members of the Langham Place set, as they have been called, a group of middle-class women concerned to improve the lot of women on all fronts. Their name comes from the Ladies' Institute at 19 Langham Place in Kensington, a reading and luncheon room – a modest female equivalent of the gentleman's club – which opened its doors in 1860, supported by these women, and where they often met. Among the leading lights were yet another of Mai's nieces, Barbara Leigh Smith Bodichon, Bessie Rayner Parkes, daughter of another distinguished Unitarian family – and Emily Davies, daughter and sister of Anglican clergymen, Annie's complete opposite in every way, yet someone whose life would move increasingly in counterpoint to hers.[52]

The ladies of Langham Place and their periodical, the *English Woman's Journal*, campaigned on a number of fronts: for reform of the law relating to married women's rights and property; for wider employment opportunities for women; for votes for women. In the early 1860s they were focussing increasingly sharply on the inadequacies of the education offered to women, especially middle- and upper-class women. Elementary schools, schools for the working class, the only schools which received any state funding, were mixed, open to girls as well as boys. Single-sex education was the norm for the middle and upper classes; and for the girl destined to become a lady, the domestic model reigned supreme. If she could not be educated at home by her mother – as Annie herself had been – then she might be sent to board at an establishment which presented itself as a second home, and emphasised its modest size, informality, intimacy and family aspect. Such enterprises could range all the way from ones offering trivial 'accomplishments', like Miss Pinkerton's Academy, caricatured by Thackeray in his novel *Vanity Fair*, to the cultivation offered at Avonbank, the school outside Stratford-upon-Avon run by the Byerley sisters, which Elizabeth Stevenson, later Elizabeth Gaskell the novelist, and Samuel Smith's sister Julia had attended.[53] For those girls whose parents could not afford the fees of a boarding school – like the group identified by Annie in and around Ambleside – provision was essentially random, depending on the accident of an Annie, or a Selina Fleming, in the neighbourhood. Only two exemplars of an alternative approach, the large institutional day school for girls, were in existence, both in London: Queen's College, Harley Street, founded in 1848 by F. D. Maurice, and the North London Collegiate School, founded in 1850 by Frances Mary Buss. A first large girls' boarding school had been founded at Cheltenham in 1853 and grew rapidly once Dorothea Beale became Principal in 1858.

Those concerned with the education of middle- and upper-class boys in this period had no ideological difficulty with large institutional frameworks and structures. Instead they focussed on problems of resources, the use and abuse of existing endowments for education, and the unevenness and randomness of provision across the country, an important issue for those parents outside the metropolitan area who could only afford day school fees. Agitation on these matters was growing at the end of the 1850s and the beginning of the 1860s; and the campaign for boys and the campaign for girls fed off each other. The forum which the campaigners shared was the National Association for the Promotion of Social Science, founded in 1857 and intended, as John Stuart Mill was to put it, to 'bring together persons of all opinions consistent with the profession of a desire for social improvement'.[54] Its annual meetings gave members of the Langham Place set opportunities to air their thoughts on law reform issues and women's employment and for men and women to combine to address issues of middle-class education. In the late 1850s the Universities of Oxford and Cambridge had begun to arrange 'local examinations', intended to raise standards in boys' schools around the country and provide parents with some measure of the curriculum and its adequacy in a given school. In October 1862 the Social Science Association formed a committee of men and women to campaign for the opening of these examinations to girls and girls' schools. In 1863 the Cambridge Local Examinations Syndicate experimented with a scheme for girls only; but the Langham ladies, led by Emily Davies and including Annie, petitioned in 1864 for common examinations, and the next year Cambridge agreed.[55]

The Social Science Association had also brought together the voices demanding an investigation of the management of existing educational endowments and resources, resulting in two Royal Commissions, the Clarendon Commission, set up in 1861, to look at the nine foundations of Eton, Winchester, Harrow, Rugby, Charterhouse, Westminster, St Paul's, Merchant Taylors and Shrewsbury; and the Taunton Commission, set up in 1864, to look at all other schools between Eton and its eight 'co-respondents' – Matt Arnold's phrase – and elementary schools for the working class.[56] The assumption had been that this inquiry would look at boys' schools; but there was nothing in their terms of reference so to limit them. Emily Davies took soundings among Commission members and, in the light of these, she and Eliza Bostock organised a Memorial that autumn, asking that girls' schools be included, to which, in January 1865, the Commissioners duly agreed. Among the signatories of the Memorial, led by Arthur's friend A. P. Stanley, biographer of Dr Arnold, Dean of Westminster and Principal of Queen's College, was 'Anne J. Clough, late Manager of the Middle Class School, Ambleside'.[57]

Annie did not put herself forward to give oral evidence to the Commissioners, as did some of the other signatories; but she submitted a short paper, an expanded and rewritten version of which was then published in *Macmillan's Magazine* in 1866, as 'Hints on the Organization of Girls' Schools'.[58] Over twenty years later, she recalled that the ideas in the paper had first been formulated and put down while she was staying with Lucy Cumming, now Lucy Smith, and her husband William, at Dolhyfryd, their cottage on Derwentwater, in the summer of 1865. It was then 'revised by Lucy & taken & published by Macmillan in his journal'.[59] A detailed comparison of the two texts is illuminating: it shows Annie's intense practicality but it also shows how her blunt simplicity might lead to the under-valuing of her and her ideas. The core ideas are exactly the same, but in the article they are not only more fully framed, set in the context of recent provision for girls' education and the work of the Commission, so as to be intelligible to uninformed readers, but also more fully elaborated, as if Lucy had interrogated Annie at length, drawn out the possibilities of her proposals and played them back to her.

The brief text for the Commissioners begins modestly, disclaiming knowledge of the general situation and offering only the fruits of Annie's own experience: 'I am entirely ignorant of the state of education in London, and am therefore not qualified to judge whether my scheme would be either practicable or popular there; but I have some personal knowledge of schools in the country, having managed one for the upper classes in Liverpool, and at Ambleside I conducted one for the children of the tradespeople and farmers.' After further brief remarks on the needs of parents who cannot afford boarding school fees but want something more than the elementary school for their children, the general inadequacy of the teachers in middle-class private schools and the case for the intervention of government, not so much to provide funds as to offer a framework and set standards, she goes straight into her 'Plan'. The article for *Macmillan's* begins by explaining what the Commissioners have been doing and then provides a survey of 'the present state of female education', going on to 'its special defects', 'want of standard' and uneconomical use of resources.

The core of the 'Plan' is the same in both texts. First Annie expresses a hope for the establishment by government of a central supervisory body to coordinate local activity and set standards. In encouraging local initiatives, whether by local government corporations or by individuals organised into proprietary bodies, she sings the virtues of cooperation between schools, to the point where, in larger towns, it might be possible to create one or more central schools, 'with lecture halls and playgrounds attached, and also a library of books of reference for the use of teachers, and another of reading books for the use of the pupils in the schools'. Finally she proposes the attachment to such larger towns of professorships on subjects of general interest – English language and literature, history, science and art – the visiting holders of which might deliver their lectures to groups of schools and their teachers. There are minor variations of detail between the two texts: for example, scholarships to existing schools disappear from the article, but the possible role for the central body in supervising the effective use of any monies available for girls' education is developed there. Both texts suggest that the visiting professors could help to create 'a taste for higher studies and collective instruction', 'a means of bringing both the teachers and the taught under the influence (it is to be hoped) of superior men, who would probably be led to take a greater interest in female education with such increased opportunities of knowing something about it, and using their influence in directing it'.

The largest and most significant difference between the two texts is the elaboration in the article of the proposals for local initiatives and central schools to the point where they substantially qualify if not challenge the accepted image of the good middle-class girls' school as small, intimate and quasi-domestic, not marked by competition or emulation. Small schools, she argues, attempting to teach everything, can waste resources and mean that some things are taught badly. Envisaging the collective study of subjects like history, English grammar, arithmetic, geography, drawing, gymnastics and singing at a central school, she suggests in the article that, 'by thus collecting a considerable number of pupils, it would be possible to pay the teachers more liberally, and to secure a more efficient staff'. Such shared activities, if properly supervised, need in no way undermine the moral authority and example of the teacher in the small school, to which such importance has been attached in the education of girls. In both texts she suggests that 'Assistance would thus be given to private efforts in conducting small schools, and the pupils would still enjoy those advantages of personal influence and personal character specially desirable for girls, united with superior instruction and the pleasurable excitement of receiving it collectively.' So much importance does she attach to these points that, in the article, she repeats them in concluding this section of the discussion, although careful to acknowledge the force of the prevailing ideology:

The encouragement of small schools and private education at home under the care of parents and governesses is of great consequence. The latter, where due attention can be given, is most desirable for girls, especially as they grow older; but there is, we may venture to repeat, always a need of superior guidance and the excitement of collective instruction and companionship to call forth the higher intellectual powers, and give a zest to studies that might otherwise seem dull. Collective instruction also gives the opportunity and the power of securing greater excellence in the teachers.

In writing thus, Annie was being both practical and prescient. The decades of the 1850s and 1860s were the watershed decades in the education of middle- and upper-class girls in England. Before 1850 the domestic model had dominated; from the end of the 1860s schooling for 'ladies' would increasingly be delivered through formal institutional structures, not dissimilar from those delivering schooling for 'gentlemen'. Annie's words capture the period of transition and some of the arguments used to bring it about.[60]

Annie's proposals were also prescient and practical in addressing the question of 'higher studies'. Those campaigning for systematic schooling for girls had already realised that this was integrally linked to the provision of higher – university level – education. Should the bright girl's hopes and ambitions end with secondary school? How were the women teachers of the future to be prepared? Queen's College, Harley Street, had indeed had ambitions to offer 'higher' education; but had found the preparation of its pupils so deficient that it became a school instead. Bedford College, launched a year later, in 1849, by the Unitarian Elizabeth Jesser Reid and her two friends Jane Martineau and Eliza Bostock, began with similar ambitions but met the realities of ill-grounded and ill-disciplined young women students by splitting into two, to form a school and a college.[61] This Bedford strategy, evolved by painful trial and error, in fact pointed the way forward: women would need to proceed on the two fronts simultaneously, and the rise of formal schooling for girls and the provision of higher education for women would feed off each other through the last third of the nineteenth century.

Attempts had already been made to find shelter and support for higher studies for women under the umbrella of the University of London. This body, established by government in 1836, was until 1899 an examining body only, examining and thereby validating the work of students from a variety of institutions, not only in London but also elsewhere in Britain and in the Empire. Why, it was reasoned, should institutions for women – like Bedford College – not come under this umbrella also? There was a series of attempts to secure the admission of women to London examinations and degrees in the course of the 1860s: meanwhile in parallel Emily Davies and her allies were beginning to think about connexions with Oxbridge. The admission of girls to the Cambridge Local Examinations not only had intrinsic importance in setting standards for schools; it was also the first shot in a campaign to engage the interest of Cambridge more generally in the advanced education of women. London, after all, was the parvenu. Cambridge and Oxford were the acknowledged elite institutions, targets of enormous symbolic as well as practical importance for the women. As Janet Browne has put it, 'To attend this kind of university was to step purposefully into the English ruling classes.'[62]

Annie's proposal for visiting professors giving some lectures in large towns was a more modest affair than any of these initiatives; it required neither frontal assault on the Senate and Convocation of the University of London, nor positive support from a Cambridge University Syndicate [Committee]. But it had an immediate practicality: it could be piloted on a voluntary, informal basis virtually straightaway. Similar initiatives were already being shaped in Oxford, by a group led by Mark Pattison, the Rector of Lincoln College, and including Jowett; and the publication of Annie's article generated 'a great correspondence on the subject' and letters of introduction to a host of interested parties.[63] Buoyed up by all of this, in the autumn of 1866 Annie herself set off for Liverpool, the city she knew best, to see what could be done on the ground.[64]

One of her letters of introduction was to Josephine Butler, whose husband, George, had just become the headmaster of Liverpool College. Both Butlers were keen supporters of Annie's proposals; but despite their help, it rapidly became clear that efforts to get local schools for girls to associate and combine would not succeed. The one part of her plan which did command general enthusiasm was the scheme for visiting professors or lecturers. A small committee, with Annie as secretary, was formed and efforts were made to run a trial series of lectures that winter. The lead-time was too short, however, and Annie retreated back to Surrey somewhat disheartened.

Nevertheless Annie's ideas and a visiting lecturers scheme in particular continued to attract interest. In January 1867, at Emily Davies' invitation, she talked to the recently formed London Schoolmistresses' Association; and in March, invited by the Manchester headmistress Elizabeth Wolstenholme, she gave the same paper to the Manchester Schoolmistresses' Association. Elizabeth Wolstenholme, later Elizabeth Wolstenholme Elmy and a redoubtable campaigner for women's suffrage, proved a valuable ally. She had an excellent network of local contacts, was organisationally competent – and counterbalanced the Butlers. For although Annie was always warm in her public praise of Mrs Butler, privately she was anxious. Josephine Butler was elegant and charismatic, and always pursued her own path regardless of others. She had already begun the work of succouring prostitutes which would from 1869 take her into all-out attack on the Contagious Diseases Acts, the legislation which rendered women suspected of prostitution in port and garrison towns liable to compulsory medical inspection and, if infected with venereal disease, to compulsory medical treatment.[65] In the course of this campaign she would be prepared to talk in public about matters of which ladies were supposed to have no cognisance, let alone the vocabulary to describe them; and campaigners on other women's issues increasingly gave her Ladies' National Association a wide berth. Privately they may have applauded her bravery; but publicly they could not risk being smeared by association. This was to come; but Alice Bonham Carter described Annie even in the early days as endeavouring to keep Josephine Butler interested in the lecturers scheme, 'yet afraid of her going too far & mixing other elements; thought too that she liked very much the admiration of the surrounding young men'.[66]

Ladies from Leeds and Sheffield were also represented at the Manchester meeting; and from this emerged agreement to try to organise a course of lectures the following autumn in four cities, Manchester, Liverpool, Leeds and Sheffield, and to associate the schoolmistresses' and educational associations in the four cities in a single body to support and promote such lectures and comparable schemes in the future. This year there proved to be sufficient time and momentum to make a real beginning. They secured their very first lecturer, James Stuart, Fellow of Trinity College, Cambridge, who undertook to deliver a course of lectures on Astronomy in each of the cities. Annie spent August and September of 1867 in Liverpool, staying with Margaret Calder, another old friend who shared her Charleston links, and together they did their utmost to publicise the lectures and to drum up an audience. Supporting reading and written work were set, presenting the local circulating libraries with a new challenge; and before the courses were complete, 'the existing editions of at least two scientific works were exhausted by the demands of the students'. Together the audiences in the four cities totalled 550 people. 'It was pleasant and encouraging to see so many diligent and interested students, and to hear how small knots of young people collected to read together', reported Annie happily.

By the time the North of England Council for Promoting the Higher Education of Women held its first meeting in Leeds in November 1867, Newcastle had joined the other four cities. Educational Associations in the five cities elected two representatives each to the Council, Annie and Josephine Butler being elected to represent Liverpool. The nominated members of the Council were George Butler, J. G. Fitch HMI, a particular ally of Emily Davies, Thomas Markby, Fellow of Trinity Hall, Cambridge and Secretary of the Local Examinations Syndicate, and James Bryce, lawyer and political scientist, Fellow of Oriel College, Oxford, Assistant Commissioner for Lancashire under the Schools Inquiry Commission, who had been advising Annie all year on organisational matters and the search for suitable lecturers.[67] Also in attendance, by special invitation, was another Cambridge man, F. W. H. Myers, psychologist and psychical researcher, who would leave his Trinity Fellowship to become one of Her Majesty's Inspectors of Schools in 1872. Mrs Butler was elected President of the Council and Annie its Secretary; and rules and a prospectus were adopted. The rules declared the function of the Council to be 'to deliberate on questions affecting the improvement and extension of the education of women of the upper and middle classes, and to recommend to the several associations and societies therein represented plans for the promotion of these objects'.

The obvious first step in pursuit of such objectives was to secure and extend the lecture programme. Initially the Council attempted to direct this from the centre; but the associated towns and cities, of which there were soon more than five, all had their own ideas on what and whom they wanted and how things should be arranged. By 1870 the Council had bowed to the inevitable, and although the President and Secretary were on hand to advise and adjudicate when asked, localities were allowed to do their own thing. This acted as no check on growth. In the autumn of 1868 three lecturers lectured in nine towns; by the winter of 1870 lectures were being given at twenty-three centres and some places had begun classes as well. Recognising the extent and buoyancy of demand, Owens College, Manchester, the fledgling university college, opened its lectures to women students in 1869 and Newcastle's College of Science would follow suit a few years later.

The North of England Council's other principal initiative in these years proved a more controversial one. The Cambridge Local Examinations, which could now be taken by girls and girls' schools as well as by boys and boys' schools, were aimed essentially at fifteen- and sixteen-year-olds; there were no examinations of a universally accepted standard for older girls and young women, those over eighteen, a situation which bore particularly hard upon those who wished to enter the labour market as teachers and governesses – and upon their prospective employers and pupils. Annie continued to attach high priority to the adequate training and certification of young women who needed as well as wanted to teach, and addressed the North of England Council on the subject in January 1868.[68] The first suggestion which emerged from the ensuing discussion was that a voluntary examining body, composed of Oxford and Cambridge men favourable to the idea of women's education, should be constituted; but that was soon dropped when it became clear that the Cambridge Local Examinations Syndicate might be persuaded to develop more advanced examinations for women to create a sequence with their existing Local Examinations. For Emily Davies and her close collaborators, however, anything for women only was anathema: equality could only be achieved and be seen to be achieved when what was on offer to women was identical to that offered to men. She found the notion of an equality of difference entirely implausible and rejected also the 'half-a-loaf' argument, that an examination for women only was a beginning and better than nothing at all. Such inflexibility was foreign to Annie's nature; temperament and experience both disposed her to seize any opportunity presented, however imperfect, and make the best of it. Emily Davies did her best to intimidate her and organised furiously against the plan; but Annie stood firm, only commenting ruefully to Blanche, 'If it is possible Miss D will out general us. She is a most formidable and skilful antagonist.'[69]

On this occasion, however, the big battalions were with Annie. The North of England Council submitted two Memorials to the Cambridge Senate, the second supported by the signatures of 550 teachers and 300 interested ladies, and borne to Cambridge by Mrs Butler in person. After further discussion a scheme for women's examinations was drawn up, to begin in 1869 and given a trial for three years. The first results were anxiously awaited. Myers' friend Henry Sidgwick, the Trinity College philosopher, who was one of the examiners, wrote confidentially to Blanche, asking whether Miss Clough knew anything about a Miss Gardiner. 'She is the only one that I have "distinguished" and her work is so good that I am curious about her.' The rest were less exciting; but Sidgwick summarised the eventual examiners' report to the Syndicate for Annie as 'on the whole not discouraging'. Thomas Markby was more expansive, reporting that, in general, the women had done well,

> but they are utterly unpractised in Examinations & consequently commit two great errors – they look at the questions from the first point of view that strikes them, without waiting to think whether it is the right one – and then criticise instead of answering them. Secondly they introduce irrelevant matter. It is very odd that it seems nearly impossible to convince the feminine mind that every question presents two sides, and that the infirmities of human nature are such that every order of things will have its drawbacks.[70]

The young women rapidly mastered the conventions for successful exam answers and both numbers of candidates and standards improved steadily. In 1871 the examinations were confirmed in their existence. Two years later in 1873, in response to public demand, they would be opened to young men as well as to young women and rechristened Higher Locals.

In 1864 Annie had rather diffidently given Emily Davies permission to add her name to the petition asking for girls to be allowed access to the Cambridge Locals, remarking: 'I confess to having an objection to publicity – My school was a very quiet one & grew up slowly. However if naming it will be of use I suppose I must not mind.'[71] By 1870, although she would never – and never wish to – imitate Emily Davies' style or tactics, Annie was prepared to stand up to her in a public arena. The decision to give up her school and to commit herself to the care of her orphaned nephew and nieces had brought fewer personal rewards and opportunities than she had hoped. Yet the larger family circle of which she had now become a part offered many compensations: it was liberal and progressive in its outlook, especially with regard to opportunities for women; and it was affluent and extremely well connected. These enabled her to begin to put her practical experience and her passion for education to work in sketching schemes for a larger, a national canvas. Men like Jowett and Sidgwick, who had been drawn into correspondence with Blanche as she shaped and burnished the icon that was A. H. Clough, poet, now also sent messages to and corresponded with Annie on educational matters. Jowett added a postscript to a letter of August 1868, 'I am glad to see Miss Clough is writing about education. Her scheme has been remarkably successful.'[72] As the organisation and activities of the North of England Council expanded through 1869 and 1870, she was supported by the help and companionship of Elinor

Bonham Carter.[73] Serendipity marked not only Annie's engagement with a new family network but also her emergence on to the national scene. The 1850s and 1860s were the decades in which the dominance of the domestic model for the education of gentlewomen was at last being successfully challenged, when there was an interest in, an eagerness for new ways of addressing this. They were also decades which saw a general questioning of educational structures and provision and the first stirrings of a concern about wider access. Middle-class women were part of this and among the first beneficiaries; but the ripples would spread wider, eventually reaching men and women of the working class. Annie had not aggressively sought her opportunities: but when they presented themselves, she recognised and took them. By 1870 she was becoming nationally known as an authority on the education of women and one who quietly, with disarming modesty, could make things happen.

CHAPTER 5

The beginnings of Newnham

Acquaintance with Jowett had come about through Arthur: Arthur's life and work also provided the means for Blanche and Annie to get to know Henry Sidgwick, although in a much more complex way. The two men did not meet during Arthur's lifetime. Henry, born in 1838, was of a later generation at Rugby, and went from there to Trinity College, Cambridge in October 1855. Certainly he knew of Arthur: apart from any Rugby stories, the Sidgwick sons and their widowed mother had rented Eller How from Annie for some weeks in the summer of 1861; and Henry knew Arthur's poetry well.[1] Learning of the private publication of the *Letters and Remains*, he asked his friend, the barrister Godfrey Lushington, who had married Blanche's sister Beatrice in 1865, if Blanche might be prevailed upon to send him a copy, which she was pleased to do. The warmth and sensitive intelligence of his response was all that she could have wished. Henry Sidgwick wrote that he saw Arthur as 'the one true disciple of Wordsworth, with a far deeper interest than Wordsworth in the fundamental problems of human life, and a more subtle, more cultivated intellect'. In Arthur's poetry, he continued, 'irony and sympathy – for all that is not base – seem indissolubly blended, and he never loses that judicial fairness in balancing conflicting influences, which we demand from a philosopher, but hardly expect from a poet'. Arthur's unique quality, he concluded, was his capacity to interpret exquisitely 'one phase of human nature – the youthful mind anxiously considering the life that is before it'.[2]

From this first exchange in 1866 grew regular correspondence and visits. Henry took a great interest in the preparation of the volumes published in 1869, especially as J. A. Symonds, who had been sent by Jowett to help Blanche, had become a particular friend of his; and he arranged to review them at length in the *Westminster Review*. He was stalwart in his insistence on the outstanding quality of *Amours de Voyage* but critical of the unfinished *Mari Magno* tales. Blanche, who was seriously unwell in the autumn of 1869, characteristically took issue with him on various points of emphasis and detail – without persuading him to shift his position very much. With cheerful politeness, he had predicted in August, 'How you will dislike my article'; yet their friendship was unimpaired.[3] Unlike Jowett, who failed to keep a note of irritation out of some of his letters to Blanche, Henry sustained a tone which was unfailingly polite, taking her seriously intellectually, never patronising yet occasionally gently teasing. It helped that he knew Arthur's poetry so well and valued it so highly. In Balliol circles the elegant scepticism towards enthusiasm, both emotional and political, which is so distinctive a feature of *Amours de Voyage*, had been seen as dangerous cynicism. It helped, too, that unlike Jowett, Henry was never drawn into Florence Nightingale's highly charged and often destructive orbit.[4]

A cornerstone of the relationship, however, was that Henry moved away from orthodox Christianity as Arthur had done, shaping a similar trajectory. In thanking Blanche for *Letters and Remains* in 1866, Henry had remarked, 'to no one, out of the range of his personal friendships, could Clough be an object of more intense individual interest than to myself'. This was more than mere politeness, as she would discover. Through the decade of the 1860s Henry too was journeying away from the Anglicanism of his upbringing and education into all-pervading doubt: in 1869 he resigned his Fellowship, as Arthur had done, because he could no longer subscribe to the Thirty-Nine Articles. Arthur Clough's story in this respect, Henry told his friend Myers, was *his* story. A year later, responding to some of Myers' own poetry, he endeavoured to explain how Clough's poetry had resonated with and helped shape his own thinking:

The truth is – if Clough had not lived and written, I should probably be now exactly where he was. I have not solved in any way the Gordian Knot which he fingered. I can neither adequately rationalise faith, nor reconcile faith and reason, nor suppress reason. But this is just the benefit of an utterly veracious man like Clough, that it is impossible for any one, however sympathetic, to remain where he was. He exposes the ragged edges of himself. One sees that in an irreligious age one must not let oneself drift, or else the rational element of oneself is disproportionately expressed and developed by the influence of environment, and one loses the fidelity to one's true self. This last is the point: I do not feel called or able to preach religion except as far as it is involved in fidelity to one's true self. I firmly believe that religion is normal to mankind and therefore take part unhesitatingly in any social action to adapt and sustain it (as far as a layman may). I know also that my true self is a Theist, but I believe that many persons are really faithful to themselves in being irreligious, and I do not feel able to prophesy to them. If I have any complaint against them, it is not that they do not believe in a God, but that they are content with, happy in, a universe where there is no God; but many of them are not

7 Henry Sidgwick

content, and to these I have nothing to say, not being able to argue the matter on any common ground.[5]

Their positions were not identical; and doubt would lead Henry into investigating the paranormal and psychical research. However, Henry and Arthur were not far apart from each other in separating support for a Christian morality from support for its theology. Thus in 1869 Blanche saw Henry make the same public act of renunciation that Arthur had made twenty years earlier, before she had known him. When she wrote to Henry in

July that year, enquiring anxiously what the consequences of resignation would be for him, she received a resoundingly up-beat reply. 'Personally I feel no doubt that I have done right. For long I have had no doubt except what arose from the fact that most of the persons whose opinion I most regard think differently. But one must at last act on one's own view.' It was, he concluded, 'an act of mere honesty'.[6] The interval of time did make a difference. Whereas in 1848–9 Arthur had put himself in an exposed social and intellectual position, with serious financial and material consequences, twenty years later the admission of doubt was an acknowledged, even a respected, feature of the intellectual landscape. The publication of Charles Darwin's *On the Origin of Species* in 1859 proved decisively to broaden critical discussion of biblical accounts of creation and the Bible's status as the revealed word of God. Public debate grew and grew through the decade of the 1860s, helped by skilful orchestration from a number of Darwin's fellow scientists; and the ecclesiastical establishment found itself on the defensive as never before.[7] The structure of employment amongst university teachers was also about to change.[8] Henry suffered no serious professional consequences. In the short run his private pupils sustained his income; and two years later, in 1871, Gladstone's government legislated to abolish all religious tests for university degrees and most university posts. In 1875 Trinity elected him to a Praelectorship and in 1883 he would be elected the University's Knightbridge Professor of Moral Philosophy. Blanche, who always cared dreadfully what people thought, must have been sustained by the clear signs that the brave but lonely course of action which Arthur had followed was now recognised as an acceptable and honourable one.

Annie had never needed external or public endorsement of Arthur's conduct: she was absolutely secure in her own judgement of him. Yet she, too, warmed to Henry Sidgwick, recognising in him someone not only as passionately committed to education (and mountains) as she herself was, but also a practical politician of very considerable skill. In January 1869 he had powerfully defended the new examination for women in a letter to *The Spectator*:

Whatever may be said in favour of a different school education for the two sexes, the present exclusion of women from the higher studies of the University is perfectly indefensible in principle, and must sooner or later give way. When this barrier is broken down, whatever special examinations for women may still be retained will be very different from any that we now institute. At present we have two distinct classes to consider: students who wish for guidance and support in their studies, and professional teachers who wish to obtain proof of adequate capacity. The first class will be composed of specially intellectual girls, and all these will try to obtain honours. It is only the inferior portion of the second class who will try merely to pass. In their case we shall be distinguishing the competent from the incompetent by examining them in the few subjects which they will certainly profess and be required to teach. We cannot expect parents in general suddenly to alter their views of what girls are to be taught; and we shall probably have more immediate effect in improving education by raising the quality of what is demanded, than by attempting to supply something else.[9]

It is a very clear commentary on the inflexibility and limitation of the stance taken by Emily Davies and her allies in opposing a new examination for women only. By that summer, as we have seen, Henry was sending Annie bulletins on the progress of the first examinations under this scheme; and she, in turn, was providing reading on infant education for his sister.[10]

The symbolic importance of the University of Cambridge, at the apex of elite structures of male education, has already been noted. Practically, Cambridge, with its concentration of intellectual talent, was an obvious place in which to run a lecture scheme, on the model already developed by the North of England Council; and the admission of women to the Local Examinations had signalled a willingness to consider their claims. Looking back in 1894, Henry Sidgwick situated this willingness within a larger agenda: 'the younger University men were in those years from '60 onwards very much under the influence of Mill. They were ready to help the cause of women's education just as one of the branches of liberal progress and reform.'[11] The autumn of 1869 saw the publication of a prospectus for a first set of lectures in Cambridge, to cover both the subjects of the women's examinations and more advanced work, fee one guinea per lecture, in the Lent (spring) Term of 1870. It went forward over the names of a grand committee of management, packed with university luminaries; but the real work was being done by a small executive committee, which included Henry Sidgwick and Thomas Markby of the Local Examinations Syndicate as secretaries, Anna Bateson, wife of the Master of St John's as Treasurer, and several other formidable Cambridge ladies, including Millicent Garrett Fawcett, wife of the Professor of Political Economy, Henry Fawcett, sister of the first woman to qualify as a doctor in the UK, Elizabeth Garrett Anderson, and future campaigner for women's suffrage.[12] The response was immediate and positive and over seventy women attended these first lectures.

However Cambridge, the place, was a small market town, with a thinly populated agricultural hinterland. Almost immediately, 'letters came from

8 Millicent Garrett Fawcett

women at a distance anxious to know whether any suitable accommodation could be found for them in Cambridge if they came up to attend the Lectures'.[13] Henry and Millicent Fawcett had already foreseen this and the need for a house or hostel. Emily Davies had pointed the way by opening her university college for women at Hitchin in 1869, an enterprise which would move to Cambridge in 1873 and become Girton College.[14] Even so, the members of the Cambridge lectures committee, discussing the matter in Millicent's drawing room, had been frightened by the responsibility which creation of a residential institution would bring. Millicent neatly outflanked them by proposing that money should be raised for scholarships, awarded on the results of the women's examination, and entailing residence in Cambridge to attend at least two courses of lectures – and promptly secured the promise of an award of £40 per year for three years from John Stuart Mill and his step-daughter Helen Taylor.[15] This and the other donations that followed generated enormous pressure to find appropriate accommodation for the successful young women: it was very difficult to ignore the claims of merit, wherever in the country it might be located. Some of the young women looked for lodgings but this was clearly not a satisfactory or stable arrangement; and in the spring of 1871, Henry decided to take the initiative and lease a house, approaching Annie to see if she would be willing to take charge of it or knew of someone appropriate who would. Perhaps he guessed that she might be missing the close contact with young people; certainly he felt she would be wholly in sympathy with the gradualist approach to improving educational provision for women which the lecture scheme represented. He had got to know her well enough to recognise that while 'desiring with a quiet intensity, which I gradually came to understand, to throw open the advantages of University education to women without limit or reserve, she cordially welcomed the new examination, with its liberal scheme of options, as adapted to the actual condition of girls.'[16]

Henry had been anticipated in the wish to draw Annie back into more systematic educational work. The promoters of a middle-class girls' school in Bishopsgate in London had already secured her agreement to become its headmistress, once they had raised enough funds to start; and she had given up the Secretaryship of the North of England Council in preparation. Regretfully, she declined Henry's invitation. Fund-raising for the new school did not go well, however; and a couple of months later Blanche suggested to Henry that he approach Annie again. This time she agreed, undertaking to come for at least the first term or two, to get the enterprise off the ground.[17] Henry took a lease on 74 Regent Street, and the prospectus for the next academical year's lectures, issued in June 1871, contained the additional information that 'A house will be opened in October for the accommodation of persons attending the lectures over which MISS A. J. CLOUGH has promised to preside. The terms are £20 for each term of eight weeks: with a reduction of £5 for persons preparing for the profession of education. For further particulars apply to MR SIDGWICK or to MISS A. J. CLOUGH at Combe Hurst, Kingston-on-Thames.'[18] The enterprise so provisionally and modestly begun would involve the most demanding but also the most rewarding work of Annie's life.

That October, Annie received five students in the house, which backed on to the green space of Parker's Piece in the centre of Cambridge. They were of disparate ages, ranging from the stately, thirty-year-old Ella Bulley, another daughter of the Liverpool and transatlantic cotton trade, through the beautiful twenty-six-year old Mary Kennedy, Mary Paley, just coming up to her twenty-first birthday, the eighteen-year-old Annie Migault, Augusta's daughter, and the baby prodigy, Edith Creak, much the plainest, dumpy, diminutive, aged only fifteen and really too young to be there – except that she had carried off the first Mill-Taylor scholarship in the women's examination.[19] Annie had hoped, perhaps naively, to conduct life as in a private household, without formal rules and with some flexibility in the treatment of individuals; whereas the students, whether fifteen or thirty, were all revelling in not being at home and inclined to think of themselves as entirely grown up and without need of supervision, motherly or otherwise. To these tensions was added another: a very real anxiety among their seniors that if the demeanour and behaviour of the young women generated any accusations of impropriety, the whole experiment would be in jeopardy. Annie fussed; they played up, one or two of them tending to treat her more as housekeeper than Principal; and in the early summer of 1872, it all came to a head. How and about what exactly, no one would afterwards say; but Mary Kennedy wrote to Henry and he came to talk to the students – without telling Annie first. It was the only time in their long friendship that she lost her temper with him. Henry wrote ruefully to Blanche in late May:

I do not know quite how much you will have heard from Miss Clough about the house; but I daresay you know as much or more than I do. This term has been rather a trying one; and it seems clear now that we were wrong originally in not establishing Laws and Ordinances for our institution, depending on the sanction of external authority. There is such a strong impulse towards liberty among the young women attracted by the movement that they will not submit to maternal government. However, I think also that we have been more unlucky than we had any reason to expect in one or two points. Of course we keep all these troubles secret.[20]

Responding to a gossipy Cambridge acquaintance, Oscar Browning, Fellow of King's, he played it all down, suggesting that it was a storm in a teacup which he had handled tactlessly. Annie, however, had been distressed by the idea that the episode had its funny side: 'The Scheme is her life at present, and it is so little a piece of mine.'[21] Long after, Edith Creak, by then a distinguished headmistress, offered Blanche a measured judgement on the whole episode:

You know probably that our first year was not altogether a happy one. I can understand & sympathise better than I did then with Miss Clough's intense anxiety over the working of such a daring experiment as it seemed then; but I still think our wishes were reasonable & the College could not have prospered under the regime of the first year. But while many women might have made such mistakes at the outset, few, if any but Miss Clough, could have executed so complete a change of front with the wonderful magnanimity that she showed.[22]

In the summer of 1872 the whole enterprise migrated to Merton Hall, a larger house on the edge of the city, quieter and with its own garden. This gave them all more space and lessened the opportunities for friction. Meanwhile the prospectus showed how the lessons about the need for some rules had been learnt. Annie, described as the Principal, was now reinforced by a committee of management, composed of Cambridge ladies. 'The domestic arrangements are left entirely to the discretion of the Principal' but general rules were laid down by the committee, as follows:

1. Students are expected to inform the Principal what place of worship they choose for regular attendance, and to mention to her when attending any other.
2. Students are expected to consult the Principal on receiving invitations from friends, and also if they wish to make excursions in the neighbourhood.
3. Students are expected to be home, during the Michaelmas and Lent Terms, at 6.30 p.m.
   During the Easter Term at 8.30 p.m.
   On Sundays, throughout the year, at 8.30 p.m.[23]

The rule in respect of a place of worship points to a distinctive and enduring feature of the embryo institution: the absence of religious affiliation. Henry and Annie were united in their determination to protect freedom of conscience, and when they came to build there was never any question of setting aside space for a chapel. In the mid-1880s they would politely decline the offer of monies for a scholarship with a preference for members of the Church of England.[24] At the same time they were well aware of the damage that could be done by accusations of godlessness and Annie was punctilious in discovering from each student which was her chosen place of worship and encouraging her to attend regularly. When the possibility that a student might not wish to attend any place of worship was raised, Annie responded that if the student were under twenty-one, she would normally seek the views of the parents before assenting.[25]

The move to Merton Hall was a consequence of the steadily growing demand for both attendance at the lectures and residence in Cambridge, which showed no sign of levelling off. This growth had various consequences. The lectures were put on a more formal but also a more broadly based and democratic footing in 1873, with the formation of an Association for the Higher Education for Women, whose Ordinary Members were subscribers of not less than one guinea per annum and donors of not less than £10, and whose Honorary Members were the Lecturers appointed and Professors of the University who opened their lectures to women.[26] The inclusion of this last group, three-quarters of whom had opened their lectures to women by 1875, points to one of the ways in which the women, although marginal – indeed, non-existent, as far as the University was concerned – were already beginning to make a contribution to the changing pattern of teaching and learning in later nineteenth-century Cambridge, in enhancing the importance of lectures. Much teaching still took place in very small groups; and since fellows of colleges were not obliged to teach, young men who wanted to shine in the Tripos, the degree examinations, often paid for the help of private coaches. This was how Henry had sustained his income after resigning his fellowship. This was what Arthur had done in the Oxford of the 1840s, before he gained his Oriel Fellowship. Professors were the only persons obliged to lecture; and often it was dreary work, with negligible audiences. The addition of the women cheered the lecturers – and attracted more of the young men. Some college fellows were also beginning to lecture; and those of them who also lectured to women often duplicated or recycled material offered to the men. A symbolic breakthrough would come, however, at the beginning of the academical year 1878–9, when the Governing Bodies of Christ's College and King's College gave permission for the women students, both those under the aegis of the Association and those now based at Girton, to attend the lectures being given in their colleges to men students.

Women students attending lectures were invariably chaperoned; and they were not allowed into the market place to seek private coaches. Considerations of propriety, if nothing else, required that the Association and its successor bodies kept as tight a hold on the provision of small group teaching, classes and supervisions as on lecture arrangements, and often the same people contributed both. There were also educational arguments for such control and integration, ones which Henry and like-minded colleagues at Trinity and other colleges were urging on their own institutions. In this respect too the experience of the women contributed to another important shift in teaching and learning in late nineteenth-century Cambridge, the recapture of teaching by the colleges.[27]

Packing lecture halls and finding supervisors was relatively straightforward: the more intractable problem was finding places for the young women to live. Merton Hall was rapidly over-subscribed and the owner had anyway given notice that in the summer of 1874 he wished to return to reside there himself. Two houses were found in Bateman Street, for the year 1874–5; but already in the course of 1873 the decision had been taken to put an end to this unsettling nomadic existence: the Girton example must be copied to the extent of having a purpose-built building. It was established that St John's College would grant a building lease on a parcel of land in Newnham, on the edge of the city. A limited company, the Newnham Hall Company, was formed; shares were issued, donations solicited, an architect appointed, plans drawn up and building work started.

Annie was in the thick of all of this. As a member of the Association and Principal of its residence, wherever located, she sat on both its committee of management and that committee's standing sub-committee. Her contribution to the work of the Newnham Hall Company would be a central one, as we shall see. This committee work proved to be altogether more congenial and rewarding than that associated with the North of England Council, which anyway was now being wound up with honour. Having stood down as Secretary at the end of 1870 and been succeeded by Margaret Calder, Annie remained a Council member until she herself succeeded Josephine Butler as President in 1873. By now the affiliation of individual associations to the Council was a loose one and they were developing their programmes in a variety of ways suited to their own localities. Meanwhile James Stuart, the Cambridge engineer and astronomer, their very first lecturer, had seized the model offered by the lectures and made it the basis for University Extension lectures, open to women and to men. Both of these developments and their success signalled that the Council had achieved its ends, and in 1874 it was formally dissolved and the remaining funds donated to what would become the Newnham library.[28] The University Extension model was to grow and thrive nationally in the years up to 1914 and beyond, representing the first serious effort by the institutions of higher education in England to address questions of wider access. In celebrating its work, too few remembered Annie's crucial pioneering role.

The Cambridge committees working to make provision for women from 1873 onwards were energetic, intensely democratic, but with a developing camaraderie. The women shared equally with the men, a pattern not common in the period. In the girls' schools just beginning to be established, for example, Boards of Governors might be all-male, leaving simply the details of domestic management to a 'ladies committee'.[29] The small standing sub-committee which largely managed the affairs of the Association for the Higher Education of Women met most often in St John's College Master's Lodge, by the invitation of Anna Bateson; but it could and did meet in Henry Sidgwick's rooms in Trinity; in a committee room attached to the lecture rooms rented from the YMCA at 1 Alexandra Street; and in Newnham Hall, once the building was complete. If present, the President took the chair; otherwise the most senior committee member present presided, which could and did include the women members.[30] The Council of the Newnham Hall Committee included key figures of the Association, Annie, Henry, another Fellow of Trinity, Coutts Trotter, and John Peile, Tutor and later Master of Christ's, but also London-based members: Alice Bonham Carter, her sister Elinor, now married to the Oxford jurist A. V. Dicey, Dicey himself, Godfrey Lushington and Mary Ewart, daughter and heir of the wealthy Liverpool MP William Ewart, founding father of public libraries in Britain. This Council doubled as the building committee and met frequently in both Cambridge and London, in Cambridge meeting at Merton Hall, then Bateman Street, before Newnham Hall itself was completed. In London they most often met at Miss Ewart's house, 3 Morpeth Terrace, but occasionally also at the Diceys', 107 Victoria Street, and at the Lushingtons', 16 Great Queen Street. Alice Bonham Carter, Elinor Dicey and Mary Ewart were very active on financial matters and Mary Ewart did a lot of the work of liaison with the architect they had chosen, Basil Champneys, another Trinity man, whose practice had its headquarters in London. So sympathetic and responsive to the needs of the embryo institution would Champneys prove, that he was to serve as architect for all of Newnham's buildings up to 1914, an exceptional relationship which also gave those buildings a marked aesthetic and physical coherence. A. V. Dicey, in turn, conducted many of the dealings with their solicitor, William Shaen, of Shaen, Roscoe and Massey, who were also the long-standing advisers to Bedford College, the pioneer London college for women.[31] The finance committee consisted of Alice Bonham Carter, Henry and Annie, who also became a standing sub-committee 'responsible for administering the affairs of the Company generally'; and in Cambridge Annie and Henry took the lead, being formally appointed in March 1874 'to transact all business connected with the lease of the land'. When it came to a signatory for the agreements with St John's College and with the builders, Henry was empowered to represent the Company; but all the detailed negotiations with the Bursar of St John's, Dr George Reyner, from the first informal enquiries to identify a suitable plot, to the completion and approval of the building, were conducted by Annie.[32]

The work of raising the money to pay for the building had begun even before its planning. The Company duly issued its shares; but that only provided a nucleus of capital. When the plan had first been formulated in 1873, Henry had written only half in jest to Blanche, 'if anyone should call and ask your advice as to a Philanthropic Investment of Four Thousand Pounds – please refer him to me'.[33] In the autumn of that year Henry and Annie compiled a fund-raising brochure, which went out under Annie's name. It began with a history of the Lectures, intended to

give to Women an opportunity of gaining a more exact knowledge of the subjects taught in schools; and also of pursuing their studies further, in any department which they may select.

It is well before saying any more, to draw attention to the remarkable fact, that these Lectures were a free-will offering of Higher Culture made to Women by Members of the University . . .

The leaflet went on to characterise the community of residents created since 1871:

In this way a number of women of different occupations and different stations in life, and different religious persuasions, have been brought together to receive at least some share of academic education. So far the result has been very satisfactory; there has been much kindly feeling and good fellowship among the students: and their close proximity to the town, while opening to them a much greater variety and extent of teaching than they could otherwise have obtained, has also enabled them to attend their own places of worship.

£1500 had already been subscribed in shares and a further £1320 promised in donations; and the lists of shareholders and donors included many familiar names, from Cambridge and elsewhere, including all the Bonham Carters and Blanche.[34] Thanking Myers for a list of possible targets, 'millionaires', as he hopefully described them, Henry reported that he was waiting for the printing of the leaflet, 'a curious document in style, patched of me and Miss Clough: her naïve, earnest, slightly incoherent appeals intercalated with the colourless, ponderous, semi-official prolixity with which I inevitably

treat such matters'.[35] The two passsages quoted above sound more like
Annie than Henry. Nevertheless the patchwork brought in money; the
next, undated, appeal brochure reports £4650 raised, towards a target of
£6000.[36] The builders' tender in June 1874 came in at £7136 and could
only be pared down to £6922; bravely the Council members committed
themselves to going ahead, but it must have been a relief in October 1874
when Mary Ewart offered a loan of £2,000 at 4%, secured as a mortgage
on the building.[37]

Newnham Hall was – is – a south-facing building, then in a field at
the end of a lane which ran past a large Victorian house, The Pightle,
built in 1864 by Professor Liveing, a Professorial Fellow of St John's and
fortunately a supporter of the women's cause. The right of way continued
as a path beyond the back of the Hall, eventually to form a T-junction
with Grange Road. The Hall was designed to accommodate the Principal
and up to thirty students. The Principal was to have a sitting room and
two bedrooms at her disposal; there was to be a common dining room, one
large and two small common sitting rooms, and each student would have
a bed-sitting-room of her own.[38] Like all building projects, it over-ran; and
the difficulties of getting it finished in time for the Michaelmas Term of
October 1875 were compounded by a dispute between the workmen and
their employers. Annie dealt with this as only she could. She went first to
the builders and secured their permission to talk directly to the men; she
then offered the strikers the difference between their wages and their claim
out of her own pocket, if they would return to work and get the building
finished in time – and they accepted. It was one of those situations in which
the aspects of her style which led some of the students to under-estimate
or patronise her, her unfashionableness, homeliness, anxious concern, and
talent for beginning a sentence in the middle, were distinct advantages in
dealing with the world outside. People were often utterly disarmed and
no one could possibly feel threatened by her. As her niece put it, her
appearance was 'unimpeachably feminine, and her timid, hesitating manner
dispelled all idea of the "capable woman" who is an object of antipathy to
many'.[39]

Yet under the hesitancy and the occasional verbal muddle lay a continuing commitment to the intellectual needs and ambitions of women.
In September 1875, three weeks before Newnham Hall was due to open,
she had been invited to address a meeting of sympathisers and potential
donors in Yorkshire. The frantic last-minute preparations meant that she
was unable to go; but she wrote a short address to be read on her behalf. It
concluded:

It is often asked 'Why should women leave home?' 'Is not home Education best for them?' and these questions deserve a careful answer. A little reflection will, I think, shew how much more effectually, & with how much less mental strain, a woman can study, where all the arrangements of the house are made to suit the hours of study, – where she can have undisturbed possession of one room, – and where she can have access to any books that she may need. How very rarely, – if ever, – these advantages can be secured in any home we all know, and it is surely worth some sacrifice on the part of parents to obtain them for their daughters at the age when they are best fitted to profit by them to the utmost.[40]

This is the central argument of 'a room of one's own', almost sixty years before Virginia Woolf set it out. Behind it, we catch a glimpse of a twenty-year-old in Liverpool at the beginning of the 1840s, getting up very early to work on her German, her Greek and her Euclid when the house was quiet.

They did just manage to get the builders out in time, Annie taking up residence in one of the finished rooms to urge them on;[41] and at the beginning of the Michaelmas Term she welcomed twenty-seven students to the new Hall. Four other students, for a variety of individual reasons, remained as out-students; and with Annie was the first-ever Resident Lecturer, Mary Paley, who had been one of the original five at Regent Street in 1871.[42] Mary Paley's experience was a microcosm of the shift that was under way in the attainments and ambitions of the women students coming to Cambridge. When she first arrived, she had no idea of reading for a Tripos, wishing simply for 'general cultivation'. Persuaded by Mary Kennedy to go with her to a lecture on Political Economy for the Moral Sciences Tripos, her attention was caught and such was the quality of the work of both that soon Alfred Marshall, the young lecturer, was encouraging 'the two Marys' to aim for the Tripos standard. Mary Kennedy had to take a year out at the end of her second year, because of serious illness; but Mary Paley was then joined by Amy Bulley, sister of Ella, who had migrated from Girton because Miss Davies, determined as ever that the women should do exactly as the men, would not let her take an additional year to prepare for the Tripos. Mary and Amy were informally examined in 1874; Amy was placed in the second class but the examiners could not agree about Mary, two placing her in the second class and two in the first. Returning home to her father's rectory must have been something of an anticlimax after this triumph, although he rejoiced heartily in her success. Her first use of her knowledge and skills was to offer a short course of lectures locally. But when Alfred Marshall wished to stand down from lecturing to the women students, the Association for the Higher Education of Women authorised Henry to invite Mary to take his place.[43]

9 'The Two Marys', Mary Kennedy and Mary Paley

Gradually the women's examinations – or Higher Locals as they had already become – were ceasing to be the primary objective and beginning to be seen as the gateway to more advanced work. The numbers attempting Tripos examinations, and performing creditably, slowly increased; and the continuing excess of applicants over places available forced both the Association and Newnham Hall – essentially the same group of people but with different hats – to select, among obvious criteria being maturity and academic merit. The terms of admission rehearsed in the first report on Newnham Hall excluded all those under seventeen and noted that 'The Principal may require any Student to withdraw who, in her opinion, is not profiting by the course of study at Newnham Hall.' The Association's standing sub-committee noted in November 1877 that the students had not done so well in the past round of Higher Locals, primarily because many had delayed coming into residence until the Lent Term, almost half-way into the academical year. Henceforward they would normally be required to come into residence in the Michaelmas Term and an entrance test for admission to the lectures would be devised. Henry Sidgwick was asked in 1877 by the Newnham Hall Council to prepare a paper on the subject; and the Council's Report in December 1878 stated that in future, 'Unless under special circumstances, Students who intend to pass the Cambridge Higher Local Examination will be required to pass in English History, English Literature, and Arithmetic, before coming into residence. Those who have taken honours in the Cambridge Senior Local Examination will be exempt from this rule.'[44]

The continuing growth of demand and a preparedness to jump ever-higher hurdles are marked features of this first decade, pointing to a large and hitherto unsatisfied appetite for learning among middle-class women. Nevertheless, the taking and passing of examinations was not compulsory; and publications were careful regularly to stress that. The Principal's report to shareholders in the Newnham Hall Company in June 1878 noted that about one-third of the present students were preparing for a Tripos; but it also recorded the presence of two American visitors for the Michaelmas and Lent Terms.[45] Annie always particularly enjoyed welcoming American students, who would in 1883–4 include the two daughters of Henry Wadsworth Longfellow.[46]

Annie was also always alert to the needs and interests of those students for whom Newnham and Cambridge might be a crucial stage in preparing to earn their own living. The Newnham Hall Council had resolved in the summer of 1875 that, once in residence in the new Hall, Annie should have paid assistance and she was asked to propose a scheme. She proposed in

November that she should be allowed 'to receive a student to whom the whole or a portion of her expenses at Newnham Hall should be allowed in return for assistance given to her' and this was agreed. But it did not prove practical; and in February 1877 Elinor Dicey and Mary Ewart secured agreement instead to the appointment of a paid assistant.[47] From the very beginning there had been a Fund for Governesses, a fund to assist 'persons (especially those engaged in or preparing for the profession of education) who may be desirous to come to Cambridge in order to attend these lectures, but unable to do so for want of means', to which Mary Ewart was a major contributor.[48] By the time the Association was formed in 1873, there were two funds: one now described as a 'Fund for Teachers' and the Aikin Fund, created by Anna Bateson's brother, James Aikin of Liverpool; and in 1874, to stretch the money even further, Annie persuaded them that the Teachers' Fund could be used for loans as well as grants.[49]

There were also fee rebates for intending teachers. As Annie explained in 1875, it was 'an essential feature of our whole scheme that women who are making or who intend to make teaching their profession should share in all the advantages which it offers on the lowest possible terms. To them the Lecture fees are reduced by one half & the fees for board at Newnham by one fourth.'[50] But such reductions were perpetually in tension with the necessity to make ends meet and balance the books; and Annie's personal generosity and commitment, which as well led her consistently to refuse all salary for her work, made her a soft touch. The Newnham Hall Council had to struggle to contain the concessions within manageable bounds. In November 1875 they resolved that not more than fifteen students should be admitted at the lower fee without the permission of the Council. In June 1877 the absolute ceiling was set at fifteen and it was agreed that even if that ceiling had not been reached, no new student should be admitted after 10 August in any given year – obviously to stop last-minute derailment of the budget. At the same time lecture fees were consolidated into a single charge and charges for board were put up. Then in 1878 they changed tack. Instead of fee reductions, a fixed sum was to be set aside to provide thirteen bursaries, to be awarded by the Principal to the needy, but having regard also to their academic standing. This had a number of merits: the total sum involved was known in advance and could be budgeted for; it gave Annie both time and discretion to identify the really needy; and it was harder to construe such help as demeaning to the recipients.[51]

The advanced examinations, the lectures, residence in Cambridge all had an impact on the flow of more systematically educated women into the teaching of girls. And formal schooling for girls was itself expanding rapidly. It had been alleged by contemporaries that the powers given to the statutory commission created to remodel educational endowments under the 1869 Endowed Schools Act were wide enough to enable them to take a boys' school in Northumberland and turn it into a girls' school in Cornwall. Although they did nothing quite as spectacular as this, they certainly brought about the creation of a number of girls' schools. In addition the Girls' Public Day School Company was formed in 1872; and by 1880 it had opened twenty-two schools, eleven in London and eleven outside.[52] In reporting annually to the members of the Association and to the shareholders of the Newnham Hall Company, Annie dwelt proudly on the ever-growing list of teaching appointments secured by former students, taking pleasure not only in the individual achievements but also in the transformation which the work as a whole was bringing about. In December 1877 Newnham Hall hosted a first-ever national conference of schoolmistresses. Writing to report its success to his mother, Henry remarked that it had been largely Annie's idea and marvelled at the way in which she was always considering the work in Cambridge 'in its bearing on national education, and planning how its beneficial effects on the country at large might be improved and extended'.[53]

The building of Newnham Hall brought no flattening or slackening of demand from would-be women students. If anything, the signals of substance and determination sent by a purpose-built building encouraged ambitions, ambitions both to extend and to enhance the provision. As early as spring 1875 the then students had made a donation of £75 to building funds, towards the cost of a 'covered court' for games. This was not included in the first work and its precise form, location and cost were a cause of continuing concern for the Council. Eventually, with a further contribution of £30 from the students towards the escalating costs, a covered gymnasium was built in the summer of 1878 and the first work was done for the provision of a new lawn tennis court. As pressing as the need for the students to take appropriate physical exercise was the need for laboratory space, to enable the students studying natural sciences to do practical work. At this stage the male University was only just beginning to build laboratories – and there was widespread reluctance to let the women in. Individual colleges were more enlightened and the early Newnham students had benefited enormously from the generosity of St John's, who allowed them to use their laboratory. But the Newnham Hall Council were determined the women should have their own; and a chemistry laboratory was also built in the summer of 1878.[54] No sooner was that complete than discussion started on the needs of physics and biology. Meanwhile gifts of books to form the nucleus of a College Library were being solicited and accumulated, housed for the time being in one of the sitting rooms.

Threatening to swamp all of this work was the continuing pressure to build more student rooms. Lodgings still had to be found for some students; and when, with money left her in 1876 by her old friend Louisa Crofton, Annie built two cottages nearby, they served to house students too.[55] Annie finally brought the Council to face the issue formally at the end of November 1878, when she asked for authorisation to begin to raise money for a second hall. In its turn this request raised the relationship between the Newnham Hall Company and the Association for the Higher Education of Women – who faced the pressure equally. The Council went through the formality of asking the Association – essentially themselves wearing different hats – whether they would consider building a hall; and the eventual outcome was the logical one, a merger of the two bodies to create a single not-for-profit association under the Companies Acts of 1862–7, Newnham College. Even before these formalities were complete, the fund-raising for a second hall had started in the spring of 1879.[56]

As ever, Annie and Henry were at the centre of the work, although powerfully helped with the legal form and technicalities of the actual merger by Dicey and Shaen. And by now they had acquired additional hard-working reinforcement within Cambridge and within Newnham. In 1876 Marion Kennedy, daughter of Benjamin Hall Kennedy, Regius Professor of Greek and author of the *Public School Latin Primer*, became the indefatigable Secretary of the Council and continued as Secretary of the College.[57] At the same time, Eleanor Balfour, who in April 1876 had married Henry Sidgwick, was becoming entirely indispensable. Eleanor, born in 1845 and always known as Nora, was the elder sister of Arthur Balfour, one of Henry's pupils at Trinity who had become a great friend, sharing not only his philosophical concerns but also his interest in the paranormal and psychical research. The Balfours were landed, rich and eminently well connected: the third Marquess of Salisbury was their uncle, and Arthur, a future Conservative Prime Minister, entered Parliament in 1874. Nora had been educated at home and in the process had discovered a considerable aptitude for mathematics. After her mother's death in 1872 she kept house for her brother in London and it was probably at a séance there that she first met Henry. In June 1875 she joined the Council of Newnham Hall, and at Annie's invitation she spent most of the following Michaelmas Term at Newnham, helping with the mathematics teaching.[58] In June 1876, when Alice Bonham Carter resigned the Treasurer's post, on the ground that the amount and nature of the business was now such that it really ought to be done by

10 Nora Sidgwick

someone based in Cambridge, Nora succeeded her. She did the work brilliantly. She was orderly, methodical and precise; she had immense tact and she had a self-confidence in handling money, debt and the planning of schemes long-term which had been nurtured through her involvement in the management of her family's resources and estates during much of her mother's widowhood. The 1878 bursary scheme for intending teachers was her work. In 1881 it was she who persuaded the College that they should lease a further large area of land from St John's both against their own future needs and to protect themselves from undesirable neighbours.[59] Financial operations hitherto had been somewhat hand-to-mouth, involving some major acts of faith: nothing in Annie's own experience had equipped her to operate in any other way. These had enabled the fledgling institution to hop: now it had to fly properly. Nora Sidgwick's contributions, strategic, administrative and financial, to that achievement cannot be over-stated.

Nora Sidgwick and Marion Kennedy contributed very real administrative and financial talent. In addition they and Annie had the support of a slowly growing band of resident lecturers, all of them young women who, like Mary Paley, had been given the opportunity to develop their intellectual strengths through the lecture scheme and Newnham and who, as they helped to share the responsibilities of being a senior member with Annie, like Mary, came to appreciate the complexities – and the person – much more.[60] Mary herself did not stay long. In the summer of 1877 she married Alfred Marshall and they went off to start the new University College in Bristol; but she was to return to Newnham and to Cambridge teaching in 1886, when Alfred succeeded Henry Fawcett as Professor of Political Economy. However others were already coming forward. By Michaelmas 1880 there were four: Ellen Crofts, Penelope Lawrence, Mary Martin and Margaret Merrifield.[61]

The final formal meeting of the Newnham Hall Company could not be held before 1 February 1881. By that time the new Council of Newnham College had already met and the new hall, the other side of the right of way, was accommodating students. Presiding over it as Vice-Principal was Nora Sidgwick; and Nora and Henry lived in one of the sets of senior members' rooms. In proposing this arrangement to the Council in May 1880, to run for a year in the first instance, Nora had suggested that it would enable everyone to discover from experience what issues had to be faced in running a second hall: whether it should be a wholly separate enterprise, or should the two be linked in some way and if so, how. The rent which the Sidgwicks would insist on paying would also assist with the building debt. She recognised that 'objection may be felt to giving charge of the house to married people'; but Henry would actually continue to work in his college rooms in Trinity. The Council gratefully accepted; and the new hall was duly named North Hall, while the original Newnham Hall became South Hall.[62] With two substantial buildings, a Principal and Vice-Principal, four lecturers and over seventy students in residence, the 'family' who had begun the decade at 74 Regent Street had already become an institution. Two testimonies, of very different kinds, bear witness to this. One is a badly faded multi-graphed sheet, headed 'House Rules for Newnham College', which deals with matters everyone who has ever lived in a residential institution will immediately recognise: the fixing of pictures to the walls – where nails could be used and where drawing pins; provisions available to students in the common pantry; quiet study hours; the hours in which piano practice was permitted, etc. etc.[63] The other comes from Henry, who in December 1881 wrote jubilantly to his sister that they had finally liquidated all the debt and Newnham was 'now a business paying its way ... In fact, for the first time for ten years I feel that the institution can really stand alone, altogether independent of my fostering care.'[64]

Earlier in that same letter Henry had also rejoiced that two of the Newnham students were the only students to reach first class standard in the Moral Sciences Tripos. The achievements of the decade 1871–81 were not confined to bricks and mortar and organisational stuctures. The women had begun to make their mark intellectually and a first measure of recognition was won from the University. It was in 1881 that the Three Graces, three votes of the Senate which gave formal permission for women to take University examinations and have their performances certificated, were carried. At the beginning permission for women candidates to sit Tripos examination papers and have the resulting scripts marked had had to be separately and informally negotiated with each of the examiners. Mary Paley described how in 1874 she and Amy Bulley sat their papers in the drawing room of the Kennedys' house in Bateman Street, under the eye of Professor Kennedy. 'He was rather excitable and hot tempered (we called him the purple boy). He invigilated and sometimes went to sleep and we had to wake him up to light the gas.' The examination papers were brought by most distinguished 'runners' – Sidgwick, Marshall, Sedley Taylor and Venn – from the Senate House; and Amy Bulley drew Sedley Taylor, rotund, capped and gowned, almost in flight as he carried his share.[65] After the marking was done, the examiners then wrote separately and informally to the Newnham authorities and to the Girton authorities about the performances of their charges; and subsequently all that the candidates could offer about their achievements were confidential letters of reference from their own institutions. As newspapers speculated about the extent of Mary Paley's achievement in December 1874, the only thing her proud father, Rev. Thomas Paley, could do was to write to *The Times* as follows:

She was submitted to the same examination as the men, with an understanding that her place in the classes should not be divulged, but only certified to her immediate friends. I am therefore not at liberty to say where she stood. It is sufficient to say that the result of the examination gave great satisfaction to her tutors, and proved that without any very extraordinary ability and without any strain on her health, a woman is capable of the highest mental culture.

Forwarding the cutting to Annie for safe-keeping, Henry noted, 'Please remember that *we* are not to publish in newspapers.'[66]

The secrecy, the repeated need for informal negotiations, constituted a most unsatisfactory situation and, as the numbers of women candidates for the Tripos grew, more and more of a time-consuming nuisance to operate. The relative injustice was underlined in 1878 when the University of London opened its degrees to women and dramatised in 1880 when Charlotte Scott of Girton was informally bracketed with the 8th Wrangler in the Mathematics Tripos – yet received no public recognition. An earlier Senior Wrangler, T. S. Aldis, now Professor of Mathematics at Durham College of Science in Newcastle, and his wife organised a monster Memorial, with over 8000 signatures, asking for the admission of women not only to the University's examinations but also to its degrees and membership. The Cambridge activists knew nothing of this until it arrived; and the first instinct of the supporters of Newnham was that it was premature and could be counterproductive. Degrees and membership carried with them participation in University government; a backlash against this could sink the whole scheme and render even the *status quo* untenable. If implemented, it would also represent a serious check to the Higher Locals, since young women wanting a Cambridge degree would instead have to matriculate by taking the Previous or 'Little-Go' Examination, which still included compulsory Greek, a step which Henry and his allies considered seriously retrograde for the women – and which they were trying to change for the men. Emily Davies and the supporters of Girton, still essentially being run by a London-based committee, had their own doubts about the timing of the Newcastle Memorial; but its objectives were their objectives: they had always wanted the women to do exactly the same examinations as the men, from Previous to Tripos, and on the same timetable. They rejected all invitations from Newnham to negotiate jointly with the University, following the reception of the Memorial.

This was a situation, however, in which the involvement of so many senior University men in the creation and governance of Newnham worked very powerfully to its advantage. Henry had no difficulty in manoeuvring himself on to the University Syndicate, the committee set up to consider the Newcastle and related memorials, and its report early in 1881 was a great deal more acceptable to Newnham than to Girton. The Syndicate simply ignored the question of degrees. They proposed the formal opening of Tripos examinations to women who had fulfilled the normal residence requirements and been recommended by their college. On successful completion of their examinations these women would be given a certificate and their names would be published in a separate class-list. Certain passes in the Higher Local could be substituted for the Previous Examination. Emily Davies raged; but retaining the *status quo* was no longer an option and this time the Newnham half-a-loaf had to be accepted. When it came to a vote in the Senate House on 24 February 1881, the proposals, in the form of three motions or Graces, were carried by suprisingly large majorities.[67]

The excitement of the Newnham students was intense. Eleanor Andrews wrote home to her sisters that evening, describing the scene:

Mrs Sidgwick's sister Lady Rayleigh was at the Senate House with her pony carriage & was to drive with the news at once. But some of the students had another plan. One was to get the news directly it was out, she then went to Clare Bridge, waved her handkerchief to another on King's Bridge, who signalled to another on horse back, at the back of King's. She then galopped [*sic*] here at once with a white handkerchief tied on the end of her riding whip. Whereupon two others hoisted a flag on our roof, the gong was sounded & everyone clapped.

As they stood waiting for the news of the second and third votes, 'Mr Sidgwick came in sight [and] we clapped still more, & he not knowing the cause ran on into the house, but afterwards waved his hat violently & seemed too delighted to keep still. After that we came into the house & clapped Miss Clough.' Two days later, writing as Principal and Vice-Principal to thank one of the non-resident MAs who had taken the trouble to come up from London to vote for them, Annie and Nora reflected on

the benefit we feel you have done to the cause of woman's education. Could we have foreseen the almost total collapse of the opposition we should of course have begged friends who could only come at great trouble and inconvenience, not to do so.

At the same time we feel not only that that collapse was due to the strength we were perceived to have in the enthusiasm of distant friends, but that the overwhelming majority by which the graces were carried will be of lasting advantage to us in strengthening our position here, and throughout the country.[68]

In this decade 1871–81 Annie, with Henry, Nora and their powerful and supportive team of friends and colleagues, had achieved an institutional and a public presence in the University of Cambridge. The symbolic importance of this is hard to over-estimate. Newnham and Girton together signalled their determination to make the elite education of the country available to women as well as to men. And even in this short time they were beginning to make a practical difference to the lives of middle-class women. Already between 1869 and 1880 a total of 113 women had entered Girton; between 1871 and 1880 258 had come to Newnham, the larger number reflecting the college's flexibility over length and type of course. Of those 371 women, at least 230, 63 from Girton and 167 from Newnham, went or would go on to teach at one level or other, some in universities, many more in the girls' secondary schools now mushrooming around the country.[69] This was indeed the work of national importance of which Annie had dreamed.

CHAPTER 6

Enter Blanche Athena Clough

At her birth in August 1861 Arthur had named his second daughter, whom he was never to see, Blanche Athena. To family and friends she was always Thena; to her students she would be 'B.A.' Although she grew up during the two decades which saw a transformation in her Aunt Annie's life and work, it is difficult to catch more than an occasional glimpse of her or of her siblings, Florence and Arthur. It is only when Thena comes to Newnham in 1884, at the age of twenty-three, that her voice begins to be heard.

Through the 1860s the children were largely based at Combe Hurst in Surrey, the home of their grandparents, Sam and Mai Smith. As we have seen, Annie took a share in their early education, although not as much as she would have liked; but she was undoubtedly the anchor-woman as a succession of governesses and tutors came and went. Probably it was after one Christmas during these years that the little Florence wrote painstakingly and laboriously to Alice Bonham Carter, to thank her 'very much for the little hearts[.] I wore them last night and Grandmama liked them very much [.] Aunt Beatrice gave me a pair of slippers which I have got on now[.] Aunt Bertha gave me a douzen white buttons. Please give my love to Mama & Artie has written to her he has got some new skates & Aunt Annie gave him.'[1] Artie, the young Arthur, was in due course sent to Eton and eventually, after extended consultation with Henry, to Trinity College, Cambridge. [2] In 1874 the family base moved from Combe Hurst, to Embley, near Romsey, in Hampshire; for in January 1874 'Uncle Night', Florence Nightingale's father, died and, following the complex entail created by Peter Nightingale's will, Mai inherited the estate from her brother: it would pass in due course to her son Shore. By this stage Sam was bedridden and Mai, although seventy-six and severely hampered by arthritis, ruled the roost. Kitty Duff, Thena's first cousin once removed and ward, was born thirty years later but faithfully absorbed the family tradition that Embley was a matriarchy, with Mai at the centre, flanked by two of her daughters,

Blanche and Bertha, who had married W. B. Coltman, and the Clough and Coltman grandchildren.[3]

Embley Park was then a large house of the late Georgian period, on the borders of the New Forest.[4] It is a sheltered site and has a fine garden and park, with views of the Forest beyond. Here, much more than at Combe Hurst, Thena developed a passionate love of the countryside, and of the New Forest in particular, which was to sustain her throughout her life. She tramped and rode in the Forest and embraced its solitude. Looking back on her childhood, she reflected,

I can't think I had any affection for anyone except perhaps A[rthur]. I remember quarrelling with him at Robertsbridge & minding very much. I remember how we went across the park every morning and the row when I lied about the India rubber & how he & I planned to run away. I wonder if I had any morals at all. A and I used to wrangle about religion. I don't remember being much concerned about being good. I wanted to do the things I wanted to do. I wanted to go out & bird's nest & chase the cock & always wanted passionately tragically to be a boy.[5]

A visitor who did notice the aloofness, the determination and the sense of not quite belonging was Henry Sidgwick. He had first corresponded with the eight-year-old Thena in the late summer of 1869, when she had written to let him know her mother was ill. In 1872, after staying with the family at Combe Hurst, he remarked to his mother that the two Clough daughters were 'such a curious contrast, the eldest [Florence] exhibiting the old type of womanhood in rudiment, and the youngest [Thena] very decidedly the new type. I keep wondering what she will be wanting to do in ten years if the world goes on moving.' Twelve years later, visiting Embley, he was still wondering: '"Thena" perplexes me a little: she gives one the impression of having a decided character; but I cannot make out that it is decided in any direction in particular.'[6]

'I . . . always wanted . . . to be a boy': the sharp contrast between the scope allowed her and that allowed to a brother or brothers was a common theme in the experience of many of the able women of the period. Another part of Thena's sense of not quite belonging had its roots in a distance between her and her mother. Kitty Duff always understood that the warmth and the gaiety in the household came from Mai and from Bertha, rather than from Blanche, and reported Thena as saying that Blanche could never bear to talk to the children about their father.[7] She wanted to be close to them, but her efforts with her younger daughter were counterproductive. Thena wrote in July 1885, the reason it seems why I am so disinclined to talk to M[other] is that I don't want to surrender my keys to her – She wants as she says to know what I'm about – M wouldn't be content to leave me as she found me – if she didn't like me she'd alter me – when I look for people's keys I only want to know about their dispositions – to understand how they work sufficiently to know when I can go and talk to them.

Later she added that her mother 'expects to be treated with frank confident realness as a companion but she still retains the attitude of moral pastor and master'.[8]

As befitted a daughter of a leading Unitarian family, Blanche had been well educated, first by governesses and visiting masters, then as a boarder for three years at the school run by Rachael Martineau in Liverpool, and subsequently as a *pensionnaire* in Lausanne and Geneva.[9] Florence, however, seems to have been educated entirely at home, although she did come to Newnham for two terms in 1877.[10] Thena was granted – or asked for – rather more. She was sent to Highfield, the Misses Metcalfe's school in Hendon, a well-established and highly regarded boarding school with impeccable Evangelical Anglican credentials. Fanny Metcalfe, who had founded the school with her sister in 1863, was an energetic member of the London Association of Schoolmistresses and her declared aim was to follow in the footsteps of Arnold of Rugby.[11] Thena's schoolfellows at Highfield included Katharine and Henrietta Jex-Blake, daughters of the then Headmaster of Rugby and later respectively Mistress of Girton College and Principal of Lady Margaret Hall, Oxford. After four years as a boarder, Thena returned to being a daughter at home.[12] But Florence was already occupying that role. Arthur, on the other hand, had been thriving in Cambridge since 1879, taking a first in Classics in 1881 and then a first in Moral Sciences in 1883, that same year also being invited to join the Apostles – the secretive, elite intellectual society. Following these triumphs, he began to read for the Bar.[13] To Cambridge in the autumn of 1884 Thena followed him; and 'After only 3 weeks at Cambridge I realized I liked society and that to turn my back on it and to devote myself to parish & schools would be a most fearful piece of uphill work.'[14]

Thena's very first encounter with what would become Newnham had been when she was twelve, staying with Annie at Merton Hall in the summer of 1873. 'It was a very nice place for a summer holiday; the garden was full of gooseberries and currants, and a great deal of jam-making went on alongside of the studies of the few students who were up.' She remembered too being taken by her aunt to gaze at the field which it was hoped to lease from St John's for building. Subsequently she visited the new buildings two or three times, to take the qualifying groups of the Higher Local Examinations; 'and finally in the May Term of 1884 I was taken in for some weeks to prepare for the last Group for my certificate, the once celebrated Group C, Mathematics. I always held that the examiners must have mixed up my papers with someone else's, as this alone could account for my having passed, but anyhow, my name appeared on the list and all was well.' She became a student proper in October 1884, intending at first to stay for only a year.[15]

The community Thena joined was, as we have seen, now a sizeable one. Annie still took a leading share in all contriving and planning; but the reinforcement provided by the other officers and the resident lecturers had freed her a little more to do what she did best, provide outstanding pastoral care and support. The students had always to be chaperoned to lectures outside Newnham and doing this gave her ample opportunity to observe them and see how they were faring. She was no more coherent or stylish than she had ever been: as Thena was to remark, 'she dressed like a bundle'.[16] But few of the students could resist her real interest in them as individuals and her transparent concern. That October Annie was especially anxious about the asthmatic Winnie Seebohm, who wrote home to her sister, 'She *is* so thoughtful of me, I could fill a letter with her little kindnesses.'[17] Thena, one suspects, would fiercely have resisted any mothering and looked for support to her friends and contemporaries rather than to her elders. Among her particular friends were Lucy Silcox, who had come up in 1881 and was now preparing for Part II of the Classical Tripos, and the teacher of them both, Edith Sharpley, the newest resident lecturer, who had only just taken a first in Part II of the Classical Tripos in 1883. Winnie Seebohm described her as 'a little thin pale girlish creature – younger than many of the students, but when she talks and laughs she looks so nice and clever'.[18]

Thena's friendships with Lucy and Edith would last for the rest of their lives, as would the friendships which followed, with Margaret Verrall, née Merrifield, who also taught her, with Katharine Stephen, Philippa Fawcett and Pernel Strachey. This was an era of intense female friendships; but Thena had a particular talent for friendship, for drawing people to her. She both craved this – and despised herself for doing so. For behind the social assurance and the deep voice lay a profoundly insecure and lonely person. In the autumn of 1885 she wrote that,

The real ruination is the desire to be liked. One ought to be indifferent to the whole world. – I think I don't only want to be liked but to be fit to be liked – where I am not indifferent I am always satisfied and uneasy unless I myself am the subject of the conversation, unless attention is turned on me.

And then a little later:

The consciousness of independence which is another word for isolation is the
opiate which I am driven to –, to dull the horrid pain of the fleetingness of things
– the only stable constant factor in my life is myself – my enjoyments my feelings.
My friendships are like beautiful funguses which grow up and delight the eye and
then decay and rot and become heaps of corruption loathsome to look upon.

And soon after:

It seems to me a simple fact that intercourse with other people is far more productive
of pain than pleasure. The stages of friendship now are something like this. 1st a
time of anxiety, uncertainty, excitement, pleasure in one's new found friend, very
largely mixed with restlessness when away from the person and uneasiness when
they are present owing to the feeling that one must restrain and contain one's most
prominent feelings – Then 2nd the excitement dies away & there is no very keen
pleasure nor any pain – one's friend has become a pleasant responsive instrument.
Then thirdly comes the stage in which one no longer desires the person's society.[19]

Yet this bleak view of human relationships and overpowering sense of her
own monstrous egotism stayed largely inside Thena's head. She did not
drive her friends away by sharing it endlessly with them. She gave vent to
such ferocity only in what she came to call her 'black books', a title apt both
literally and figuratively. Between 1885 and 1916/19 she maintained an intermittent dialogue with herself, mostly in a set of black-covered notebooks,
but sometimes on loose sheets of paper, setting down thoughts, ideas, emotions and engaging frequently in excoriating self-criticism.[20] These notebooks and sheets make extraordinary yet profoundly sad reading. Time
and again she belabours herself for inadequacy, for selfishness, for laziness:
there is clearly some relief in setting all this down on the page, yet there is
never catharsis or resolution. Months or sometimes years later, the whole
cycle begins again – and again. Comparison of these notebooks with the
journal her father kept in Oxford in the 1830s and the one her aunt kept
in Liverpool in the 1840s is illuminating and instructive, throwing up both
similarities and sharp contrasts. Here too is a sort of moral accounting; but
it is far from the Evangelical model which influenced her father and which
her aunt explicitly invoked. Although the self-criticism eerily echoes the
self-flagellation and self-abasement before God which characterise Puritan
diaries of the late sixteenth century,[21] God played no part in Thena's world.
If she had ever had any faith, she had certainly lost it by the time she
became a student; and, as her father's daughter, she was hardly open to
challenge on this. Another part of her inheritance is also revealed by the
comparison. Annie's diaries have a balance, a buoyancy, which the other

two lack. Both Arthur and Thena dig deep into wretchedness and try to use their diaries to manage and contain that wretchedness. Thena, like her father, was a depressive. In the days before 'talking cures', pouring it all out in her notebooks or whatever sheets of paper came to hand, was often the best she could do.

On occasion violent physical exercise and solitude helped too. At the beginning of February in her second year at Newnham, she had been grappling with a particularly bad bout of depression and set down in detail how she felt and how she tried to cope.

I don't believe I was ever much more entirely miserable. Of course I've tried the blues pretty well before . . . but this time I hated my fellow creatures so fiercely & I went about longing so constantly for & picturing so vividly & fondly the sensation of a long knife going into my left side.

I've been trying to find out what produced this state of things & also a good deal what dispersed it. I believe it wasn't unreasonable. I think it began or at least got intense last Friday, that's a week ago. I hadn't done any work to speak of, & felt clearly how futile & incapable I was, & how inevitably bent towards the dogs, it was Friday I wrote down my last remarks here . . . Then on Saturday I being already in a bitter mood, I was attacked[,] my 2 lecturers told my conduct was disgraceful etc etc etc, I went out for a walk, a rush rather, pretty frantic. I couldn't tell what was the matter, I couldn't think, I couldn't understand, I only knew I was wild & could only rush along with a sort of desire to get unconscious. I suppose at home I should have rolled in the heather & torn at it – & shouted. I generally get calm in those wet tramps at home but I was just as bitter & sore when I turned back this time. What happened on the walk home turned my mind certainly & it was a different kind of discomfort[,] this very acute discomfort indeed down till that Sunday evening. My discharging the matter to M deG V [Margaret Verrall] was so great a relief that I the & it [*sic*] was all right & the next day kept me happy till Tuesday when the whole thing came back with twice as much force & for 2 days & more I had it hot. It doesn't seem long but it felt so. When that sort of thing is on I can't understand or think at all[,] I can only feel in a sort of bitter hot way & it's the not being able to think which makes it so bad, for I can't get on or get better till the feeling is removed & I can consider it dispassionately. I only know that I am quite futile & incapable, that I haven't good, right respectable feelings about friendship or anything & that I plunge & am bound to plunge deeper & deeper in the mire as I go on in life.[22]

On this occasion Thena did find relief in telling Margaret Verrall a little of what she was feeling; and as her friends, particularly Lucy and Edith, shared their joys and anxieties with her, so they must have developed some awareness of her moods. Edith, less flamboyant and a better listener than Lucy, knew Arthur Hugh Clough's poetry well: it had tipped the balance for her in the choice between Newnham and Girton.[23] In the early autumn of 1885 she wrote to Thena,

Did you see the two lines Mr Chamberlain quoted in his speech yesterday? [evidently a quotation from AHC's poetry] I wonder how many of his hearers or his readers recognised them. I was afraid, not exactly afraid, but I never could all last year, speak to you about your father, though I wanted to often; something always stopped me, partly a kind of reluctance to touch a beautiful unspoken of bond, & partly that I wanted to cope with your personality plus no glamour. I don't know whether you understand; it doesn't matter.[24]

There is both perceptiveness and delicacy here. Even so, heavy use of the black books in the worst patches seems to have enabled Thena to keep the full extent of her black moods to herself – indeed, almost to take pride in doing so – and there is no sign that her friends wearied of her company or were repelled by the recurring ferocity of her depressions. As she grew older the intensity and frequency of the depressions diminished somewhat: her strategies for managing them became well tried and there were real achievements in which to take pleasure and pride – as we shall see. But her vulnerability to what Dr Johnson called 'the black dog' never entirely disappeared. Deep inside the capable administrator, staunch friend, diverting companion and supportive tutor that she became, there remained a person who never quite believed in herself.

How much of this Thena's Aunt Annie knew or guessed is unclear. Writing to her old Charleston friend Maria Bacot, now living in Wisconsin, in sadly reduced circumstances, Annie drew a sharp contrast between the characters of her nieces Florence and Thena: 'The elder is very practical & useful & very sweet tempered [.] The younger is very clever & bright.' And writing to Thena just before she came back for her second year, Annie urged 'do cherish and make much of your Mother in these last days. When I look back I wish I had done more for my Mother and there is a little sore in my heart that won't heal – though I know that she has forgiven all.' If she did guess, she had the good judgement not to press further – not to seek for 'the keys'; and those of her letters to Thena which survive are cheerfully breathless budgets of news about common concerns. When Thena was preparing to go to Florence in the Christmas vacation of 1887–8, Annie's letter, crammed with snippets of news about friends and arrangements for servants, was brisk about which churches to see and advised against a visit to her father's old friend and one-time poetic collaborator, Thomas Burbidge and his Italian wife, who had long lived north of Florence, on this occasion, simply because it would be too cold.[25] It is difficult to imagine that Thena did not plan to visit her father's grave; but Annie was wise enough to keep silent about aspects of the journey which might be seen as pilgrimage.

During her student days Thena was treated as much as possible like any other student, although she could be called upon to help out socially from time to time. Knowing, for example, that Thena would not attend any church on Sunday, Annie asked her to spend a little time with the ailing Winnie Seebohm, who was delighted to discover that they both knew the Lionel Tennysons and Anne Thackeray Ritchie.[26] Whatever its disadvantages, student life at Newnham provided Thena with a great deal more stimulus and variety than life at Embley Park; and although she had only intended to be a student for a year, she remained one for four years. She took a considerable and well-informed interest in contemporary politics and enjoyed debating them. 'The Political Society', she wrote,

was started in my first term and was an immediate success. It almost at once took the form of a Parliament, with Speaker and Government and Opposition and members for constituencies, and for twenty years and more it flourished like a particularly green bay-tree . . . Much time and thought was spent by members of the Government in preparing bills and by the Opposition in discovering their weak points. We learnt to be familiar with parliamentary procedure, and we learnt a good deal about public questions. We were full of zeal and fury and fought joyfully and hard.

She served twice as 'Prime Minister', first as a Liberal and then as an ardent Liberal Unionist, opposed to Gladstone's commitment to offer Home Rule to Ireland, a position which she shared with Margaret Verrall, Millicent Fawcett and a number of other politically active women.[27]

Edith Sharpley worked hard to keep Thena's Latin up to scratch and to build up her Greek – 'To throw any doubts on your being able to do Greek in Group B [of the Higher Locals] next June would be to insult you.' At one stage she played with the notion of proposing Thena as an additional resident lecturer in Classics, as a way of keeping her at Newnham, although that would have been difficult to justify on either economic or academic grounds; and Thena herself torpedoed it by not doing a Tripos.[28] Keeping her a third year entailed some special pleading: the General Committee agreed on 5 May 1886 'that Miss B. A. Clough should be allowed to stay a third year at Newnham if this were recommended by her Lecturers'. The fourth year was even more of a fudge: on 5 October 1887 Miss Clough's report to the General Committee 'that she had allowed her niece Miss B. A. Clough to return as a student for a fourth year, Miss Sharpley having given up her second room for the purpose, was received with approval.

Miss B. A. Clough is to pay for her board & lodging and to make her own arrangements as regards instruction.' Eventually a longer-term solution was found: on 17 November 1888 the Council resolved that Miss B. A. Clough be appointed Secretary to the Principal at a salary of £50 per annum.[29]

Subsequently people were to praise Thena's selflessness in taking on the role, praise which in her black book she firmly rebutted – 'my object in staying was still my own development. I remember Alice Lloyd telling me I was wasted on such menial work & I said yes I knew, but it was in exchange for the freedom which came of living away from home.' But to herself and Edith she acknowledged that there was more to her commitment to Annie than that. 'To me she began by being an aunt whose points had been shown me – (i.e. some of her points, as it were her active doing part) but whom I could not find, something like a bore for a long time.' Then having stayed up one summer, either 1886 or 1887, to help with the August correspondence, 'I remember saying to Edith she seemed to me so nearly perfect I was sure I could not see all there was – I think I meant in her breadth of view & sympathy.' From this she moved 'gradually into the position of slave companion valet[,] first taking it in exchange for the advantages it gave me then recognising more & more fully that it was a really great thing to do. But I did not often get great pleasure from the doing of it.'[30]

The work was difficult and demanding in two quite different ways: managing and supporting her sixty-eight-year-old aunt and engaging with a fresh phase of the institution's development. By the time Thena became her aunt's secretary a third hall had been added to the first two. Applications from would-be students continued to flow in and as Henry explained to J. A. Symonds in May 1885,

Important matters will come before the Newnham Council on the 16th. It will be proposed to take a decided, though not irrevocable, step towards the building of a third Hall, by taking a temporary house to receive additional students. Miss Clough, whose mind is always peculiarly open to the logic of facts, has yielded to the pressure of applications, and set her thoughts toward a third Hall: and as 'ce qu'elle veut, elle veut <u>fortement</u>', I expect that we shall begin building in about two years, if the pressure continues.[31]

It all fell out exactly as he had predicted. A large new hall, to the north of the road which divided the two existing halls, running west towards Grange Road, and costing £20,000, most of which had to be borrowed, was built and ready for opening in June 1888. The Prince and Princess of Wales did the honours, accompanied by their children and Nora's uncle, Lord Salisbury, then Prime Minister; and Thena found herself drafted into presenting the bouquet to the Princess of Wales.[32] By then the Council had also addressed the issue of names for the halls. The simple geography of North and South Hall would no longer suffice and 'ignores the personal element which has been so powerful in the establishment of Newnham College. It rejects the opportunity of commemorating, in the simplest and most obvious way, the names of those to whom the College principally owes its existence and success.' So wrote the historian and Council member G. W. Prothero to Annie, and no doubt to Henry and Nora too, seeking permission to raise the matter of renaming the halls in the Council at the end of 1887. They agreed; and so the new hall was called Clough Hall, North Hall was renamed Sidgwick Hall, while South Hall, the very first building, became Old Hall.[33]

The creation of the third hall brought the issue of the ancient right of way which bisected the grounds to the top of the agenda. A right of way could only be abolished if another could be substituted for it. Henry and Nora embarked on laborious negotiations with the private owners and the two colleges, Selwyn and Corpus, owning land to the north of the new hall, to create a road there. It took nearly four years to complete these negotiations. It was not until 7 November 1891 that Henry could report to the Newnham Council that all objections had been withdrawn; and in the process he and Nora dug deep into their own pockets to compensate owners and then to contribute to the making-up of the road and the planting of trees along it.[34] It was entirely appropriate that the new road should be called Sidgwick Avenue; and its importance in allowing the integration of the College's site and buildings cannot be over-estimated.

With the opening of Clough Hall the College was accommodating 150 students and had at last a dining hall in which they could all gather. Looking back from the 1920s, Thena considered that this, complemented by the moving of the right of way, marked the watershed between Newnham as domestic enterprise, a pair of over-grown country houses, still on occasion managing things by improvising, and Newnham as institution, with rules and structures.[35] The group of senior members which she formally joined was now a substantial one. The growing company of lecturers, resident and non-resident, were being increasingly supported by administrative and tutorial staff, and some of them combined the duties. When Nora Sidgwick had taken charge of North (later Sidgwick) Hall in 1880, she had brought with her as her secretary Helen Gladstone, the younger daughter of the Liberal politician, who had been a Newnham student 1877–80. After two

11 The Newnham staff in 1890. Thena stands behind Annie, notebook at the ready. Back row, left to right: Alice Gardner, Thena Clough, Rebecca Saunders, Mary Ellen Rickett; middle row, left to right: Helen Gladstone, Annie Clough, Katharine Stephen, Jane Lee; front row, left to right: Margaret Tuke, Edith Sharpley, Agnes Collier

years, the Sidgwicks decided that residence in the Hall and the tutorial responsibilities thereby entailed were something of an over-load, and Helen was appointed Vice-Principal in charge of the Hall in Nora's place. In 1886 Helen recruited Katharine Stephen, daughter of the distinguished lawyer James Fitzjames Stephen and niece of Leslie Stephen, founding editor of the *Dictionary of National Biography*, to act as her secretary. Jane Lee, daughter of Archdeacon William Lee, Professor of Ecclesiastical History at Trinity College, Dublin, had been appointed resident lecturer in modern languages and literature in 1882. In 1884 she became Librarian and in 1885 she also took charge of the house temporarily leased in Barton Road while Clough Hall was being built. When, on its completion, Annie moved from Old Hall to reside in Clough, Jane became the Vice-Principal in charge of Old Hall. Annie meanwhile was given the support not only of Thena as her secretary but also of Katharine Stephen as Vice-Principal of Clough, the biggest of the three Halls; and Katharine took over as well the responsibility for the growing Library from Jane Lee.[36] Invaluable help was still being given by devoted volunteers, male and female, like the Kennedy sisters, Anna and William Bateson, Annette and John Peile, Neville and Florence Keynes, and Mary Ewart, and would long continue; but the developing structure of posts sends institutional much more than domestic signals. The families here represented also indicate the responsiveness of the liberal intelligentsia and their daughters to the opportunities that institutional structure was beginning to offer.[37]

By this time too, the organisation of committees had become settled. The Council continued to deal with matters of policy and grand strategy; but effective use was being made of sub-committees, both standing and occasional. From 1880 the Education Committee dealt with regular admissions and teaching arrangements, while the General Committee picked up a host of miscellaneous matters, including non-standard admissions, overall numbers, buildings and other domestic issues. From 1882 successive Librarians had the support of a Library Committee. The road negotiations of course had their own sub-committee. When in 1888–9 it was decided that the College needed its own entrance examination, a special examinations committee was constituted to do the detailed work. Once the scheme was up and running, the committee was disbanded and oversight of admissions reverted to the Education Committee. At the same time the steadily growing group of old students were formalising their structures for meeting regularly and keeping in touch with and supporting the College. The Newnham College Old Students' Club was founded in April 1881, holding its preliminary and first full meetings in the coffee room of the Working Women's College in London, at 7 Fitzroy Street. They settled into a pattern of one business meeting and two or three social meetings a year and published an annual Letter. Once they had sorted out the business of collecting subscriptions they began to think about ways and means of contributing to Newnham financially; and their first project in 1887 was to have both Sidgwicks painted by J. J. Shannon.[38]

Thena was at first a small cog in this machinery but nevertheless a distinctive one. Her passion for landscape was recognised in her appointment to the very first sub-committee of the General Committee to deal with the gardens alone, in the autumn of 1888.[39] Once the Old Students' Club had decided in 1889 that their committee needed a member who was a Cambridge resident, she it was who was elected in 1890 and she would serve through the decade.[40] As Annie's secretary, she was the general dogsbody in the rush to get Clough Hall habitable and ready to receive students in the early autumn of 1888, and she was for ever mortified about her miscounting, which left one room unfurnished and one student without a room.[41] This was the part of the work which she found hardest and about which she complained most vehemently in the privacy of her black book. Brought up in an affluent, large household, with ample numbers of servants, managed by someone else, it came as a shock to have to cope in so economical and pared down a fashion. Looking back on it four years later, she remembered it as

A horrid time. I had not grown out of Embley ways [,] thought Cambridge and Newnham squalid . . . The new hall was of course peculiarly squalid [,] half the furnishing to do, no housekeeper & then worse than none. I knew nothing & had all to do that Aunt Annie didn't do herself & she I think must have felt the loss of MMM [her previous secretary] & felt me very inadequate & unhelpful – I wasn't in the least broken in & she was I thought very cross to me [.] I know I hadn't cried for years and she used to make me cry with her sharp little words & I used to go at night & cry away in my bare-boarded bedroom. I felt very much that I was turning my back on Embley & the old clean dainty easy life with reading & thinking & solitude & expanses of garden & country that had been my life till now & that now it was this squalor & labour & no leisure.

While it was happening, however, she was also honest enough to admit, 'I dare say if I had leisure it would turn to dust and ashes in my hands. I do at intervals believe in and feel enthusiasm for my present pursuit.'[42]

  Gradually Thena learned to manage the household, displaying the practical skills that put her in November 1889 on a special Council sub-committee looking at the drainage of all the buildings and then involved with the garden and road committees in sorting out the fences and railings needed as a consequence of the new road.[43] Gradually too she learned to work with her aunt, forcing herself to be patient and not to fuss, especially over small matters, and choosing more carefully and effectively the points at which it might be possible to intervene to try to curb and limit Annie's inveterate tendency to involve herself in everything. Annie's talent for 'always being so much interested in anything one told her that she made all one's plans for one'[44] had its drawbacks as well as its advantages. The summer of 1889 was a particularly anxious one for the Newnham senior members, as Katharine Stephen was having to cope with the first manic-depressive outbursts of her brother J. K. – Jem – Stephen, a Fellow of King's, who had been going around Cambridge waving a revolver. A letter from Nora about Katharine's continuing difficulties with Jem arrived while Annie and Thena were staying with Augusta Migault in Germany. Thena was driven to prepare a speech to make to Annie about conserving her energies and not attempting the impossible '& made it too down in the drawing room there & she laughed a good deal & said dear me, but she attended somewhat

& was I think somewhat influenced'.[45] It was an uphill struggle and there were times when Thena not only resorted to her black book but also to great long tramps through the countryside, eventually coming to rest under a tree, sitting and smoking and trying to bring her feelings into some sort of equilibrium. A turning point came in the summer of 1890, at Embley, when

I tramped through those near woods without stopping for a minute, not even smoking, till I got to where those wild roses are all over the bushes then up to those splendid beeches on Whitebridge hill I think it is – & I sat down against one close to a stump with water in & smoked one after another & threw the hot things into the water & heard them hiss & wrestled it out & saw that her life was more valuable than ruin, that to keep her alive was more worth doing than to develop myself and that if I did nothing else I should have done far more for the ideas I care about than by anything else.[46]

There would still be difficult patches; but after this crisis Thena felt that she never thereafter wholly lost sight of the larger objectives and all that could be learned from working closely with other people, with all their demands and imperfections.

Amongst the events which may have helped Thena achieve a degree of balance and reminded her of the long-term goals and aims were those which made 1890 'Philippa's year', as Thena christened it:[47] 1890 was the year in which Philippa Fawcett, Millicent Garrett Fawcett's only child and a Newnham student since 1887, was placed above the Senior Wrangler in the Mathematics Tripos. Through the 1880s the women students at Cambridge had continued to improve their academic performance; and there was great and general rejoicing in 1887 when Agnata Ramsay of Girton was the only candidate of either sex deemed to be fit to occupy the first division of the first class in Part II of the Classical Tripos. Emily Davies and her supporters set out to use this achievement to reopen the question of degrees for women. Henry was dismayed: he thought it was premature and it once more raised the question of compulsory Greek. He devoted all his considerable political skills and weight to block the Girton schemes – and succeeded. It is an episode in his long and distinguished career as a university reformer that reflects little credit upon him.[48]

It was common to concede that women might display talent in literary and linguistic studies; but not to expect them to do so in Mathematics. Yet until 1824 the Mathematical Tripos had been Cambridge's only Tripos and its status was still immensely high: Wranglers – those who topped the first class of the Mathematical Tripos, ranked in strict order of marks –

12 Philippa Fawcett (standing) and Edith Sharpley *c*.1890

remained the *crème de la crème*. Philippa Fawcett's father Henry, who had died in 1884, had also read mathematics, being seventh Wrangler, and her parents recognised early on that she had mathematical aptitude. She attended the Girls' Public Day School Company school in Clapham but also had additional coaching in mathematics organised by her parents. When she came up to Newnham in 1887 her work was directed by the resident lecturer, Mary Ellen Rickett, who had herself been Newnham's very first Wrangler equivalent, and Philippa's male coaches were chosen with especial care, as those who usually worked with the high-flyers. Tripos candidates at Newnham were invariably cosseted during the examination term, fed additional delicacies, encouraged to exercise and rest properly as well as working; but Philippa was the object of particular hopes and attentions in the spring and early summer of 1890. Annie wrote to Millicent Garrett Fawcett on 30 May, 'I am glad to tell you that Philippa is keeping up her strength and spirits – she really seems very well and has slept well.' The Senate House was packed for the reading of the Mathematics examination results on Saturday 7 June: Philippa, Annie and Helen Gladstone were among those in the gallery and the crowd downstairs included Philippa's grandfather, Newson Garrett. Protocol required the reading of the whole of the men's list before the women's list, but finally they got there and pandemonium erupted once Philippa's name, with the statement 'above the Senior Wrangler', was read. Eventually some order was restored, the remainder of the women's list read and Philippa, more composed than her grandfather, processed out. Millicent was summoned by telegram from London and the whole of Newnham was *en fête* that night: a dinner, bouquets, speeches, a bonfire on the hockey field and dancing. The celebratory lay began:

> Hail the triumph of the corset
> Hail the fair Philippa Fawcett.
> Victress in the fray
> Crown her queen of hydrostatics
> And the other Mathematics
> Wreathe her brow in bay.

The national press made much of the achievement the following week and the *Pall Mall Gazette* and the *Women's Penny Paper* organised a subscription fund for Newnham in her honour.[49] Philippa took it all with her usual calm and later that summer was to be found learning elementary Dutch with Thena, before they carried Annie and Alice Bonham Carter off with them for an expedition to Holland.[50]

Such exaltation could do much to make drudgery worthwhile. But Thena also saw and was fiercely proud of the fact that Annie had become an iconic figure in the campaign for women's education not only in Britain but in the world at large.[51] In the 1870s those Oxford women developing the plans that would become Somerville College, including her former pupil at Eller How, Mary Arnold, now the novelist Mrs Humphry Ward, had sought advice and made visits.[52] The two Misses Longfellow fed what they learned as students at Newnham in 1883–4 into their contributions to the Harvard Annex, later to become Radcliffe College. American visitors as well as students were always warmly welcomed to Newnham, and Grace King, the New Orleans novelist, would write a happy account of a visit in 1891 in her memoirs: she had dinner in Clough Hall and the next day Annie invited her to talk to the students about the poet Sidney Lanier. Contacts with Germany flourished. Queen Victoria's daughter, the Empress Frederick, had sent Helena Lange to visit both Newnham and Girton. Then in 1884 she appointed one of the early Newnham students, Alix von Cotta, who had come up in 1876, the Directress of the Victoria Lyceum in Berlin, the only institution in Germany which offered higher education to women.[53] In December 1891 Annie also took a major share in the work of the London committee for the selection of the first Lady Principal of the University of Sydney's Women's College. She wrote references for the three Newnham candidates. She advised crisply – and without favouring Newnham – on the candidates to be shortlisted from the total field of sixty-five, recommending a first group of four, with a further two in reserve, if the other members of the committee were prepared to consider any younger candidates.[54]

The Newnham students had already once made a collection in 1882 to have Annie's portrait painted by W. B. Richmond; and in 1889 the Old Students' Club collected more funds for a second portrait by J. J. Shannon, to hang in the Clough dining hall and complement his portraits of Nora and Henry. Annie's style was no more polished than it ever had been – she used to irritate Thena by always referring to 'the higher education', sometimes, one suspects, to tease[55] – but nothing now daunted or over-awed her. The economist Alfred Marshall had begun his career in support of the higher education of women; and Mary Paley, his wife, remained its staunchest supporter. Alfred, however, increasingly took fright at its implications and in January 1889, having heard that the Newnham students had been debating issues relating to women's suffrage, wrote Annie a long, convoluted and worried letter, deprecating the association of her name and Newnham's name with 'any movement for altering the social & political relation of men and women'. Annie was fully capable of dealing with weasel words like this. She declared herself 'gratified by receiving so many closely written sheets from you about Newnham' and acknowledged that the work of the College required great watchfulness and discretion: 'I have always done my best to preserve a womanly character & regard to home duties among my students & I think with a good deal of success.' She herself had never felt strongly about suffrage, being much occupied with other things. She could, however, understand why some felt strongly and there were

many fearful evils that women suffer from that might be mitigated if they had the sufferage [*sic*].

But I do not wish that the sufferage should be won by violent speeches & excitement. It should come like a great wave of public opinion – steady & strong but gentle & these waves will I hope one day land the bark of Women's sufferage and bring it safely to port. Women are anxious to be fellow helpers and feel they can be such. And so dear Alfred I went to the Sufferage meeting on Saturday to help on quietness & peace.[56]

These words were meant to disarm, but there was nothing disingenuous about them. Thanking Mary Paley Marshall and all the others who wrote to her at the end of February 1891, the tenth anniversary of the Three Graces, but almost the twentieth anniversary of the beginning of Newnham, Annie returned again to the importance of quiet steady work together:

It is a great satisfaction to have had the opportunity of helping in work of this kind and especially as it has proved successful and has led towards the opening out of new careers & a broader life for Women with wider interests. To me the fact that all this has brought me into communication with so many young women has made my own life much fuller and happier. As the evening of life has come upon me may I hope and venture to ask that those who have benefitted [*sic*] by the Higher Education & social union of College life, will do their best, as time goes on, to guide the movement wisely and to help to keep up some degree of intercourse among the members of this College. I cannot but think of the future and I feel that I must appeal to the students especially to the ablest, the most experienced and the ablest, to be ready to give their counsel and their help in developing the work of the College both internally and externally.[57]

In the summer of 1891 Thena and Annie travelled together to Ireland, to stay with the Stephens and then spent time in Ambleside. They were 'happy and comfortable together' and 'laughed over things & people a good deal'; although Thena worried afterwards that it might have been too physically demanding.[58] She had begun her work as Annie's secretary with the thought that she might be able to help her wind down and retire. She soon came to see that that would be impossible and concentrated instead on minimising the possible sources of stress and stopping Annie's timetable becoming overloaded. At times she was afraid that her efforts to prevent everything coming to Annie – and Annie from involving herself in everything – inhibited their relationship and 'made as it were a barrier of silence & secretiveness between us' but she could see no alternative course of action.[59] The autumn term went fairly smoothly until Annie became ill; she recovered to a degree but it left her fussy and irritable – and perhaps a little frightened. She came increasingly to depend upon Thena for almost everything, including getting dressed and undressed each day. Thena remembered that,

Once or twice at night when I went to see her into bed, she was all of a fuss & angry with housekeepers or us & our stupidity & I had grace given me to agree & assent & not contradict & then she got quiet & gentle again. It was then one night she said to me those things about her not being strong & one night I told her, but I was very much afraid of saying much for fear of stirring up & preventing her sleep, that I knew I was a troublesome self-willed niece, but I did always want to do what she wished & she just laughed as she always did when things were getting nearly sentimental. I am so glad now that I did say that for I think she must have known then that it was true & perhaps forgiven me my contradictiousness.[60]

Edith Sharpley supported Thena in the work of caring for Annie, cheering Thena when she told her that Annie 'had more real comfort in my being there than anyone else's when she was ill'. When they were both being told off, Thena comforted Edith by suggesting that 'it was all right for us to get her bad temper if we could keep the best of her going for the world in general'.[61] In the Christmas vacation Blanche bore her share by taking Annie to Hastings for a fortnight; and she tried in vain to persuade her not to return to Cambridge and afterwards to return to London to be nursed. At the beginning of February 1892 a bad attack of breathlessness showed how weak Annie's heart had become. Her bed was moved permanently into her sitting room and Thena and Edith were reinforced by a trained nurse. Annie was not in pain, and as she became less and less mobile she took pleasure in being read to. When Thena and Edith read George Moore's *Esther Waters* to her, she teased them that Esther would not have acted as she did, had she had 'the Higher Education'. At the same time she demanded to be kept up to date with all the news of the College and it proved not practicable to keep the tragic news of Jem Stephen's death and Katharine's consequent absence from her for more than a day.[62] Physically she grew steadily weaker and became aware, as did Thena, that there could be only one outcome. Thena was anxious that her own lack of faith might be a barrier between them as death approached; but Annie did not find it so.

The two or three times she spoke to me about dying in her gay way, the way she looked up at me smiling with her eyes very brown and bright & said 'It doesn't matter you know' & then the last night I can't forget when nurse said 'Now Miss Clough you must try & be quiet & get some sleep' & she said so very touchingly 'I <u>will</u> try' & I was down on the floor by the bed holding her hand & I kissed it quickly when she said that & she gave her little laugh again – I'm glad she knew it. Then at the end, the end when she was so tired her head couldn't rest & she moved it always to the side for something to lean against & I put my face there for it to lean against her nice dear white hair – I think that was a faint comfort for a moment – Then came that bit of time not very long while I was kneeling there frightened, very frightened lest before the end there should be more breathlessness, more distress, frightened for her, frightened to see her die, I was over on her right side nurse on the other sometimes fanning sometimes chafing her hands. Edith kneeling lower down that other side & her breath began to come slower & slower she all the time with her eyes very bright looking straight out of the window. I could hear Edith crying quite quietly. I was watching her too hard to cry & it came slower and slower & at last it didn't come again & we laid her back.[63]

Anne Jemima Clough died in the early hours of 27 February 1892, aged seventy-two. The Provost and Fellows of King's College hastened to offer their chapel, in which she had often worshipped, for the funeral service on 5 March, after which her body was buried in the churchyard of the village of Grantchester, just outside Cambridge. At a special meeting on 12 March the Council recorded its sense of the greatness of the loss, describing Annie as one

who during the greater part of her life held a foremost place in the advancement of the education of women: who for twenty-one years at Cambridge guided the movement from small beginnings to assured success; who presided over the College with self-sacrificing devotion to its interests and with unfailing wisdom and dignity alike in its internal administration and in its relation to the University: and who by her noble character and loving sympathy left a lasting mark on the many generations of students committed to her charge.[64]

The eager young woman who had confided to her journal in 1841, 'if I could only do something to benefit my fellow creatures', had succeeded beyond her imaginings.

CHAPTER 7

'An ought which has to be reckoned with'

As soon as the Lent (Spring) Term of 1892 ended, Thena fled to Italy, first to Florence and Siena and then on to Venice. She made heavy use of her black book, trying to set down all her recollections of the last four years, trying to gain some grip on the turmoil of her feelings. As usual, she was savagely self-critical, convinced she was a fraud, as she accepted the condolences that flooded in: 'I know I don't feel the things everyone expects me to feel.' Yet the poignant detail of her memories, as the previous chapter shows, reveal the depth of her emotion. As she contemplated a future in which she would not have to dance attendance on a demanding old lady, she recognised that the prospect of leisure and choice had lost much of its savour: and firm atheist though she was, the imagery of John Bunyan's *Pilgrim's Progress*, perhaps a legacy from her schooldays, cast a long shadow.

My life will be easier now of course far less arduous laborious anxious – there will be in it now some of that leisure some of those possibilities I have so often wished for But how curiously the whole face of it has changed – it is on a lower greyer level a flat uneven arid thorny country through which one has to pick one's way with a new portion of responsibility on one's shoulders. It was an uphill road before & stony & one fell down & groaned & despaired often but one did somehow believe in its leading in the really best way . . . The centre of interest the source of inspiration, the representative of so many insufficiently represented ideas, of so much truth that I have, recognise and more than half admire, curious touchstone of genuineness, all this is gone out.[1]

On Thena's return to Cambridge, there were many practical matters to address. Annie had appointed her one of her executors, with A.V. Dicey, Elinor Bonham Carter's husband, and Thena's brother, Arthur. Part of Annie's modest estate of some £14,000 went to create a trust for her brother Charles' children and grandchildren, the rest in a series of legacies, the recipients including Thena, Blanche, Alice Bonham Carter, Marion Kennedy and her sister Julia, Margaret Calder, Mary Claude and Mary Paley Marshall. She left £1000 to Newnham College, 'if at the time of my decease it shall remain an

Unsectarian Institution as it at present is'.[2] Thena contributed substantially to the discussions of old students about a suitable public memorial to her aunt; and the eventual result was a handsome set of bronze gates, designed appropriately by Basil Champneys, at the head of Newnham Walk.[3] The question which exercised Thena most, however, was that of a memoir of her aunt. She had begun by feeling that anything written would be but a 'shadow' on the paper – 'the lamp has gone out' – then wondering whether it would be possible to convey the force of 'that curious character in which there burnt so strong a flame forcing its way out in so many ways lighting up so much'. A decision was precipitated by a suggestion that Blanche, her mother, should write the first half of a memoir, drawing on the work she had already done on the Cloughs' childhood for the memoir of Arthur Hugh, while Thena wrote the second half, about Newnham. Thena reacted strongly against this: 'the first part in M's hands would be merely repetition of the other book – that tho' she knows a good deal about it there is a good deal she doesn't know – that what I wrote about the last 20 years would fit in very badly with the first half'. Either she had to stand clear of the project entirely, or write the memoir herself. She chose the latter course – it is the one debate with herself in all the black books that is swiftly, decisively, positively resolved; and by the middle of 1893 she was compiling a first list of enquiries to make in gathering information.[4]

Work on the memoir occupied Thena for over three years, in the interstices of her duties at Newnham; and its fruits were finally published in 1897. She had access to her aunt's contemporary manuscript diaries as well as to the manuscript memoirs written later for her mother to use, and to her father's letters up to the beginning of the 1850s. She also had the inestimable advantage of access to many of Annie's friends and collaborators. She was systematic and thorough in interviewing them and gathering their written comments: her black books for these years include preliminary lists of questions, notes on the responses to them and her own musings on what she had learned.[5] For the work was not only a voyage of discovery about her aunt, it was also a journey to find the father she had never known, by routes that did not lead through her mother. As she put it obliquely, 'it has so many collateral or incidental attractions'. She saw for herself how close Arthur and Annie had been to each other in their early years, saw how Annie almost hero-worshipped him, remaining always convinced of his utter moral rectitude. Yet she saw also how Arthur's rigid self-control, reserve and exact, sometimes over-nice, sense of taste formed a growing barrier between them, often making Annie feel inadequate. In January 1894, reading Annie's diaries, Thena directly posed the question,

What was AHC really like? She [Annie] describes him as always sweet & even tempered very kind in helping her but she was often acutely discontented – says how much he does for them & yet I sometimes think he is careless of her & again – sometimes he thinks all women a pack of fools & me the greatest of them – but always rebukes herself for being unjust to him – She is self-conscious with him & shy & speaks of talking a lot of show-off nonsense about poetry wh Arthur did not seem to approve of – but all this alongside of her intense admiration & adoration of him . . . He was evidently very reserved & silent – He is described later as being very much the scholar & the Oxford man & he was from the beginning extremely fastidious. She was certainly different – she was vehement, full of hot feelings, eager for her own way probably rather hot & hasty in temper. She was very much not fastidious & had rather a difficulty in understanding fastidiousness. She had an immense curiosity & never wearied or satiated interest or appetite.[6]

Such fastidiousness posed for Thena a dilemma. She saw herself as sharing her father's commitment to the best and finest in thought and sentiment; yet watching his manner of deploying it in his relationship with his sister, she could see how chilling and inhibiting it might become. Equally, she could see how her aunt's absorbing interest in people, underpinned by her own rock-like moral sense, bred a different kind of sensitivity.

What was it carried her through her life – what was it that worked inside her & got itself expressed at last? For one thing, there was her clear determination to succeed in being as good as she could be – from the first she meant to win her crown – then came her hobby her passion for her fellow creatures, all of them as individuals. This is as clear as daylight.

Her intellectual tools, as it were, were her moderation, power of seeing the other side – her memory which was perhaps part of her interest, & her inventiveness, resourcefulness . . . What made her so wise, thinking much, caring & sympathising . . . Then her vitality – really that was quite half the battle.

She had a fiery nature at bottom & a fundamental belief in her ideas . . . But in detail she was gentle & patient & ready to believe herself mistaken.[7]

Annie's responsiveness to people was crucial, Thena thought, in enabling her to cope with the discontents of the first five students. As Thena herself accumulated administrative experience in the running of a new kind of institution for young women, she wholly recognised her aunt's dilemma: 'she had to make all the tradition to fix how far the authority of the Principal should go . . . she had to create the idea of what a women's college should be, how it should differ from the restraint of a school & from the freedom of a men's college'. Annie's real efforts to understand the students' viewpoint and her complete lack of concern for her own dignity enabled her to change tack without rancour and, indeed, with grace. It didn't matter if Annie started an argument in the middle or things came out in a muddle: 'she didn't mind making suggestions she was quite ready to accept correction & bow to superior knowledge – And 1 out of 3 or 4 of her suggestions might hit the mark.' At the same time her capacity to imagine herself in someone else's shoes did not blind her to their foibles: she was amused in a wholly unmalicious way by people's 'pretensions & extravagances, oddities'. She and Thena laughed at the same things, which could include their own predicaments: Thena, the atheist, being swept off to church by their hosts at Abbeyleix in Ireland; the efforts of both of them to cope with a disruptive baby on a train to Holyhead. Thena was a considerable mimic and could reduce her aunt to tears of laughter in capturing the mannerisms of a colleague or replaying a scene in which they had both been involved. At bottom they were fundamentally in sympathy and at ease with each other, an ease which Thena never found herself able to achieve with her mother; and Thena's 'simple almost involuntary' response to her mother's plaintive enquiry as to why she behaved so much better to her aunt than to her mother, 'Because she never talks nonsense', conveyed that fundamental sympathy.[8]

Thena's *Memoir of Anne Jemima Clough* was published at the end of 1897. Her father's old friend J. A. Froude had done his utmost to thrust aside the 'Damocles' sword of *Respectability* [which] hangs forever over the poor English life-writer' – Carlyle's own words – in writing the life of Thomas Carlyle, another of her father's friends, at the beginning of the 1880s. But the conventions which had bound English biography were only gradually beginning to loosen.[9] The tone of the *Memoir* is even, a little flat; and the judgements and characterisations muted, especially by comparison with those recorded in the privacy of the black books. Thena did not attempt, for example, to try to convey Annie's sense of humour. Yet it is comprehensive, balanced, clear, accurate not only in its extensive direct quotation but also in its account of political and institutional developments – Henry had read it very carefully in proof, as had Frank Darwin and his wife Ellen, formerly Ellen Crofts – and readers of the book as diverse as Anna Bateson and Herbert Bell, the distinguished Ambleside photographer, wrote enthusiastic letters. A critical note was struck only by one of her Leigh Smith cousins who felt she had not accorded sufficient weight to the contribution of Barbara Leigh Smith Bodichon to the foundation of Girton.[10] Thena had allowed herself one sharply personal comment in the *Memoir*, in choosing as a frontispiece not a reproduction of either the Richmond or the Shannon portrait of Annie, but a photograph by Eveleen Myers, the wife of F. W. H. Myers, Henry's friend and fellow psychical research worker. She chose it because it showed the Clough dark eyes, so often hooded in repose, gazing directly at the camera. These eyes were a family characteristic Annie shared with her brother Arthur and with Thena herself. The Myers photograph shows a sombre but above all a strong and determined face – too strong for some of the audience; and in the second edition of the *Memoir* it was replaced by the Shannon portrait – a more conventionally benign image.[11]

In preparing the *Memoir*, Thena had learnt a great deal about her family and about the institution in which she lived and worked. In the longer term this knowledge would contribute to a degree of resolution of her uncertainties about her own life and the direction in which it should go; but it would take time for these effects to be felt. She gained great intellectual satisfaction from the process of writing; and her deft handling of a mass of material showed the superb administrator she was in process of becoming. She also learnt much not only about Newnham but also about Cambridge and the general campaign for the higher education of women, in all its political complexities and institutional manifestations. As she put it, 'I don't want to write a history of the WM [Women's Movement] but I think I ought to understand it.' She noted with interest Henry's view that education for women was but part of a reform agenda. Discussions with Henry, Nora and Marion Kennedy had helped her to appreciate the political uses of the gradualist, incremental approach within Cambridge; at the same time she was fair-minded enough to recognise the intellectual coherence of the Girton stance and the case for treating women identically with men. This depth of knowledge and understanding would prove a major resource in the years to come and underpin her administrative skills. Yet none of it was enough entirely to vanquish the demons of depression and insecurity. She endured a particularly bad patch, for example, in the summer of 1894.[12]

Thena was not the only member of her generation in the family to suffer depression; her brother Arthur was likewise afflicted and awareness of the burden they both shared may have strengthened the bond between them. After a starry undergraduate career, Arthur had read for the Bar but then in 1885, like his father, he accepted an appointment in the Education Department of the Privy Council Office, work which he did not much enjoy.[13] This was followed, according to family tradition, by deep disappointment in love. Travelling in the United States he visited the family of his father's old friend Charles Eliot Norton and fell in love with Norton's daughter Sally, only to be decisively rejected.[14] Whatever the impact of this rebuff, he did eventually recover sufficiently to pay his addresses and propose marriage to Eleanor Freshfield, the daughter of the distinguished Alpinist Douglas Freshfield (yet another Trinity man) and his wife Augusta, née Ritchie. Nevertheless, throughout 1892 Arthur was not at all well, debilitated by insomnia and beginning to suffer from the heavy doses of barbiturates which were all the doctors could offer to help him sleep. Gradually he tapered the medication off and in the Christmas vacation, shepherded by Thena, he took leave in the Mediterranean, first North Africa and then the South of France. Florence Nightingale's comment to Blanche on all this offers a vivid glimpse of Thena's public persona. 'What a power brave Thena is – so striking her calmness, her complete self-possession, her wasting no words.'[15] The leave and the climate helped Arthur gain further strength and he was well enough to go through with his wedding to Eleanor on the long-arranged date, 9 February 1893, supported by his anxious best man, a Trinity friend and contemporary, Henry Babington Smith. However full recovery took most of the rest of the year.[16]

Playing an important part in the rebuilding of Arthur's life in the longer term was the creation of a Clough estate in the New Forest. His grand-mother, the matriarch Mai, had died in January 1889, when under the Nightingale entail, Embley and its estate passed to Blanche's brother, Shore Smith, who duly changed his surname to Nightingale. Sadly, he did not long outlive his mother, dying himself in the middle of 1894, and at this point the estate was broken up and the house sold. By this stage Arthur and Eleanor were already trying to buy a plot of land – some eight acres – at Burley, not far away, on which they hoped to build a house. Burley Manor was also in process of being broken up and Blanche decided to add her not inconsiderable resources to those of Arthur and Eleanor, to buy a total of 125 acres for £3698. On this they were to build first two cottages, next a large house for Blanche, Florence and Thena and then a house for Arthur and Eleanor, who had been using one of the cottages at weekends and holidays, while living in a rented house in London during the week.[17] Life as a gentleman farmer and conscientious country landlord suited Arthur far better than the administrative work of the Education Department. He also rather fancied himself as an architect and was much involved with the design and construction of Castle Top, the house built for himself and Eleanor, and then with that of the additional cottages built in the village. In June 1898 he took the plunge, resigning from the Education Department and henceforward devoting himself to Burley and its affairs.[18]

Thena continued to take pleasure in the landscape of the New Forest, as she would for the rest of her life. But she had no intention of spending more than the vacations at Burley Hill, as her mother's new house was called. Relations between them were no easier than they had ever been and she tried yet again to sort out the reasons for this in a fragment, undated, but almost certainly belonging to these years.

I seem as if I must consider for the 100th time my uneasy existence with my parent. I sometimes think it is very doubtful whether I ought to grumble so much. I wonder if it's true as she says that I'm cruel to her. After all, she does let me follow my so to speak career & it doesn't seem very unreasonable that she should expect me to attend on her the rest of the time. What's really the matter I suppose is the way it's done – I have about an hour and a half generally for my own purposes in the morning & perhaps 2 hours most evenings besides any time I like to take out of the time between 11PM & 9AM. It really is a good deal. The thing that makes it feel like bondage is the way it's demanded of one the way one is somehow expected to be always there whenever she wants one & only as a favour allowed off . . . I suppose what is really irksome to me that unless I make a great struggle & go away as I did last year for 2 nights I am never my own master for a day.[19]

Poor Blanche! She had already learned that the name of Clough had a resonance in the world which did not depend only upon her husband's poetry and her own work as keeper of the flame. She came to acknowledge this with grace, serving several terms on the Newnham Council between 1892 and 1897, and generously endowing a scholarship, named for Arthur Hugh.[20] Her son, for whom she would have done anything in the world, lived near at hand. She had the company of one daughter permanently at home, the sweet-tempered Florence, whose voice, except in that one childish thank-you letter to Alice Bonham Carter, we have lost. Yet not content with all this, Blanche never ceased to crave as well the affection and approval of her younger daughter; and her ways of seeking it never failed to irritate that very different individual, clever, reserved and able to be very spiky when she chose.

Thena might have coped with Blanche's self-pity more equably and even robustly if she herself had felt more consistently positive about her 'so to speak career'. Living at close quarters with women and men who were, she knew she was not an academic; and although widely read, with a powerful analytical intelligence, displayed in her commentaries on her reading in the black books, whether John Morley *On Compromise*, the novels of Thomas Hardy or Abbott and Campbell's biography of Benjamin Jowett, she always played down her own intellectual strengths. She had difficulty believing that the growing institution that was Newnham had as much need of administrative and tutorial skills as it had for good teaching and distinguished research. In the trough of depression in the summer of 1894 she questioned whether she should continue there: 'I spend my life there in an ineffectual attempt to do properly a miscellaneous assortment of small practical duties.' At the same time she acknowledged the pull of her immediate obligation to Nora Sidgwick and her awareness of how much her involvement had meant to her aunt: 'I care about that & I care very much about the place.' And as she began to recover her equilibrium, she was able to recognise that large institutions are always supported by 'a miscellaneous assortment of small practical duties'. Coming out of the church at Embley after Shore Nightingale's funeral at the beginning of September 1894, she and Arthur 'loafed' in the sun, watching horses in a nearby field. It brought back all the comfort and stability of life at Embley, which her Newnham experience had subsequently taught her were dependent on the hard work of a host of people. 'I don't say I've been on the hard ground but I have looked through my platform & climbed about among its beams & looked down at the ground. I suppose in plain English this is the very simple matter that I felt my peace & comfort were dependent on an elaborately organized household & that I knew nothing about household things & now I know a little more.' A women's college needed the underpinning of sound administration even more than a large Victorian country house.[21]

The Newnham responsibilities about which Thena was so disparaging were steadily accumulating. She was the key member of the Garden Committee, an active member of the General Committee, an important link with the Old Students' Club and the new sub-set of old students, the Associates, created in 1893. Formally she was described as Assistant Treasurer and Assistant Secretary; and as Nora, the Treasurer, was also now the Principal, having been appointed by the Council to succeed Annie in 1892, her Assistant carried substantial responsibility. In the first half of 1893, for example, when Nora was unwell following a bad fall, Thena simply took over sections of the work, including the correspondence with the Bursar of St John's about the exact delineation and fencing of boundaries consequent on the closure of the path and the creation of the new road.[22] Her name was first canvassed as a possible Vice-Principal, that is, carrying tutorial responsibility for one of the three halls, in 1894, when Jane Lee resigned, but by a majority vote, the position was offered to Mary Ellen Rickett. When the next vacancy occurred, a year later, in November 1895, when Helen Gladstone had to step down in order to become 'the daughter at home' for her ageing parents, the Council were unanimous in offering the post to Thena. At that point she was on leave from college duties for a term, as she pulled the final draft of the *Memoir* together, and inevitably the offer triggered a great bout of soul-searching and self-abasement in the current black book: 'am I the sort of person who would really be wholesome among the students & is this the sort of occupation which would make me the best sort of person I can be' – to which her answer was predictably 'no'. Margaret Verrall briskly cut through all this: 'There is no-one I am more anxious to see definitely & permanently connected with the College.'

She continued, 'the fact that you are who you are & have had so much to do with Newnham is of course important but I don't put it in the same class as the fact that you are *what* you are'. By this she meant two linked things: first, that Thena had the highest intellectual standards; and second, that her atheism made it easier for her not to confuse moral worth with intellectual distinction. For Margaret, Christianity tended to breed such confusion, especially among women, a recipe for mediocrity. Whether or not Thena entirely shared this view, she allowed herself to be persuaded and accepted the post. Nearly ten years earlier, she had reflected, 'My life is one of self-indulgence but there is in my composition an ought which has to be reckoned with.' This was an occasion when 'ought' prevailed. Atheist she might be, but her sense of duty was as powerful as that which had animated her aunt – and burdened her father.[23]

Thena became involved in the inner councils of the College in time to share one of the biggest setbacks to face the institution so far, the emphatic rejection by the University of any degree of recognition for the women students beyond the permission to take examinations granted by the Three Graces of 1881. In the process she saw at close quarters not only the issues facing the College but also the labyrinthine workings of the University in which they were trying to gain a foothold. It proved a hard but important apprenticeship.[24] Baulked in 1887, Emily Davies and Girton had felt it worth reopening the question of degrees for women in the summer of 1895, encouraged by the fact that such proposals had surfaced in Oxford. The Sidgwicks again dragged their feet, wanting to wait until a vote had been taken in Oxford; but the Girton initiative found a more positive response from a new Newnham constituency, the Associates, the body formed in 1893 to give a degree of representation in the government of the College to former students and members of the staff. Thena was one of the first group of Associates to be elected and their first President was Margaret Verrall.[25] At their AGM in November 1895 they agreed to send forward the following resolution to the College Council: 'that in the opinion of the Associates of Newnham College, the Senate should be asked to admit women to membership of the University and to University degrees', acknowledging that the issues of membership, which would bring participation in University government, and the titles of degrees were distinct although by no means unrelated issues. The Council responded by creating a committee to confer with the Girton Council and with resident members of the University, about the right timing for such an initiative.

At first all the omens seemed positive. Both Girton and Newnham recognised that they had to present a united public front and worked hard to sustain it, not, for example, letting disagreement about the relative merits of the Higher Locals and the Previous Examination get in the way. Discussions with sympathetic resident members produced a Memorial to the Council of the Senate asking for a University committee or Syndicate to consider upon what conditions and with what restrictions women might be admitted to degrees, which in six weeks at the beginning of 1896 attracted over 2000 signatures. But then things began to unravel. In March 1896 first the Oxford women were defeated and then the proposed membership of the Cambridge Syndicate, which included Henry and John Peile, was challenged on the grounds that it was already *parti pris*. Both promptly withdrew their names and a new Syndicate was proposed and graced; but it was the first signal of storms to come. Over the summer both sides mobilised supporters and arguments. Expounding the fundamental intellectual inferiority of women, Alfred Marshall was prominent among the root-and-branch opponents, a prominence which must deeply have hurt Mary Paley Marshall; and he was also one of those proposing a separate women's university, a safe distance from Cambridge, Oxford and London.

Neither Newnham nor Girton would have any truck with the notion of a separate women's university: they recognised it for the ghetto it was intended to be.[26] They concentrated instead on explaining the real problems that having no formal qualification from an established university presented for women. Thena, a member of the main Newnham committee, took responsibility for gathering the views of old students. The Newnham Associates and the Girton Certificated Students combined to form a special committee to do this and to mobilise signatures for another Memorial to the Senate from these students, and Thena and her former school-fellow Katharine Jex-Blake acted as joint secretaries. In the end they secured 1234 signatures out of a possible total of 1539, all the old students of both institutions to date. Providing supplementary evidence to the Syndicate when it began to meet in the autumn, they explained that, 'since women leave college without proceeding to a degree, a very general impression exists outside the University that the course of study they have pursued is inferior to that pursued by men'. As all other UK universities apart from Oxford were now admitting women to degrees, this put the Cambridge women at a material disadvantage, particularly in the search for employment. There was a world outside Cambridge, which knew little – and perhaps cared less – about its fine distinctions. As Thena and Katharine delicately put it, 'Educational and other appointments are sometimes in the hands of persons not conversant with University affairs, who do not recognise the value of a Tripos certificate and prefer the qualifications of women who have graduated.'[27]

The Syndicate took evidence and deliberated through the autumn and winter of 1896–7. Fairly early on, in November 1896, by a majority vote, they took the crucial decision that women were not to be admitted as undergraduate members of the University, but might be given the title of the BA degree – in other words, they might have a formal piece of paper from the University but no share in University government. By February 1897 the Syndicate were irretrievably split; and Majority and Minority Reports followed. The Minority – five members – recommended a new, made-up title for any degrees to be granted to women – MLitt or MSc, 'or some other title of a degree, not being the title of a Degree in the University'. The Majority – nine members, including the current Vice-Chancellor – recommended that the women should be granted the titles of their degrees, first BAs and then MAs but made no mention of official access for women to lectures and laboratories, to the University Library and to competition for University awards and prizes.

Three days of formal discussion followed the publication of the Reports, on 13, 15 and 16 March; but the vote could not then be held until the Easter Term and in the intervening two months the battle raged in the press and by correspondence and fly-sheet. The Majority Report proposals were a meagre half-a-loaf, compared to the whole loaf so optimistically looked for at the beginning of 1896. It was, nevertheless, half-a-loaf and not a stone; but when the women signalled their acceptance, their earlier petitions for more were deployed against them and it was claimed that passage of the measures would simply encourage them to go on agitating. It was a classic illustration of 'the principle of the wedge', as set out barely a decade later by that consummate analyst of academic politics – and staunch supporter of Newnham – F. M. Cornford: 'you should not act justly now for fear of raising expectations that you may act still more justly in the future'.[28] Thena and Katharine Jex-Blake did their best with another dignified memorandum at the end of April, claiming that 'the proposed measures will, if passed, remove the chief incentive to agitation'.[29] But it was a difficult position to sustain. Who could deny that the granting of these concessions now *might* form the basis for further demands in the future – as the Three Graces of 1881 had preceded the proposals being discussed in 1897?

By the time the vote in the Senate House was due on 21 May 1897, argument had long since given way to *grand-guignol*. The undergraduates had already joined the fray with gusto, the Union voting by 1083 to 138 on

13 The declaration of the result of the ballot on the titles of degrees for women, 21 May 1897

11 May against the proposals; and on the morning of 21 May, many met the special trains from King's Cross, bringing non-resident MAs to vote, with fliers – one-horse hackney carriages – to bring them more speedily to the Senate House. An anonymous spectator described the scene, as the streets in front of the Senate House filled with excited young men:

A vigourous cockcrow emanating from the roof of Caius College and done with marvellous fidelity, was the signal for the commencement of operations. Forthwith, the occupants of the front rooms at Caius began to hang out their banner on the outer walls and a roar of laughter went up as there slowly descended from the upper window the lay figure of a woman with aggressively red hair dressed in cap and gown . . . Up till about 2 p.m. nothing worse than confetti and flour had been thrown. The dons, after voting, stood in solemn and serried array, within the Senate House Yard, waiting for the verdict. Someone threw a cracker over the palings and this was the signal for the commencement of a general bombardment. Cooped up like sheep in a pen, the devoted dons, some thousands in number, were pelted with fireworks of every description, while the smoke rose in clouds above their heads. The noise of the explosions and the cheers and counter-cheers were deafening.

When the voting figures were announced, 1713 against and 662 in favour, there was absolute pandemonium. A mob of excited undergraduates set off for Newnham – closer than Girton – and a Newnham student of the time still remembered over fifty years later 'listening from the roof of Sidgwick Hall, to the distant roar from the town, which increased in volume as the "attacking forces" gradually approached'. The Clough Memorial Gates were firmly closed and behind them stood the grim-faced Newnham staff.[30] The mob had the sense to retreat – but spent the rest of the night celebrating wildly in the Market Square, shop doors, shutters and fencing being wrenched off to feed a huge bonfire. Over £100 worth of damage was done – several thousands of pounds in today's terms.

CHAPTER 8

Regrouping

The likelihood of defeat, even on the modest proposal of the titles of degrees, had begun to emerge once the Syndicate split. However its scale, the extravagance of the language and at the end the actual violence with which it was accompanied, deeply shocked the Cambridge women. Despite the 2000 signatures asking for the creation of the Syndicate in 1896, they had not, a year later, secured the votes even of a majority of resident members of the University. There was understandable apprehension about what might happen next. The Newnham Council discussed the issue on 26 May and agreed that there was no action they themselves could or should take. They just had to wait and see. A first sign of the kind of action they feared, designed to dislodge them from the precarious foothold they still had, came at the beginning of August 1897, when it was reported to the Education Committee that 'Mr Sedgwick had intimated to Mrs Sidgwick his desire to close his lectures on biology & morphology to students of Newnham and Girton Colleges as soon as this could conveniently be done.' The committee wondered whether all lecturers to whose lectures the College proposed to send students in the coming year should be asked whether they would accept them. Nora suggested that she should discuss tactics with Dr Peile, as President of the Council. He felt that a blanket enquiry might be needlessly provocative, but agreed that 'in any doubtful case great care should be taken not to assume that women would be admitted'.[1]

Adam Sedgwick, the geologist, was, like his better-known geologist uncle, also Adam, a well-known misogynist and had been one of the most vociferous opponents of the women. In the event, his example was not widely followed and the pattern of teaching went on much as before, although the women remained always conscious that they were there by grace and favour. Nor did all the press coverage and the public spectacle appear to have put off intending candidates, as Nora reported, in a slightly surprised tone, to the Annual General Meeting in November 1897.[2] Gradually, as the drama receded, it became clear that although they had gained nothing, they were to lose nothing of substance either; and slowly Newnham began to move back into a posture of quiet long-term planning and development on several fronts, physical and organisational.

Building plans are by their nature long-term; and the 1890s had seen no slackening in College building. The windfall of a share of the bequest to women's causes of the poet Emily Pfeiffer had meant that they could move earlier than would otherwise have been the case, to link Old Hall and Sidgwick, following the closure of the right of way.[3] The Pfeiffer Building was completed in 1893, including a flat for the Principal and incorporating an archway, finished later in the year, by the Clough Memorial Gates. It was under this archway, behind the closed gates, that the senior members stood on the night of 21 May 1897. The next plan was a purpose-built library; and in May 1896 the bibliophile Henry Yates Thompson, another Trinity man and an active member of the Newnham Council, and his wife Elizabeth, daughter of George Smith, the great Victorian publisher, offered to give the whole building, to be designed, as always, by Basil Champneys.[4] This handsome structure was actually opened in 1897, the year of the great rebuff. The Yates Thompsons continued to be generous in their gifts of rare books and manuscripts; and in 1906–7 they would provide an extension to the Library.[5] At the beginning of the new century the Council also came to realise that they could not continue to house resident lecturers in pairs of student rooms. At the end of 1903 the staff lecturers politely pointed out that their rooms were on the small side for all they were expected to do in them. The next year, extensions, where possible, were made to rooms in Sidgwick; and by 1906 Kennedy Building, a dedicated building for resident lecturers beyond Clough Hall, giving both greater space and greater privacy, was completed and named.[6] The question of buying the freehold of the land from St John's College had, meanwhile, been rumbling on for years. It looked as though St John's were finally prepared to consider a serious offer at the beginning of 1897, but a nervous Newnham Council decided to defer their own decision until after the vote.[7] It was the clearest indication possible of recovery of nerve that, in February 1899, they agreed to offer £18,000 to St John's for the freehold, provided the payment could be made in two instalments. By the end of May 1900, with generous help from the Sidgwicks, from the Yates Thompsons and from Mrs Winkworth, a leading member of another of the Unitarian families who supported them so staunchly, they had mobilised all the funds needed.[8]

As important as material consolidation and expansion was the work that went on to develop and shape institutional structures. As we have seen, Newnham by now was already an institution, no longer an over-grown domestic operation. However, organisationally it still resembled a school more than a university college. Conceptually and psychologically crucial in the recovery from the events of 1897 were the beginnings of a move towards the structure of a self-governing academic corporation, in the form of support for research and the articulation of a salary and pension structure for lecturers. The historian Alice Gardner, lecturer from 1884, always cherished warm memories of the personal support Annie had given to her research work.[9] However the first collective steps were taken in the autumn of 1897 and the early spring of 1898. At a Council on the day of the AGM, 6 November 1897, it was reported that the artist and suffragist Christiana Herringham wished to give £100 a year for three years – anonymously – to support a research post.[10] Acceptance was speedy and grateful, although there was a short, fierce wrangle about whether the post should be called a research 'fellowship'. It was, and the first fellow was elected the next year.

At the same time, informal conversations, in which Margaret Verrall probably played an important role, had been going on with the classicist Jane Ellen Harrison. Jane had been a Newnham student between 1874 and 1879 and was the unsuccessful candidate when Margaret was appointed lecturer in 1880, although mercifully this did not undermine the friendship between them. With the assistance of a modest private income, Jane lectured, taught and published from a London base through the 1880s and 1890s, launching work on Greek art and Greek religion which made her celebrated. Not unreasonably, she hankered after a degree of academic recognition; and having twice lost out to male competitors in appointments to professorships in the University of London, she was not averse to a move. In February 1898, the Council agreed that she should be invited to reside in Newnham free for two terms, in return for which she would give two courses of lectures.[11] This arrangement, with minor variations, would be extended and extended until 1922. Meanwhile the search was on for funding to put the research fellowships on a secure and permanent basis. The Associates came to the rescue in the short term; but more endowment was needed and at the end of 1902 it was agreed to go to public appeal. Christiana Herringham again was generous and at the end of 1904 undertook to match the funds raised from the public at large.[12] By 1909 the College was in a position to elect at least one research fellow a year by open competition, and in some years two.

Research fellowships were fixed-term appointments, for a maximum of three years, often held by those embarking on academic careers. Yet active research work was increasingly coming to be expected of university teachers

14 Jane Harrison as a student

throughout their careers and the Newnham lecturers from time to time presented themselves as candidates in the research fellowship competition, often successfully; conversely some of those successful in the competition went on to appointment as college lecturers.[13] Formal acknowledgement of the interdependence of research and teaching in higher education came in 1907, when the Council agreed to the principle of paid sabbatical leave for teaching staff.[14]

This was part and parcel of a wider consideration of the terms and conditions of teaching staff. In the years up to 1914, the abolition of religious tests and the working-out of the recommendations of the Royal Commission on Oxford and Cambridge, which sat from 1872 to 1877, gradually propelled the men's colleges in both Universities away from the old model of the bachelor clergyman tutor, watching over the moral welfare of his pupils and in due course moving on to a college living and marriage – the model which had prevailed in Arthur Hugh's Oxford of the 1840s – towards a more professional kind of university teacher, distinguished in his subject, providing intellectual as well as moral support to his students and located within some sort of career structure.[15] The old model plainly had had nothing to offer Newnham: in the first years of the new century the College moved to make the new model work for women as well as for men. Two important initial steps were taken: the formal constitution in 1907 of a regular staff meeting, discussing the Council agenda and making representations, as appropriate, before the Council itself met; and the establishment of a full salary and pension structure for staff. The latter, in which the staff themselves took a major part, was inevitably detailed and complex, immensely boring to the reader but of passionate concern to those who stood to gain or lose. The process took over four years, the final details not being settled until the spring of 1911; but it represented a major achievement, not only for the institution itself but also as a model for others.[16]

Thena, as we shall see, played an important part in the institution's work of regrouping. Yet even as this was beginning, neither the achievement represented by the *Memoir* nor full involvement in the work of Newnham were proving enough, singly or together, to free her entirely from periodic bouts of violent self-doubt, although slowly, painfully, she was learning to manage them a little better. She had by now been through the cycle often enough to begin to see how fruitless and destructive they were. At the end of 1898 she admitted, 'in a way I'm happiest when I'm obliged to be busy when I've no time to think what I ought to do & have to run about muddling over some trifle or other. But that's nothing but a sort of abstraction a relief from using my mind.' She decided she needed more intellectual stimulus – but then was honest enough to admit that she had had patches of great unhappiness while working on the book. Her current term of service as Vice-Principal came to an end at the end of 1899 and she could not decide whether she would accept a further appointment or make a break.[17] Out of all this thrashing about came a radical plan: to take leave and travel to India with Philippa Fawcett, now a staff lecturer in Mathematics at Newnham. The original scheme had been for Philippa and her friend and Newnham contemporary Margaret Tabor to go, Margaret wanting to visit her brother who was in the Indian Civil Service. Then Nora had suggested that Thena might join them; and what eventually took shape was an extended tour for Philippa and Thena, while Margaret spent time with her brother. In May 1899 the Newnham Council granted Philippa and Thena unpaid leave for the whole of the next academical year. On 5 November, Thena's brother Arthur, his wife Eleanor, and their sister Florence and cousin Tommy Coltman saw them both off on the boat train from Charing Cross, to embark on the *S.S. Caledonia* in Southampton, in company with Margaret and a missionary named Miss Fowle, although the excitement was somewhat dimmed by anxiety about the war which had broken out with the Boers in South Africa, a month earlier.[18]

Characteristically, Thena began her journey with the gravest misgivings, 'horribly afraid as I always have been afraid that the whole thing will consist merely of catching trains packing, trying to put on the right clothes & to behave suitably'.[19] But although there were bleak patches, there were also absorbingly interesting sights and encounters: and the black book of this period is a mix of the usual self-lacerations and some extremely vivid writing, a vividness carried through into the regular letters she wrote to her mother. Philippa, too, kept a journal of their travels: but she was blessed with a much more even temperament and it is a careful, systematic record of the places they visited, the sights they saw and the people they met, not without humour, and ornamented with little sketches and plans. She plainly was a model traveller. It looks as though she read the entries aloud to Thena each day or each evening, to check their accuracy, for there are occasional interpolations, in Philippa's hand-writing, but with the initials BAC.[20]

They had prepared with great thoroughness, both learning some elementary Hindustani, equipped with all the right guidebooks and a staggering array of letters of introduction. A succession of members of Katharine Stephen's family had been judges in India and all their contacts had been mobilised. Blanche had exerted herself to dig up every family connection, however remote – there are frequent references in Philippa's diary to 'a sort of cousin of Thena's', including a Shore Nightingale, and two Bonham Carters with connections to the entourage of the new Viceroy, Lord Curzon, in Calcutta. Arthur, in turn, appealed to his old Trinity friend and best man, Henry Babington Smith, who had served in India as private secretary to the previous Viceroy, Lord Elgin, from 1894 to 1899.[21] And his father-in-law, Douglas Freshfield, was already in India, to climb Kanchenjunga. Thena and Philippa would breakfast with him in Jaipur on Christmas Day 1899, on his return journey after a successful ascent.

After a reasonable voyage – some seasickness in the Gulf of Lions and relief that they were travelling second class and so spared the long-drawn-out black tie/white satin dinners of the first class, particularly in the heat of Suez – they arrived in Bombay on 19 November. They spent five days there and then began to journey across northern India, travelling mostly by train, and usually accompanied only by a male servant, Lalla, who took immense pride in the grandeur of some of their connections. In the cities themselves, they went about on foot, in carriages or on ponies, and occasionally by elephant: in Saharanpur, to their trepidation and wonder, their elephant, named Rampolia, proceeded steadily down a whole flight of steps, bearing them on her back. They stayed sometimes in private houses, sometimes in hotels or dak bungalows – guesthouses. Thena most enjoyed the private households because she was fascinated by the people, wanting 'to make a small gallery of Anglo-Indians as I have them in my mind'; but she was critical of some of the English civil servants, particularly Sir Mackworth Young with whom they stayed at Government House in Lahore, 'the first house in India where there was to my feeling some pretension & want of simplicity'.[22] Philippa reserved her fiercest comments for the missionaries, whom she thought patronised the Indians they were supposed to be converting; although she excepted the various medical missionaries, whom she felt worked primarily as doctors. Both became rather weary of the expectation that they must want to see the schools and colleges in every place that they visited. At a boys' school in Ahmedabad, Thena was required to give away the prizes, although mercifully not to make a speech: in Lucknow they realised that the pressing invitation to visit the Eurasian girls' school came because the Headmistress, Miss Gow, two years out of Girton, was desperate to 'see some people who reminded her of England and Cambridge'.[23]

In Lucknow at the end of January 1900 they rejoined Margaret Tabor, who had gone straight there to see her brother. He was unable to show them much, however, because he was going down with fever. Somewhat anxiously, they continued on to Calcutta, where their anxiety was increased by a telegram from Margaret, telling them the diagnosis was typhoid. They offered to return at once, to help share the nursing, but she insisted they continue. From Bhagalpur, where they were staying with the Ritchies, yet another set of 'sort of cousins of Thena's', connections of her sister-in-law Eleanor, they duly sent a telegram home to Newnham on 23 February, for the Commemoration celebrations, and then journeyed to Darjeeling, almost as far north as they could go, since both Nepal and Tibet were closed to travellers. Their hosts there insisted they be vaccinated for smallpox, since there were several cases in the local bazaar – one wonders why that hadn't been required before ever they left England. But they continued to worry about Margaret and her brother and came to the conclusion that instead of making an expedition into the foothills of the Himalayas on horseback, they must go back to Lucknow, to assess the gravity of the situation for themselves before leaving India. On 7 March, however, the news from Margaret was so much better that they decided they could go on.

This four-day journey, in sight not only of Kanchenjunga but also of Everest, was for Philippa one of the highlights of the whole expedition. They had to cope with extreme cold, especially as the best views of the mountains were in the very early morning, around 6 a.m., before the cloud descended: and setting off on their ponies they wore every stitch of the clothing they had with them. Characteristically thorough, Philippa set down exactly what that meant: 'I wore combinations, vest, jaeger chemise, night gown, 4 pairs knickers, Shetland shawl round middle, jaeger dressing gown, fur cloak, fur thing round neck, stockings, shoes, gaiters.' Jersey or blouse, and skirt, seem to be taken for granted; but a later entry in the journal suggests that with the gaiters went knickerbockers, which would have enabled them to ride astride – much safer.[24] Despite the cloud, the views were overwhelming and both were much moved. The descent was not without its adventures either: the local police inspector, who was meant to be their guide, kept falling off his pony dead drunk; but the two remaining man-servants coped and Thena was able to bribe the sirdar, who also doubled as cook, with cigarettes – as she remarked to her mother, 'It was very fortunate for him that I have such vicious habits.'[25]

The drama of the landscape, as always, moved Thena; but her pleasure was not as uncomplicated as Philippa's. February and March saw the return of some dark moods – and the smallpox vaccination, followed by a heavy cold, cannot have helped. Once more she used her black book to berate herself for being idle, self-centred and egotistical, incapable of real affection, good for nothing. As she emerged gradually from the trough of the mood, she acknowledged the crippling effect of this kind of self-consciousness, this kind of self-preoccupation: 'it has been borne in upon [me] increasingly for a longish time that the only way to be happy is to be keenly interested in something outside oneself – to be a specialist, to have an impassioned hobby'.[26] Yet as ever, the black book helped her contain the worst of it. Philippa's journal shows them indefatigably travelling on: by ship to Ceylon, where they docked at Colombo and Thena had her pocket picked on the train to Kandy; thence to Hong Kong, where Thena had an introduction to the Governor, General Gascoigne, provided by no less a personage than the Colonial Secretary, Joseph Chamberlain, himself. Hong Kong was the base for journeys to Macao and Canton by steamer; and then they rejoined the *SS Empress of India* to go on to Shanghai.

After Shanghai, their destination was Japan. However one of the other passengers had come down with suspected smallpox, and although he was immediately taken off the ship, they were held in quarantine off Nagasaki at the beginning of May. It was eventually decreed that they might land, provided the ship and all her 900 passengers were thoroughly fumigated: they were required to bath in disinfectant and have their clothes baked, and the entire ship was scrubbed with disinfectant. Thena was amused by the cheating that went on. 'We none of us wore the clothes we had been wearing contemporaneously with the suspect but everyone put on their oldest possibles. Smart ladies appeared with their bands pinned together & bedroom slippers on & men in pyjamas.'[27] The whole process took hours; but then they saw something of Nagasaki before cruising on through the inland sea and then landing on Honshu to take the train to Osaka, Kyoto and Miyanoshita. Here Thena confessed to a rash, no other symptoms, but a fear that it might be smallpox. An American doctor consulted dismissed this and diagnosed measles instead, telling them they could carry on as normal. However they felt it wholly unfair to spread measles among the unsuspecting Japanese and decided to go on not to Tokyo but instead straight to Yokohama, their point of embarkation, Thena doing her best to avoid other people. There they found an English doctor, who pooh-poohed both smallpox and measles and suggested allergy, possibly shellfish. Much relieved, they went off on 13 May to send telegrams to their respective students in Cambridge, about to begin their Tripos examinations. To get as much in as cheaply as possible, they used what seems to have been a contemporary commercial code: Thena's message, to all her tutorial pupils in Clough Hall, was *Assector Clypeus*, 'Compliments of the season, difficulties exist but they may be overcome'; and Philippa telegraphed the mathematicians, *Aggravo*, 'There is no cause for apprehension.'[28] Then they set off to see Tokyo after all.

Philippa was more enthusiastic about Japan than about India – apart from the mountains – perhaps in part because it was cleaner. Thena was more muted: language was a much greater barrier than it had seemed in British India. However Katharine Stephen's brother Herbert had provided an introduction to the Marquess Ito and thus they saw something of the ceremony of the Imperial court and of Japanese music and dance; and Philippa was disconcerted and immensely flattered to discover a hotel proprietor at Nikko who had read her father, Henry Fawcett's, *Manual of Political Economy*. At last on 25 May they embarked for Vancouver, arriving on 5 June to face more medical inspection but no fumigation.

The final leg of their journey took them across Canada by train, through the Great Lakes by boat and then by train to Boston, where they were met by members of Charles Eliot Norton's family, with whom they stayed in Cambridge, Mass. Here they were certainly not able to escape educational institutions, attending the Commencement ceremonies not only at Radcliffe but also at Harvard. In addition horrendous toothache and a badly swollen face cost Thena several visits to the dentist. At the beginning of July they were in New York. Did Thena reflect that these last stages, from the Great Lakes to New York, had been travelled in diligence and riverboat by an excited Annie, two-thirds of a century before? From New York they took their final boat home: they had been away nine months and circumnavigated the globe.

Almost straight away Philippa and Thena slipped back into the affairs of Newnham. Thena attended her first meeting of the Education Committee for a year on 1 August 1900. The shocking news of Henry Sidgwick's cancer, and the surgery which it was hoped would slow its growth, had already reached them by telegram in Vancouver. By the time they were back in Cambridge, Henry and Nora were staying with her brother, Lord Rayleigh, at Terling Place in Essex, and Henry's strength was visibly ebbing: he died on 28 August. Musing in the privacy of her black book, Thena was frank about their disagreements: 'I couldn't help feeling that with respect to a good many things he had carefully, very carefully thought out the question 30 years ago & that he was not prepared to reconsider.' She recognised that some people distrusted him and thought him devious: what they may have resented was 'the unconscious arrogance of the very clever towards the stupid or less clever'. They also disliked losing to him: 'When he wanted a thing he pressed on for it as in war or politics trying to out general his enemies, to give them a throw, to put them in tight places.' These were skills indeed in the world of national or imperial politics; but in the smaller world of the University, everything was more personal. 'I don't imagine he bore malice himself when he was outmanoeuvred & he didn't understand other people's doing so. I think he can hardly have accepted At [Aunt] Annie's view that it was often better to go without things than to get them by force.' Henry, for example, had been determined to call the first research posts 'research fellowships' and had carried his point in the teeth of opposition not only from Marion Kennedy but also from Richard

Archer-Hind: Annie, she thought, would never have forced the decision through. At the same time she acknowledged the stature of both: 'He & AJC do seem to me to have fought to some purpose – to have left the world better than they found it – It seems quite worth while to us who feed on the opportunities they got for us.'[29] Newnham mourned Henry as they had mourned Annie; but both had built well and the institution continued to develop.

For Thena, the question now to be faced was whether the year away had enabled her to see more clearly how she should proceed. For Philippa, the journey had bred a new self-confidence, a realisation that she was well able to cope with the world beyond mathematics and beyond the beaten tracks of Europe. In 1902 she was invited to go to work in South Africa, in the Transvaal, setting up an educational system in the wake of the Boer War. Telling Thena in confidence of the invitation, which she was minded to accept, she wrote 'If I make anything of this it will be entirely due to you.'[30] For Thena herself, things proved, inevitably, less simple. At the end of December 1900 she reflected, 'I suppose I really am rather refreshed by a year off. Last term at first I shuffled along doing the minimum with a good deal of my customary boredom, then when things became difficult it seemed more interesting.' She had learned that wherever she went, she took her demons with her; but she was becoming ever more practised in containing them. The experience had tested but also shown the extent of her 'people skills', as the twenty-first century would call them. Although there was a mordant edge to her observations which had been entirely absent from her aunt's view of the world, she and Annie were at one in finding people endlessly fascinating; and she was coming to realise that working with them was a strength that not everyone had.[31] In addition, in the next four years, changes in her family would alter the focus of her life in important ways.

In May 1901 Blanche and Florence were out driving near Salisbury when the horses of their carriage bolted and both were thrown. Blanche sustained a broken leg but Florence was much more severely hurt. Paralysed, she was taken to the nearby Museum Hotel in the village of Farnham, and there she died, aged forty-three, on 30 May.[32] It was a dreadful end, out of melodrama, for a gentle person who has flitted like a ghost through these pages. Blanche's leg slowly mended; but as she was seventy-three in June 1901, it was thought desirable she should have a companion and not live alone, except for the servants, at Burley Hill. If the possibility of Thena's leaving Newnham was ever canvassed, it has left no trace in the surviving papers. Instead Thena and Arthur's cousin Lily, the seventh child and fourth daughter of Charles and Margaret Clough, now both dead, came to act as Blanche's companion. Blanche survived Florence by only three years, dying in May 1904. Of Thena's reactions and reflections, there is no trace in the papers remaining from this decade. Yet later, during the War, when for the first time she read the letters her father had written to her mother from the United States, before their marriage, she wrote with real understanding of the developing relationship between them:

He was tremendously in love & as it seems to me in a simple way – feeling her to be good, straight without guile or affectation & passionately wanting the comfort & soothingness of her affection – he doesn't want intellectual companionship from her – he's partly tired of intellectual intercourse wants understanding of course anyway not misunderstanding – but chiefly the relief of encompassing affection from an impulsive rather simple honest & to him attractive personality.

She began to see how her mother's anxious concern and clear practical sense, intrusive and smothering as it often seemed to her daughter, had felt soothing, uncomplicated and supportive to her over-tired, over-anxious, eternally fastidious father.[33]

Lily Clough had thrived at Burley Hill, and fallen in love with John Duff, younger brother of James Duff, Arthur's Trinity friend and contemporary, who was working for Arthur as a fruit farmer. Shortly after Blanche's death, John and Lily married and Lily soon became pregnant. While she was out walking in the later stages of her pregnancy, a thunderstorm came on and in her haste to return she clambered over a stile but fell awkwardly. The fall brought on labour prematurely. The baby, a girl, named Lily Katharine but always known as Kitty, survived, but sadly her mother did not. Poor John Duff had already been widowed once and had left the daughter of his first marriage, Kitty's half-sister Frances, in California, with her mother's relations. Following this second tragedy, Thena, as Lily's relation, took charge.[34] In the days before there was any legislation regulating adoption procedures, such family arrangements could and did happen. By the autumn of 1905 thus, Thena found herself not only sole mistress of a large house but also responsible for a very young child.

Money – and the servants it could buy – made such responsibilities feasible and not crippling. Blanche had left her very considerable estate equally between Thena and Arthur, with a small trust fund for Lily;[35] and although Arthur was quite heavily mortgaged to support his work as a model landlord, both had considerable resources. Thena did not depend upon her Newnham stipend as Arthur had not depended on his from the Education Department. Thena felt that Burley Hill was the right environment for

Kitty's early childhood and employed a full-time nursemaid to look after her there, with John Duff continuing to live and work nearby, visiting his daughter frequently, and Arthur and Eleanor as additional backstop at Castle Top. The following year, she was sufficiently confident that all had now settled and stabilised, to spend five weeks travelling in the United States, her black book vividly recording her delight in the variety and drama of its landscape.[36]

Thena enjoyed being mistress of Burley Hill, taking particular pleasure in its fine garden and grounds. She was immensely hospitable, often inviting friends to stay. She had done this a little before her mother's death, but now had much greater freedom, and there are times during Long Vacations when the entire business of Newnham appears to be conducted from Burley Hill. Philippa's absence in South Africa from 1902 to 1905 had inevitably loosened that friendship; and on her return she remained based in London, as the deputy to the Chief Education Officer and the highest-ranking woman employed by the London County Council. Thena remained close to Katharine Stephen and to her brother Harry.[37] Also in these years she became increasingly good friends with Pernel Strachey, whose tutor in Clough Hall she had been. Pernel, born in 1876, was the ninth child and sixth daughter of Sir Richard and Lady Strachey, key members of a major Anglo-Indian dynasty. She came up to Newnham in 1895, beginning in the History Tripos but then switching to Modern and Medieval Languages, specialising in eighteenth-century French. After a year's research in Paris, she was appointed to a lectureship in French at Royal Holloway College in the University of London in 1900, then returned to Newnham as a staff lecturer in 1905.[38] Pernel had first stayed at Burley Hill in the summer of 1902, when Blanche was still alive, and like Thena, came to love the landscape of the New Forest. By the summer of 1907 she was sufficiently a part of the household to stay there, accompanied by her brother Lytton, while Thena was away. Pernel reported on their activities to Thena.

Lytton is in the big room and I am in the one next the nursery (which is my favourite one) and he has to do the carving and make the tea at breakfast.

Kitty is much interested and intrigued by him. Today he was sitting in the verandah and she came walking by; she stopped and looked at him and giggled faintly – he took no notice so she then sat down in the path and pretended to be very busy with some small stones but all the time she was looking at him with the most engaging smiles and it was some time before she could be induced to move on. She isn't a bit shy and visits us in the drawing room with perfect goodness. There seems to be a regular routine that we have to go through. Katharine's india rubber beasts and the scrapbook and playing on the piano and pulling books out of the bookcase. The method of experiencing everything by means of one word seems to me extremely sensible – don't you think so? Why can't we all simply say 'ba sheep' or 'piano' if that's what we happen to want? Tonight there was a frightful hullabaloo because her head had to be washed – for some reason she seems to hate it. I am occasionally called Auntie Who? – which is considered a very good joke.[39]

It is an unexpected, cheerfully domestic picture of the literary critic and ornament of Bloomsbury which Lytton Strachey would become. His *Eminent Victorians*, which changed the conventions of biography for his generation as Froude's biography of Carlyle had changed them for his parents' generation, would appear in 1918. Perhaps he talked with Thena about the one of his subjects whom she knew well, Florence Nightingale? In 1907 Pernel's vivid account of the two of them in charge of the household, and Kitty, shows us that the emotional centre of Thena's life is being reshaped. By 1911, in the black book of the time, Thena is sounding like any concerned parent, musing on Kitty's development, her apparent detachment from people, her dislike of practical things and skills, reinforced by voracious reading – 'Her head seems to be quite full of witches & fairies.'[40]

At the same time as the contours of her private life were altering, Thena was heavily engaged in the affairs of Newnham. She continued to take a large share in all practical matters: it was not uncommon, after a problem with a building or a member of the domestic staff had been aired, for a minute to conclude, 'the matter was left to Mrs Sidgwick and Miss Clough to deal with', or simply 'to Miss Clough'. When she went on leave in the autumn of 1899, her responsibilities, as Vice-Principal, for the garden and for the management of all inside repairs, had to be shared between three people. Following the death of Henry Sidgwick in 1900, a committee was formed to raise funds and make proposals for a series of appropriate memorials: an annual lecture, a bronze panel with a portrait medallion and a sunken garden with a fountain, where the old right of way had been, running between Sidgwick and Old Halls. Thena as Secretary, convened it, reported on its deliberations and oversaw the action that followed. In the spring of 1904, Thena advised the Council that they needed to address the provision of a new kitchen. Whenever there was building, she was a member of the relevant committee; and when in 1909 the decision to build a fourth hall was taken, there she was on the building committee and commissioned with Nora to find a house to rent to take the overflow of students in the meantime.[41]

Thena also took her share in the discussion of the larger context and the nature of the institution they were trying to shape. Jane Harrison had always been a supporter of hers and, as an externally elected member of

15 Thena Clough, *c*.1900

Council, had first proposed her for a Vice-Principalship in 1894. Jane was a vigorous exponent of the view that Newnham should transform itself from a company not for profit into a self-governing academic corporation, become a college like any other, so that if and when degrees for women were granted, Newnham would be on an equal footing with other colleges. Thena did not disagree with this; but she did take issue with Jane's corollary that part of this process should be the abolition of the Vice-Principals' posts and a reduction of the powers of the Principal. Jane argued that tutorial and administrative responsibilities should all be carried by the resident lecturers. Thena pointed out that in an institution that size there was an irreducible minimum of administrative work; and distinguished scholars and teachers did not all make good administrators or tutors; 'we used to be told it was important the lecturers should not have their time taken up with tutorial work'.[42] This good-natured wrangle had its particular ironies. Jane only taught her own specialism, classical archaeology, to students she liked; all the basic teaching in classics was always organised and mostly done by Edith Sharpley.[43] Jane and her allies on Council, who included the philosopher Bertrand Russell for a spell, were energetic in raising constitutional issues, but seldom followed them through. Thena's contributions were less radical, but whatever she undertook was invariably delivered.

It is to these years too that the most vivid image of Thena as Vice-Principal at Newnham belongs. Elsie Butler, who would become the first woman Professor of German at Cambridge, read Modern Languages at Newnham between 1908 and 1911 and wrote in her autobiography of her 'deep-seated desire to flout authority', especially in her student years:

I would have flouted it a good deal more than I did, had it not been for my tutor Thena Clough, whom everyone called B.A. She rode me, as indeed she rode everybody else, on a very light rein, turning a blind eye on my many lapses from virtue and laughing indulgently when I kicked against the pricks. I was extremely fond of her. I admired her looks, her voice and everything about her; but what I admired most was her extraordinary gift for conversation. Dinner at the high table with her was little short of a revelation to me. Not only did she introduce the most enthralling subjects, but she displayed a genius for drawing us all out, for making us appear supremely witty and wise, which I have never seen equalled in anyone else. We became positively brilliant, even the shyest of us. Everyone contributed to the total effect, she apparently least of all; but no one ever talked so well unless she was there. Extremely amusing in a *tête-à-tête*, she could be absorbing if the matter were serious; and to talk to her on any subject whatsoever (she welcomed them all) was to experience that liberation of the mind which is the greatest gift Cambridge as a whole has to bestow. I was intoxicated with a feeling of liberty whenever I left her room.[44]

Those who knew the energetic, effective public person were therefore less surprised than Thena herself when, in June 1910, the external members of the Newnham Council asked her to succeed Nora Sidgwick as Principal.[45] The possibility had occurred to her almost ten years before; but she had not thought about it since, encouraged perhaps by the appointment of Katharine Stephen as Deputy Principal when Nora took a term's leave in Lent 1901, and she was disconcerted to find the entry when she reread her black books in trying to decide how to reply. 'I had forgotten till I read these books that I had ever thought of it.' As so often, her first reaction was to rehearse her own inadequacies: 'I have a very slight mind, a very little bit of mind. It has a certain quality about it – a certain insistence on clearness & coherence a certain capacity for taking things in but there is very little of it. It soon fails – all life all decisions are an effort to it.' Beyond that she though her only other quality was 'a certain persuasiveness, an odd capacity for getting on with people, making them like me'. She recognised that that was what allowed her to engage so effectively with the students, made her a good Vice-Principal, with all the tutorial and pastoral responsibilities that the post then carried; but as Principal she would be, would have to be, much distanced from them. Equally weighing on her was her awareness that Katharine Stephen very much wanted the position and her conviction that Katharine, under-estimated for too long by Newnham, would do a good job: 'She has so much more mind than I have such a much greater capacity for work, for acquiring & such a much solider, better founded character – cooler judgement.' Thena admitted to herself that if Katharine were not in the running, she would accept. She saw the College as 'a great centre of opportunity – I have strong views about the management of the students, about the dangers & difficulties – the points that must be kept in sight. It is just a big enterprise that I know the working of & can't help being deeply interested in & having views about.' Briefly she considered the argument that the Council knew better than she where the interests of the College lay; but 'Who are the Council & what do they know? These men know nothing except on an outside impression, I have always known I was more showy.' She made up her mind to decline and no amount of persuasion would shift her. A week later, on 11 June 1910, the Newnham Council therefore offered the Principalship to Katharine Stephen.[46]

In 1892 and again in 1896 Thena's complex, convoluted yet powerful sense of duty, to her aunt's memory, to Nora Sidgwick, 'the ought which has to be reckoned with', had led her to accept responsibilities and commitments at Newnham in spite of her sense of her own inadequacies and a hankering to make a clean break. By 1910 she had become wholly committed to continuing to work at Newnham. However, her enduring sense of her own limitations combined with her conviction of Katharine's quality and her determination to see this recognised, to lead her to decline the Principalship. And perhaps, as she watched Kitty grow, an awareness that she had a life outside Newnham, which she was enjoying, helped her to make this choice with a freedom she had not experienced before.

CHAPTER 9

War and its consequences

The decade that began with an act of renunciation paradoxically proved to be one of the most demanding in Thena's long life. Declining the Principalship in 1910 did not lead to a reduction in her commitment to and involvement with the running of Newnham. There were two strands to this continuing engagement: observance of a convention very different from that prevailing now, and personal. In the contemporary world the also-ran, the unsuccessful candidate, and the individual retiring from a post, usually withdraw from the scene, to give the successful candidate or the successor a clear run. That tended not to happen in the Newnham of the early twentieth century. Although Nora Sidgwick retired from the Principalship in 1910, she continued as Treasurer, then Bursar of the College until 1920. Thena remained Katharine Stephen's right-hand-woman, seen by a student who came up in 1916 as 'the most striking and quietly forceful character in the College' and by some of the younger senior members as the real power behind the throne.[1] Such continuing involvement was so taken for granted that we can only guess at its rationale. It was surely fostered by a sense that they were still pioneers, still outsiders, still needing every scrap of hard-won experience and expertise to make their way. Reinforcing this were the powerful friendships forged in pursuing this shared enterprise, and finally the personalities themselves. Nora had managed the finances and resources of the College with quiet foresight and great success for over thirty years, contributing generously from her own pocket at critical moments: no one was going to ask her to disengage before she was ready to do so. Although Katharine Stephen, plain, earnest, socially concerned and devout, had been seen in her early years as a subject for caricature by her cousin, the novelist Virginia Woolf, the rest of the Stephen family relied heavily on her common sense, directness, rare unselfishness and unfailing good humour. She had borne the brunt of coping with her manic-depressive brother in the early 1890s: she was named the legal guardian of Virginia's mentally handicapped half-sister Laura: she oversaw the care of her nephew James when he was considered too young to join his parents in India: she saw much of her Quaker aunt, Caroline, who lived in Cambridge: and she wrote to her mother every day that she was not with her. The qualities which made Katharine a model eldest daughter were also put at the service of Newnham. After Katharine's death, Thena recalled that at the end of one particularly dreadful week, Katharine wrote, 'Don't forget when you write my notice in the Newnham Letter to say that I liked it all.' She was, Thena concluded in that notice, 'always gallant towards life'.[2] It is hard to imagine that Katharine did not know that the Principalship had been offered to Thena first; and although they had come to the College at about the same time in the 1880s, Thena had the inestimable advantage of having been a student before joining the staff, aside from bearing the surname 'Clough'. Yet there is no hint that they did not continue to work warmly and effectively together.

The major policy issue to be addressed at Newnham from the autumn of 1910 was a constitutional one. Research fellowships had been established; the creation of the staff committee had brought them a more systematic voice in College matters; and the structuring of appointments procedures, salary scales and pensions was almost complete.[3] However the formal legal status of the institution was still that of a limited, not-for-profit company, like all the women's colleges in Cambridge and Oxford then. As early as 1896, before the great rebuff, Jane Harrison had begun to argue that Newnham should begin taking steps to become a self-governing academic corporation, a college like any other: this, she thought, would facilitate their ultimate acceptance within Cambridge. Thena was not entirely convinced that 'oligarchy is the best organization'; but the local political arguments for such a move were very powerful, especially when both staff and the two organisations of old students were also urging that their respective positions receive more formal recognition.[4] Thena was throughout at the heart of the long process then launched, not only because she possessed an exceptionally safe pair of administrative hands, but also because she occupied several key posts. In declining the Principalship she had nevertheless agreed to become Secretary to the College Council; she had been President of the Associates since 1907 and continued as the Cambridge member of the committee of the Old Students' Club.[5]

The Associates, the privileged sub-set of old members created in 1893, set the ball rolling in the summer of 1910 by creating their own committee on constitutional matters. This group worked and consulted until in November 1912 they were ready to propose to the College Council an outline scheme for petitioning the Privy Council for a Charter and Statutes.

The College Council's response led to a joint committee of the two groups which reported with a more fully developed scheme in November 1913. After three more Council meetings the scheme was finally formally accepted in February 1914 and then sent on to counsel for technical and legal vetting. The decisions taken would shape the conduct of business in the College for at least the next half century and form important precedents for the other women's colleges when they in their turn decided to move towards self-government. It was a lengthy and complex process, of absorbing interest and importance to the several constituencies involved, but tedious to reconstruct now in detail. There is a tiny hint of the negotiating skills and patience called for when Thena suggested gently to her stubborn and combative colleague, the geologist Gertrude Elles, that the best way of responding to a particularly active fellow-Associate, Margaret Isabella Gardiner, always full of suggestions, was to write as little as possible, trying not to offer hostages to fortune: 'I feel it's alarming to enter into correspondence with an ardent controversialist who has plenty of time on her hands.'[6]

Threaded through the negotiations and the endless committees there was also for Thena the engrossing responsibility of Kitty's upbringing and education. Kitty's nanny had been succeeded by first one governess and then another at Burley Hill; but for schooling and the company of other children, Cambridge was a better base in term-time. One of Edith Sharpley's sisters, Ada, kept a very successful small preparatory school and Kitty was duly enrolled there, along with other Cambridge academic children, including Michael Ramsey, the future Archbishop of Canterbury, and her Duff cousins, the children of her father's elder brother, James. She lived during the term with Harry Stephen and his wife Barbara, née Shore Smith, Thena's cousin, in their Grange Road house. Many of the Newnham senior membership became honorary aunts, Aunt Edith, Aunt Kate and Aunt Pernel in particular joining Aunt Thena, and the College itself Kitty regarded as an extension of her play area: long afterwards she recalled the exhilaration of racing noisily down the long corridors: 'Those passages are wonderful to howl down when you're well under ten. You can career along those passages howling and it's wonderful.'[7] It was not a typical childhood but it seems to have been a happy one.

Kitty was perhaps too young to register the full import of the declaration of war in August 1914, although the war may have contributed to the decision to send her on to boarding school in 1916, to St Felix at Southwold, where Lucy Silcox, Thena's undergraduate friend and contemporary, was now the dynamic and successful headmistress.[8] The world of Kitty's elders was, however, transformed, as the anonymous student who wrote the 1913–14 Letter for the Old Students' Club explained:

The outbreak of war has cleft the college year. From the dark and near side of this chasm, we look across to days of irresponsible joyousness. We hear again the wild sounds of dissipation in the name of Suffrage during the Lent Term. We picture ourselves conscience-less on the river. We recall Triposes and Mays [examinations] as nightmares indeed, but as nightmares quickly over.

And now a new seriousness is in our college life. We have a quickened purpose of usefulness. We steel our nerves to meet the exigencies of Red Cross. We feel qualified to write several theses on the subject of ubiquitous knitting. Our rooms emit the chatter of French and the deep gurgle of Flemish. The privileged among us drink in the tall tales of wounded Tommies. Strangest of all, we do some work, and we occasionally come down early for breakfast.[9]

Unlike the men's colleges, Newnham – and Girton – were not immediately depopulated by the departure of almost all their students for the forces. But war work was nevertheless a major part of their lives. A handful of Newnham students, like the young Vera Brittain at Somerville, felt they must abandon their courses for the time being to nurse or drive ambulances and the College rapidly evolved a sensible policy whereby students were given leave to 'degrade' (intermit), provided they were enrolled in regular nursing training or doing other work authorised by government. Many more students, like Constance Tipper, née Elam, and Dorothy Garrod, later greatly to distinguish themselves in their respective disciplines of engineering and archaeology, heeded the advice to complete their qualifications before offering themselves for war service.[10] And possessing specialist and/or professional skills in short supply proved to be the key to effective war service for many of the women. The urge to do *something* had in the first instance found expression in provision for Belgian refugees in Cambridge as well as in London – hence the 'chatter of French' and the 'gurgle of Flemish'. More fruitful and far-reaching in its effects was the decision taken jointly by current and old students of Newnham in November 1914 to raise the initial capital funding and then provide running support for a 100-bed mobile unit within the Scottish Women's Hospitals group. This organisation had been the brainchild of Dr Elsie Inglis and the Scottish Women's Federation of Suffrage Societies, initially scorned by the arrogant males of the British military establishment but given some facilities by the French and subsequently welcomed with open arms on the Eastern Front by both Russian and Serbian authorities. It became the main focus of fund-raising in Newnham and Girton and the destination of many of the products of the 'ubiquitous knitting' and drives for all sorts of other garments and supplies. Old students with medical and medical-related specialisms gravi- tated towards its work, like the American palaeobotanist Ruth Holden, who would tragically die of typhoid and meningitis in Kazam in 1917, and the physicist and radiographer Edith Stoney. Jane Harrison, invited to continue despite reaching the retiring age, made her own contribution by teaching Russian at Newnham to those who wanted to offer the hospital units more mundane skills. Elsie Butler, who had been teaching French and German as a temporary lecturer at Newnham, seized the opportunity, and then launched herself on an extraordinary war-time career as courier/interpreter for hospital units operating in Russia and the Balkans.[11]

Jane and Elsie's efforts make it plain that the wish to undertake some war service was not only felt by the Newnham students. Gertrude Elles became Commandant of a Red Cross Hospital literally on Newnham's doorstep in Cambridge, in Wordsworth Grove; Lorna Swain, the mathematician, spent the years 1917–19 at the Royal Aircraft Establishment at Farnborough; while Lynda Grier went off to the University of Leeds as Acting Head of the Department of Economics, to free the male incumbent for government work in London. Likewise Alice Gardner came out of the retirement just begun, to do the same job in the History Department at Bristol.[12] She had already been replaced as lecturer in History at Newnham by Catherine Firth; but the College was not so generously situated that it could manage with many absences or find temporary replacements of suitable calibre. Nor, given its finances and its role as the educator of the next generation of specialists, could it simply close down for the duration of the war. Thena took leave of absence for a term in the autumn of 1916, temporarily to provide respite for Pernel Strachey's sister, Pippa, as Secretary to the London Society for Women's Suffrage, now entirely devoted to organising women's war work. Pippa had earlier collapsed with what was first described as influenza and then suspected to be malaria, and spent most of January to April 1916 convalescing at Burley Hill.[13] Thena's work for the Society, which she would continue subsequently on a voluntary basis, gave her a great respect for the women working in industrial occupations and she became a subscribing supporter of the Society of Women Welders.[14] This brief absence apart, however, she and the other older members of the community concentrated on keeping the institution going in as good order as possible, battling not only against the attractions of war work, glamorous-sounding whatever the realities, but also against a rising tide of privation.

Living costs rose steadily throughout the war, accompanied by shortages of food, fuel, and domestic labour, imagined and real, until formal rationing of food and fuel finally arrived at the beginning of 1918. Economy was seen as an expression of patriotism and the Council held off raising fees; but the consequence was growing debt and in the winter of 1917–18 it was recognised that fees would have to go up at the beginning of the next academical year.[15] In parallel went a whole succession of household economies: the ending of free milk for students in the evenings; one meatless meal each day; the substitution of margarine for butter; students making their own beds and dusting their rooms; limitations on the depth and number of baths; the rationing of coal for fires in students' rooms; a curfew – all electric lights out at 11 p.m.[16] The student magazine *Thersites* carried the following epigraph in the Michaelmas Term of 1916:

> 'Tis but a three years' fast;
> The mind shall banquet, though the body pine.

This combination of warning and promise stayed vividly in the memory of Edith Riley, who had come up that term to read Modern Languages.

There is no denying the literalness of the *fast*. Inevitable, of course. The U-boat war was at its height. The Government had classified us as sedentary females, lowest in the ration scale. Patriotism brought a letter-balance to the breakfast table for the scrupulous weighing of each slice of bread. Our meat ration, it was rumoured, went to the maids, to persuade them not to go off and make munitions. But need the damsons in the pudding have been preserved in vinegar? Need the vegetable concoctions have been quite so revolting? C.T.A. stood for College Tummy Ache, a very prevalent ailment.

But we were a hardy generation, adding voluntary endurance tests (disguised as privileges or spiced with disobedience) to those we could not avoid. We were not allowed to sleep out in our hammocks in the garden, but we *were* allowed to sleep on the roof – not with any College bedding, of course, but with such private rugs and cushions as we could muster to mitigate the hardness. How we scorned the one Sybarite who had equipped herself with a camp-bed! We must have become inured to cold. It was not until after tea that conversations broke off with: 'Well, I must go and fight my liar.' The Spooner habit was still rampant but here the transposition was apt enough: it was a fight to get one's meagre evening fire to burn. Earlier in the day there were lectures, or a session in the Library cocooned in a rug, with all the books one could possibly need piled up within hand's reach.

The young grumbled noisily but made the best of things: the compensation for the extremely icy conditions of January and February 1917 was magnificent skating on the flooded fens.[17]

For Thena the problems of war, whether at first hand or the reported horrors of the trenches, underlined the need to seize the moment, to make the most of the world and the relationships around her. In June 1918, 'the smell of the syringa the other day gave me an acute squeeze of the heart, filled me, seizes me with poignant desires and regrets'. She mused on intense, unexpected moments of pleasure and whether they could or should be pursued: 'what is one's right in life for oneself for anyone that one cares about – for Kitty for instance – for one's friends . . . ?'. A little later she wrote,

I think I want to have enough – whatever that may amount to – of moments of intense feeling – that means after all of real personal life . . . You may get great moments in dealing with other people in wielding magnificently the weapon of your faculties – like FN [Florence Nightingale]. I once made a speech to a room crowded with students when I played on them like an instrument – I saw Melian Stawell turning white & red as I spoke & it was a fine sensation – but even in a small way I don't call that an important moment.

Aunt Annie speaking in the hall in 1888 [at the opening of Clough Hall]. That was rather a fine moment of accomplishment.

Musing then on the episodes of heroism displayed in war, she concluded, 'one result of this war is that individuals matter more than they did'. In September 1918, coping with a suicidal student, she remembered that 'I wanted to stop living at 24. I'm glad I'm still alive certainly because life is so interesting.'[18]

What is striking is that after 1911 the black books virtually cease to be used as a confessional, as what the novelist William Boyd has called 'a psychoanalytic crutch'. There are a few entries: those quoted above, horrified reflections on accounts of German atrocities in Belgium and life in the trenches, and the long entry about the relationship between her parents, triggered when she first read their letters, and already mentioned. Yet these resemble thinking aloud much more than the agonised self-criticism of earlier times; and no new black book was started after 1918. Among the surviving papers there are a number of individual undated sheets, with black-book-like reflections, some stuffed into the five notebooks, others bundled loosely together; and it is plain she never entirely lost the habit of writing out her thoughts and feelings, as she sought to manage her bleaker moods. It also seems plain, however, that in this period of intense activity she became as comfortable within herself as she would ever feel. Characteristically she herself supplied the clue: 'I have always supposed it important to find scope for one's faculties. Is not living strenuously as good as living dangerously & not very different?'[19] She was in these years fully extended and fully committed, as a powerful administrator and as a parent. Her letters to Kitty, away at school – 'Dearest Kits' – were practical, warm and up-beat. Were the suspenders she sent the right sort? Congratulations on the exam results – Aunt Edith thought the Latin paper 'quite hard';

should she stay in a hotel rather than in school when she came over to Southwold to visit, so as to be able to take Kitty out?[20]

The outbreak of war in August 1914 had temporarily halted work on Newnham's application to the Privy Council for a Charter and Statutes. Once it became clear that the war would not be over by Christmas, the process was resumed. Thena reported on it in a printed leaflet for the Annual General Meeting of the College in November 1915. The proposals agreed jointly by the College Council and the Associates had gone to an appropriately specialist KC in the spring of 1914 for vetting and translation into appropriate legal language. By May 1915 his second draft was being considered by both bodies and after further amendment was accepted in June 1915. Then it was the turn of the AGM of the limited company which the College formally still was. The AGM duly approved; the Council inserted names in the various schedules, founders and benefactors, members of the first Council of the new institution, etc. and in January 1916 the petition finally reached the Privy Council. As Thena explained to the Old Students' Club, it would have to go on from there to lie on the table of the House of Commons for three months; so the process was unlikely to be complete much before the beginning of 1917. The Charter was finally granted on 12 April 1917 and the first meetings of the new College Council and the new Governing Body took place on 2 June 1917.[21]

Newnham had been run by a Council for nearly thirty years; and although the chair was now taken by the Principal and not by one of the external male members, they were still present, as members of the Senate of the University of Cambridge. Since the University continued to ignore the women, the inclusion of members of the Senate in College government under the Charter and Statutes was a vital link and statement of intent. For the women teaching staff, however, now translated into Fellows of the College, membership of a Governing Body was a new experience and some of them had ambitions to displace or at least to limit the Council in the running of the College. The year 1918 saw the Governing Body making a certain amount of noise, flexing its muscles, trying to ensure that it had a substantial role in appointments and in the composition of committees. However the Statutes were clear on the powers of the College Council: they controlled both appointments and money. It has continued to interest constitutional lawyers that the Council in Newnham has more power than is the case in many other colleges. The explanation for this is twofold: first, the history and second, the choice of Trinity College's Statutes as a model. Newnham had a Council long before it added a Governing Body, whereas many of the men's colleges were run by the Governing Body until pressure of numbers and press of business led them to add a smaller executive body, the Council. Trinity, in the general college context, was something of an exception, for by the beginning of the twentieth century the Trinity Fellowship was already so big that its Council had accumulated significant power. This first year of the new system in Newnham, collisions between Council and Governing Body on matters of procedure even more than on those of substance were very much a feature of life. Katharine Stephen coped well with this, at one stage gracefully pleading ignorance and misunderstanding in a new situation but holding the line on the key issues, supported firmly by Nora Sidgwick, Thena, elected Vice-Principal of the College as a whole in January 1918, and Dr Parry of Trinity.[22]

The real test for the Newnham Governing Body came, however, at the end of 1919 and the beginning of 1920, when they had to elect a new Bursar and then a new Principal: under the Statutes these two appointments rested with them. They followed a standard procedure for the Bursarship, first setting up a committee to write a job description and then advertising. Although disappointed with the quality of the field, they shortlisted two and managed to appoint one of them.[23] It was much harder to write a job description for a Principal and nobody tried. Instead they set out to try to find a woman of appropriate distinction via existing informal networks – and got themselves into a fearful tangle.

Katharine Stephen announced her intention to retire at the end of the academical year at the very end of October 1919, and in November the Governing Body decided that possible names were to be gathered for discussion at the very end of January 1920. Twenty-nine names were reviewed, including Thena's, and she and several other people promptly ruled themselves out. It was decided to gather more information about a sub-set of candidates and establish whether the individuals in question were willing to be considered. This process continued through the next three months, a number of those considered also ruling themselves out and new names being introduced after consultation with other women's colleges in Oxford and London. Consistently a candidate – and present for most of the discussions – was Lynda Grier, the Fellow and Lecturer in Economics, now returned from running the Department of Economics at Leeds. Yet also developing was a 'stop Grier' campaign. The first indication of this was the late introduction in March of a new name, that of Frances Melville, a philosopher by training and Principal of Queen Margaret College, the women's college, in the University of Glasgow. She was invited to visit Newnham: then on 1 May she and Lynda Grier were formally nominated, the election to take place on 8 May. However the day before that meeting Thena and Jane Harrison, an unholy but exceedingly powerful alliance, made a new nomination, that of Meta Tuke, a former student, who had taught French at Newnham from 1892 to 1905 and was now Principal of Bedford College, in the University of London – and one of those who had already declined to stand in January. Grier promptly withdrew as both candidate and participant, Melville's proposer and seconder withdrew her name and Meta Tuke was elected unanimously by a show of hands – although it remained uncertain whether she really was a candidate. When the Governing Body met again on 4 June, Meta Tuke had written to withdraw her name definitively. Melville was once more formally proposed; but this time Jane Harrison and Agnes Collier the mathematician also proposed Thena, she firmly declaring that, if elected, she would serve only for a year. It was agreed to reconvene to vote formally on 21 June: by then Melville had withdrawn herself and Thena was elected Principal by sixteen votes to two.[24]

It was an extraordinary sequence, which must have left bruised feelings. It seems no accident that Lynda Grier went off to Oxford the very next year, to become Principal of Lady Margaret Hall. We shall probably never know what were the grounds of the opposition to her: she seems to have been competent, deeply Christian and indubitably worthy, if somewhat humourless. However the fierce determination to find a Principal who could command the support of the whole College, and Thena's decision at last to allow herself to be drafted, surely have some roots in the external demands facing the College. While the Fellows of Newnham were scouring the country for possible candidates and caballing amongst themselves, the University was yet again debating the admission of women, and a Royal Commission, of which Thena was a member, was considering the affairs of Oxford and Cambridge. In the face of such public scrutiny and only a year away from its own fiftieth birthday, Newnham could not afford to look or to be divided, disorganised, and unable to manage its own affairs in an orderly and discreet fashion.

The position of the women in Cambridge had been raised again by their friends even before the end of the War. In April 1918 a Memorial with twenty-four names appended was presented to the Council of the Senate, asking them 'in due time' to reopen the question. The climate was apparently auspicious: the Representation of the People Act of 1918, enfranchising women over thirty and allowing them to stand for Parliament, became law in June and conversations on the position of the women were known to be taking place in Oxford. In Oxford negotiations were carried on informally for two years and proposals were only brought before Congregation in the spring of 1920, when it was clear they had a good chance of going through without controversy. With the twenty/twenty vision of hindsight, such a strategy might have worked better in Cambridge, where from the first the discussion was conducted in full public view and its timetable dictated by the lengthy procedures of Senate and Regent House. However it must be noted also that Oxford had already abolished the voting rights of non-resident members, a battle which Cambridge had yet to face.[25]

The initial response in Cambridge to the Memorial of the twenty-four was ominous. The Master of St John's published a counter Memorial, deploring their timing and raising once more the idea of a separate women's university. Newnham and Girton, he urged, should seek a Charter enabling them to become a degree-giving institution. Then everything went quiet for well over a year, although in the winter of 1918–19 the Newnham Associates and the Newnham Governing Body both discussed the issue and formed a joint committee with Girton to mobilise support and lobby both the University and the public at large. The old grounds of division had by now disappeared: Newnham accepted people taking the Previous instead of the Higher Locals if they wished, and compulsory Greek had gone in 1918. The Newnham secretary to the joint committee was Pernel Strachey; but this time she and her Girton counterpart had the help of a paid organiser, Agnes Conway, who had come up to Newnham in 1893, had moved from history to classical archaeology and was working at the Imperial War Museum, of which her father, Sir Martin Conway, was Director. As he was also, from 1918, MP for the Combined English Universities, Agnes was well placed as a lobbyist.

The two Memorials from the spring of 1918 reappeared in May 1919; but the real discussion did not start in Cambridge until the end of October 1919, when the Council of the Senate proposed to set up a Syndicate to consider the matter, a decision finally taken on 6 December. The general climate still appeared a favourable one. The Sex Disqualification (Removal) Act had just gone through Parliament, removing the formal barriers to the entry of women to most professions except the Anglican Church and the Stock Exchange. In July, at the garden party to celebrate Girton's fiftieth birthday, the guest of honour, the historian H. A. L. Fisher, Minister of Education, had made much of the contribution of educated women to the war effort. In February 1920 a statute to admit women to full membership of the University was introduced into Oxford's Congregation and by the beginning of May it was clear that it would go through. However, on 7 May (the day Thena and Jane Harrison launched their final anti-Grier strike) the Cambridge Syndicate reported that they were split, six and six. The signatories of Report A favoured the admission of women to full membership: the signatories of Report B recommended the creation of a separate women's university. Newnham and Girton were at one in refusing, as they had in 1897, to have any truck with the idea of a separate university. Report A gave them what they wanted; but the split signalled clearly how hard it would be to get it accepted. The questions now to be faced were whether the women and their supporters could and should deploy the existence and investigations of the Royal Commission to bring pressure to bear within Cambridge.

The Royal Commission of 1919–22 inquiring into the affairs of Oxford and Cambridge owed its existence to the decision of both Universities to seek financial aid from the state for the first time. The War had brought not only rocketing costs but also the collapse of fee income for the men's colleges, and at its end the two joined other UK universities in going cap-in-hand to the Treasury. An interim grant was made but regular help in the future would not be forthcoming without an inquiry into both resources and structures.[26] At the end of August 1919 H. H. Asquith, the former Prime Minister, agreed to chair the Commission and H. A. L. Fisher, the Minister of Education, settled the remaining membership in consultation with him and with the Deputy Chairman, Gerald Balfour, Nora Sidgwick's younger brother, in the course of September.[27] It had become customary by now to include token women in the membership of a Royal Commission, and this one had two, Emily Penrose, Principal of Somerville, representing the Oxford women, and Thena, representing the Cambridge women. The surviving correspondence does not tell us why the Vice-Principal of Newnham was chosen instead of the Principal, or the Mistress of Girton; perhaps the Balfour connexion had something to do with it, while Fisher was linked by marriage to the Stephens and an old friend of Gilbert Murray, the classicist, who was in his turn a very close friend of Jane Harrison.

Fisher himself, married to a Somervillian, Lettice Ilbert, was sympathetic to the women's cause. He had made all the right noises at the Girton garden party in June 1919; and when Murray checked to ensure that the Commission's terms of reference enabled them to address the question, Fisher reassured him that 'the reference is quite wide enough to include women but I hope that the Universities will not wait for the Report of the Commission before they award the degree.'[28] Likewise, the Commission's secretary, C. L. Stocks, included the exclusion of the women and their slender resources in the successive schedules of reform proposals received which he prepared for Asquith in the first months of the Commission's life.[29] By the end of May 1920, Emily Penrose, representing the Oxford women, knew that the battle for admission was won; now she had to fight for the resources needed to support the institutions. The reverse was the case for Thena, representing the Cambridge women: their financial situation was much less parlous, but the battle for admission was entering its fiercest phase.

The Commissioners were due to visit Cambridge in the course of August 1920, to take oral evidence *in situ*. In addition to the statements of needs which Newnham and Girton had been asked to provide in advance of the hearings, the Councils of both Colleges decided to prepare a joint statement on the constitutional position and its consequences, making it plain 'that at the present time the education of women at Cambridge is under a serious disadvantage owing to the fact that the Women's Colleges are outside the University'. They went on to spell out the problems not only for old students but even more for staff and their recruitment:

Apart from the disadvantages felt by the professional women who have passed Honours Examinations but have no degree, those women who are carrying on the work of the Colleges have long found themselves hampered and discouraged by their isolation and their inevitably subordinate position, and by their exclusion from all share in University affairs, even in those which most closely concern their work and on which experience qualifies them to form opinions. It has of late years been increasingly apparent that women who have achieved or who may hope to achieve distinction in any branch of work prefer to find employment in the newer Universities where these conditions do not exist, and should this continue it cannot fail to react unfavourably on the success of the Women's Colleges at Cambridge.[30]

In the interests of economy the Commission did not have made or print complete transcripts of the oral evidence given: there are simply typewritten summaries from which it is seldom possible to discover who asked what questions. The summaries of the hearings on 10 August 1920, when the Mistress of Girton, Thena's old school friend Katharine Jex-Blake, and the College Secretary, Mary Clover, gave evidence, and on 11 August, when Katharine Stephen and Nora Sidgwick followed them, suggest that the constitutional question was touched on only briefly: both sets of witnesses were asked whether, if admitted to membership of the University, they would wish to be treated as full Colleges, or would accept the lesser status of public hostels. They replied that they would accept either. The remainder of the questions focussed on resources in money and buildings, although Katharine Stephen did succeed in making the point that Newnham did not wish to expand further and the numbers and quality of applicants constituted a case for a third women's college.[31]

So gingerly an approach to the issue on the part of the Royal Commission might have been defended in August 1920, when the Cambridge Senate had yet to vote on either Report A or Report B. Evasion looked a less respectable tactic six months later. The proposals of Report A, granting women full membership, were defeated by 904 votes to 712 on 8 December 1920: meanwhile Thena and Emily Penrose had found themselves constituted a committee of two, to prepare a report on the position of the women's colleges, which might form the basis of that section of the Commission's final report.[32] Yet as they explained in their opening paragraph, 'as up till now there has been no discussion of this subject formal or unformal [*sic*] by the Commission we have had no opportunity of hearing the views of our fellow Commissioners on the questions which arise in connection with it'. All they could do was to set out the very different problems of the women's colleges in the two places and propose remedies.

First the two women rehearsed the extreme financial difficulties in which the Oxford colleges found themselves. They recognised that some men's colleges were almost equally poor but went on to argue that the case for funding women was a special one, invoking both the public interest and the role of Oxford and Cambridge as elite institutions.

Highly educated women are urgently needed as Teachers and the education of girls is unquestionably suffering for want of them. A large number of women have now to earn their own living in various professions and those who show the greatest promise should be given the opportunity of obtaining the best possible education in preparation for their work. There are too, among women as among men, a select few who are capable of making contributions to knowledge or of striking out new lines in public work and for these such opportunities are plainly desirable in the public interest.

They proposed for the Oxford women either an annual grant or a single non-recurrent capital grant, and help with establishing a loan fund and conducting a public appeal.

Turning to Cambridge, there was no case for special financial help: 'but though the Cambridge women's colleges are better off financially than those at Oxford, their exclusion from the University, recently confirmed by the Senate, makes their position and prospects most unsatisfactory'. The absence of a degree was a serious hindrance to women in employment, and in the competition for the best students Cambridge would now lose out to every other UK university. A titular degree might alleviate some of these problems; but it would do nothing for the staffs of Newnham and Girton. 'It is not easy to convey to anyone who has not been in close contact with it how irksome, one may almost say how humiliating, the position of these women may be and often is.' They were excluded from curriculum discussion and decision-making and from the community of scholars; their students were admitted to laboratories, lectures and libraries only by grace and favour; it was increasingly common, therefore, for able women to turn down posts in Cambridge. They ended with a final challenge to their fellow Commissioners: 'we must add that in our opinion if the University of Cambridge is to receive financial help from the National Exchequer, justice requires that no section of the nation should be excluded from the opportunities it has to offer'.[33]

The male Commissioners were disinclined to take up the challenge. When the report was discussed on 21 January 1921, Hugh Anderson, the Master of Caius, and one of the principal workhorses of the Commission, suggested that the Council of the Senate might set up a fresh Syndicate. The crispness of Thena's response comes clearly through the secretariat's summary.

Miss Clough doubted whether any satisfactory solution could be devised, for any compromise must omit some points which the women regarded as vital, notably membership of the Senate. She feared that if the Commission left the matter undiscussed as being *sub judice*, it might have to be altogether omitted from the Report. An analysis of the recent vote at Cambridge showed that among those actively engaged in the work of the University and Colleges, a majority of 20–30 favoured Report A; taking all the residents there was a small majority against it.

The effect of this intervention – which may have been her intention – was fully to expose the men's reluctance to get involved: a generalised sympathy for the women's position was one thing, direct intervention on their behalf quite another.

Lord Chalmers, with whom the Chairman agreed, held for the time being it was inexpedient to discuss the details of the question – which must be left, in the spirit of hopes, to Cambridge.

It was decided to proceed with the remainder of the Report upon the assumption that either Cambridge would itself adopt a satisfactory solution or the Commission would have to say something on the question in its Report.

The Commissioners also failed to reach agreement on financial aid to the Oxford women. Despite support from the historian G. M. Trevelyan for the argument that women were a special case, Gerald Balfour and Chalmers contended that grants to individual Colleges rather than to the University would create a most dangerous precedent, especially as two of them (St Hugh's and Lady Margaret Hall) had clear denominational affiliations. Decisions on all the issues relating to the women's colleges were postponed.[34]

In the wake of the defeat of Report A (full membership), the Girton Council had been eager to make a direct request to the Commissioners to intervene. The Newnham Council first sought the advice of the men on the *placet* committee, those who had organised support for Report A, and then of Thena. The *placet* committee were inclined to think there was nothing to lose: presumably they thought that those who would consider any action by the Commission unwarrantable interference were likely to be opposed to the women anyway. Thena, however, advised waiting: the Commission would not return to the matter until after Easter and by then it might be clearer what kind of opposition and/or form of compromise they were facing and that knowledge could help shape the appeal.[35] The defeat of Report B (a separate women's university) by 146 votes to 50 on 12 February was a small consolation, although two Memorials proposing that women be offered only the titles of degree were already circulating in Cambridge. As the Newnham Governing Body waited to see how much support there was for these and what 'compromise' proposals might form round them, Thena reminded them that she had only intended to serve as Principal for one year and offered her resignation. It was hardly the moment to leave the helm, and Agnes Collier, who had succeeded her as Vice-Principal, was supported by complete unanimity in asking her to continue, at least for another year.[36] It is a curious episode: was there a real flash of insecurity or, having undertaken the task for a defined period, did Thena simply feel honour-bound to remind them?

Four days later, on 8 March 1921, both Memorials proposing titular degrees were finally published and the Council of the Senate at last acknowledged the pressures of the outside world: the Vice-Chancellor announced the convening of a working party to shape compromise proposals, on which the women would be consulted. These took the form of admission for the women to matriculation, degrees, University prizes, posts, membership of Boards and Syndicates, and representation, but without a vote, on the Council of the Senate. Their numbers would be limited to 500; any woman professor would not *ex officio* become Head of Department; and a separate Board would be set up to deal with discipline and other unspecified matters. It was half-a-loaf time again. The Councils of both Colleges recorded this view, but signalled their preparedness, made public in a letter to the *Cambridge Review*, to accept the proposals and not to ask the Royal Commission to intervene, if the proposals went through the Senate by the end of the Easter Term. The Council of the Senate drafted two Graces (motions),

published on 3 May: the first, Grace I, embodied the compromise proposals, the second, the fall-back position, Grace II, was a proposal for the
award of titular degrees only. The votes on Grace I would be counted first;
and only if that fell would the votes on Grace II be counted; otherwise they
would be destroyed. Voting day would be 16 June 1921.

The national press continued to take an interest in the matter, publishing
letters and interviewing those who would consent to speak, and within
Cambridge the fly-sheet war had been raging throughout the academical
year. However the procedures devised by the Council of the Senate to try
to put a term to the discussion and achieve closure caused nearly as much
trouble as the main issue. Strenuous exception was taken to the bypassing of
the usual sequence of Syndicate and Report and an unprecedented voting
procedure. The Council survived a vote on the procedures on 4 June by
just four votes, 115 to 111, but then wobbled disastrously on the timing of
the substantive vote. The post-war economic boom had collapsed in the
winter of 1920–1, unemployment was soaring and the miners had been on
strike since 15 April. Coal shortages were making train travel increasingly
unreliable and the Council finally caved in to those who argued that the
legitimacy of any decision would be suspect if sizeable numbers of the
non-residents were prevented from voting. The vote was postponed until
20 October. The women were in a cleft stick. They had undertaken not to
appeal to the Royal Commission before the vote, but they were afraid the
Commission *would* have its report already complete in draft by October.
Thena sought and secured an assurance that if Grace I was defeated, then the
Commission would be willing to receive a statement from the Cambridge
women's colleges.[37]

In the midst of all this, Newnham was preparing to celebrate its Jubilee,
its fiftieth birthday as an institution. When planning had first started the
year before, they had hoped to secure the Queen's attendance at a garden
party; but a suitable date in the royal calendar could not be found and they
settled instead for the attendance of the College's Visitor, the Chancellor of
the University, Arthur Balfour – Nora Sidgwick's brother. A short history
of the College was commissioned from Alice Gardner; Alice and Edith
also compiled a Book of Benefactors of the College; and the launching
of a Jubilee appeal for further funds was agreed. At Thena's suggestion,
Edith began in addition to gather a record of the war work of members
of Newnham.[38] The garden party was duly held on 29 June, followed by
a dinner for as many old students as could be accommodated. There is
a splendid photograph of the elder statesman at the garden party, beside
the garden which was the memorial to Henry Sidgwick, he in sober suit

16 The Jubilee Garden Party 1921

and homburg hat, surrounded by three of Newnham's Principals, past, present and future, his sister Nora Sidgwick, Thena Clough, and Pernel Strachey, who would follow her, all resplendent in hats, gloves and best frocks. Thena, in her stateliness, looks as if she could stand in for the absent Queen Mary. One can only hope that as the noise of argument continued to rage around them, the solace of reminding themselves what had been achieved, outweighed the burdens of maintaining a serene public presence throughout and organising yet another set of events.

A bare fortnight before the vote, on 6 October 1921 the opponents of the women unveiled their big gun, the argument that the half-a-loaf proposals of Grace I contravened the terms of the Sex Disqualification (Removal) Act of 1919. The only courses legal for the University, they contended, were complete admission or complete exclusion of the women. The Caius lawyer A. D. McNair, one of the members of the Senate on the Newnham Council, promptly mobilised Dr R. A. Wright KC and C. S. Kenny, recently retired Downing Professor of the Laws of England, to publish with him another fly-sheet, countering this 'legal red herring', and pointing out that the 1919 Act was permissive. But the spectre of endless litigation following the passage of Grace I was not so easily dispelled. And having earlier been sympathetic to the women, undergraduate opinion had now swung firmly against them. Although the crowds around the Senate House on voting day did not indulge themselves with effigies, banners and flour bombs, as in 1897, the mood grew increasingly excited and the chants of 'we won't have women' swelled in volume. The voting figures were finally announced at 8.35 p.m. Grace I had been defeated by 908 votes to 694: Grace II was carried by 1012 votes to 370. At this, excitement boiled over into riot. Urged on, it was alleged, by a 'grey-haired clergyman', a group of undergraduates raced to Newnham. 'Borrowing' one of the College's hand-carts, they used it as a battering-ram to smash the lower panels of the bronze Clough gates, Annie's memorial. They then tried to force entry into the College at another point, from which they were finally removed by the police. Bravely facing the mob in the Pfeiffer archway, behind the gates,[39] Thena's thoughts must have been bitter.

The institution, now fifty years old, had completed its refashioning as a self-governing academic community, the first women's college to do so; had survived the privations of war while making a significant and honourable contribution to the war effort; and still it was excluded from the determinedly male world of Cambridge, by men whose juvenile supporters were nothing better than hooligans.

CHAPTER 10

Salvage operations

The defeat of October 1921 and the symbolic act of destruction which accompanied it made deeper wounds than the rebuff of 1897. Cambridge had shown itself out of step with so much of the world around it. In other institutions of higher education anti-feminism might have gone underground rather than disappeared; but at least the formal opportunities for access were now in place, providing a platform on which the women could fight to improve practice. Efforts to construct such a platform in Cambridge had once again failed. And once again Newnham and Girton had to pick themselves up and to work to see what could be salvaged from the mess.

The proctors, the University's policemen, had not anticipated reaction of such a violent kind on 20 October, although riot and vandalism frequently characterised undergraduate Armistice Night 'celebrations' in Cambridge in these post-war years and a mock march on Newnham was a regular feature of Bonfire Night on 5 November.[1] They managed, however, to identify six so-called ring-leaders, whose respective colleges promptly sent them down. If anything, this made things worse not better, since it was seen in some quarters as scapegoating and obscurely the women's fault.[2] More constructively, an undergraduate committee was immediately formed, on which every college was represented, to apologise and organise the collection of funds to repair the damage. The Newnham Governing Body held an emergency meeting on 25 October, to decide how to respond. A. D. McNair, who continued to serve on the Governing Body as one of the members of the University Senate, suggested that acceptance of the offer of money might be misconstrued. However, it was eventually decided that rejection was more likely to be misconstrued and Thena was authorised to tell the committee spokesmen that the Newnham Governing Body would accept the offer, provided it was conveyed in a letter which made it plain it was not so much compensation as a manifestation of the indignation felt at the insults offered. The committee gratefully availed themselves of her help with the wording and the resulting letter read: 'This is in no sense an attempt to make amends by monetary compensation; we feel that by the wanton destruction of the Memorial Gates an insult has been given to the memory of Miss Clough; and we realise with the keenest sympathy the extent to which the feelings of the College have been outraged.' Thena's reply as Principal was equally stately:

You will understand that the whole college was united in the strongest feeling of indignation and grief at the occurrences of Thursday night, but we withheld any expression of our feeling, because we believed that the majority of the university shared it.

It is with the greatest satisfaction that we have received your assurance that we were not mistaken in this expectation, and we thank you, and those who passed the resolutions, very warmly for expressing your opinion so clearly and so fully.[3]

The Councils of Newnham and Girton lost no time in preparing a supplementary memorandum for the Royal Commission: drafted by Thena and Katharine Jex-Blake and signed by the latter for Girton and Agnes Collier, as Vice-Principal, for Newnham, this went in on 14 November. It rehearsed the sequence of events, described the compromises already made by the women in preparing to accept Grace I, and assessed the impact of titular degrees. They would remove some, although not all, of the disadvantages experienced by Cambridge women in the employment market; but they would leave wholly untouched the isolation of the Cambridge women teachers and their students, already set out fully in the Memorandum of July 1920. The admission of women to membership of the University of Oxford had exacerbated the situation.[4]

Aware that the women would lose no time in invoking the Royal Commission, the Council of the Senate, in its turn, rushed into action on degree titles. A Statute embodying the principle went through on 5 November 1921 and straight on to the Privy Council. The Council of the Senate's anxiety was heightened by an analysis of the voting in the course of November, which revealed that a majority of active University teachers had supported Grace I; it was the votes of the non-residents which had defeated it. The Newnham and Girton joint committee baulked at trying to block the Order in Council needed to give effect to the new Statute; but they wrote to all their old students, asking them to lobby their MPs on the unfair treatment of the Cambridge women.[5]

At the beginning of March 1922, the Newnham Governing Body managed to anticipate another attempt by Thena to tender her resignation as Principal. Lorna Swain and Jessie Slater proposed that she be asked to withdraw the time limit on her term of office, recognising her service over the last two years: 'equally at the auspicious time of the College Jubilee, and in the days of disappointment and discouragement which followed, they had in Miss Clough a leader who worthily upheld the unity and dignity of the Society, and who unceasingly worked in its best interests'. Mention too was made of her work on the Royal Commission. Thena thanked them and withdrew the time limit.[6] But some of the plaudits must have sounded hollow in her ears: she knew that the Royal Commission's Report, due to be published at the end of the month, would prove a disappointment. No notes of discussions among the Commissioners on the position of the women over the winter of 1921–2 have been found, so we do not know the details of the battles she and Emily Penrose fought. They made some gains in the campaign for money. The Commission recommended grants of £4000 a year for ten years to each University, for distribution to the women's colleges, one-half of the grant to be earmarked for stipends and pensions. Perhaps the Commissioners hoped that this would sugar the pill for Newnham and Girton; for the remaining section of the report dealing with the women at Cambridge was a curiously bodged affair.

It began with a resounding declaration of unanimity that 'ample facilities should be offered both at Oxford and at Cambridge for the education of women and for their full participation in the life and work of the University' and then continued that as Oxford had already changed its Statutes, the Oxford Commissioners wished to express no view on the situation at Cambridge. The Cambridge Commissioners' statement began by rehearsing the history of the women and their efforts to secure inclusion in the University community. Then they moved on to the present position, to consider 'Cambridge as the only British University where women have not obtained membership, although they have been granted titular degrees.' They noted that a section of Cambridge opinion wanted the women excluded altogether and dismissed this out of hand. Yet

we so far agree with this point of view that we desire strongly that Cambridge should remain mainly and predominantly a 'men's University', though of a mixed type, as it already is. To give a sense of security in this respect, we consider that the number of women undergraduates should be limited by University Statute to 500 . . .

But we are also of opinion that women should be entitled to be admitted on the same conditions as men to membership of the University, subject to certain limitations stated below.

This was Reeling and Writhing to impress even the Mock Turtle and Alice; and the subsequent paragraphs displayed a similar agility. The Cambridge

Commissioners acknowledged the reality of the women's grievances and their wider implications.

It would be a national disaster if the standard of women's education at Cambridge should decline. But in our opinion this result is inevitable in the coming generation if Cambridge is left, for the first time, in the position of the only University in the country where neither women students nor women teachers have the status of membership of the University, and where the teachers, however well qualified, are not eligible for posts or offices in the University, and are excluded from all share in discussions on the organisation of teaching.

When they finally got on to practicalities, they were in favour of women being allowed to apply for the new University posts proposed elsewhere in the Report, while not being eligible for other offices; and it was plain they wished Grace I had been carried, rescuing them from the horns of the dilemma on which they were impaled. That was certainly the view of the Master of Caius, Hugh Anderson. Even so, they were still unable to unite to urge action by Government.

The question whether effect should be given by Parliamentary legislation to the changes recommended above, or whether the University be left to deal with the matter under the new Constitution proposed in paragraphs 49–58 of our report, is one on which we are divided into two fairly equal parties.

Thena had made some headway, but not enough. She recorded her agreement with that part of the Note of Reservation entered by the solitary Labour member of the Commission, Will Graham, which began, 'It will be very difficult to justify, either in Parliament or in the country, the grant of public money to Cambridge University so long as it refuses to women teachers and students the rights which they now enjoy in every other University in Great Britain.' He called for early legislation to remedy the situation.[7]

Newnham and Girton had now to continue the salvage operation on two fronts: to see whether the government could be persuaded to be more clear-thinking and decisive than the Commissioners; and to try to use the intermittent gestures of concern about their plight from the Commissioners to shape additional toe-holds within the complex structure of Cambridge. They turned first to the government and in June 1922 Thena and Katharine Jex-Blake led a deputation to Fisher, to ask for the insertion of a clause in the bill being drafted to enable the implementation of the Commission's recommendations, making the grant of public money to Cambridge dependent upon full membership for the women. Ominously, however, even some of their staunchest supporters had reservations about this, feeling that another battle, parliamentary or local, might delay the implementation of other recommendations beneficial to Cambridge, including the abolition of the non-residents' vote.[8]

The standard form for a such a bill, containing a number of detailed rec-ommendations dealing with specific institutions, was to create a Statutory Commission, a body with a fixed life, empowered to remodel the statutes/trust deeds of the institution concerned, following general principles set out in the bill but having freedom to negotiate to deal with individual institu-tional peculiarities. It was unusual for the general principles adumbrated in such a bill to go beyond the recommendations of a Royal Commission; but there was at least one precedent, from 1868, when a little-known back-bencher had successfully carried an amendment extending the powers of the Endowed Schools Statutory Commission, enabling them to remodel endowments to create girls' as well as boys' schools.[9] Fisher returned a suitably non-committal reply to the deputation in June, but by the end of October was out of office anyway, following the fall of the Lloyd George coalition. The Conservative administration which succeeded them was less likely to be sympathetic; although more generally the steady tightening of party discipline had weakened the force of the 1868 precedent and it may be questioned whether any government, faced with an ambivalent Royal Commission, was likely to act. Although women over thirty now had votes, it was difficult to see any political mileage in an action which benefited so few of them and which would undoubtedly be seen by many men as deeply provocative.

By January 1923 the women had learnt by a round-about route that the government was unlikely to include a clause in the bill, specifically instructing the Commissioners to deal with the position of the women at Cambridge, so they turned their attention to Parliament. Thena was in regular touch with Philippa's mother, that veteran campaigner Millicent Garrett Fawcett; and both Millicent and A. D. McNair thought they were likely to have more success in the Lords than in the Commons, where the whips were less powerful and argument was sometimes heard. Nevertheless they did try their luck in the Commons, only to lose their amendment in July by 150 votes to 124. Nor did they have any success in efforts to ensure that at least one of the Statutory Commissioners, finally named in January 1924, was a woman. Once the Commissioners had begun work, they indicated that they would take account of the Royal Commission's recommendations that women might be recognised as College Teachers in the new Faculties and be eligible to apply for new University appointments created; but further than that they would not go. In a Memorandum of

8 August 1924 they announced, 'The Commission have dealt with the women in the organisation of teaching. As at present advised, they propose to leave to the University itself questions relating to the admission of women to a share in the government of the University.'[10]

Attempting to bring pressure to bear on government needed discretion, consumed inordinate amounts of time, and proved ultimately dispiriting, as it became clear how little leverage the women had, enfranchisement notwithstanding. Yet this was not the only front on which Thena and her colleagues had to work to salvage what could be salvaged from the defeat of 20 October 1921. The University had rushed through the Statute allowing the granting of the titles of degrees to women. Ordinances, giving effect to this, were a matter for the University alone and in the shaping of these detailed provisions the women might make some small gains. A first draft of the Ordinances was published on 24 October 1922 and gave away as little as possible. It omitted all mention of security of access to lectures, laboratories and libraries for the women; declared the upper limit of 500 on women to apply to all women students of less than MA status, effectively cutting the number of the undergraduates the two colleges could admit; and allowed the women only to read for and be granted the titles of Honours degrees, thereby excluding them from those subjects, Agriculture and Archaeology, which offered Ordinary degrees only and from the unclassed Diploma in Architecture, and casting into outer darkness any woman unfortunate enough to fail a Tripos. It was duly savaged by the women's supporters, led by Parry and McNair, at the ensuing Discussion in the Senate House. A second draft at the end of November grudgingly gave way on two points: women might study Archaeology and Agriculture and those 'allowed an Ordinary' on their examination performance might have its title. At a second Discussion on 7 December, Dr Parry, briefed by Thena, again led the attack, this time alleging that the absence of any guarantees of access to teaching, laboratories and libraries flew in the face of the Royal Commission's manifest wish to provide some guaranteed space for the women at Cambridge. As the bill to create the Statutory Commission was still in the making, this was a shrewd stroke. Finally in a third draft of the Ordinances, issued in January 1923, access to lectures and laboratories, except as otherwise determined by a lecturer with the permission of the Vice-Chancellor, was conceded; and in March 1923 they at last went through.[11] Again, the women had not secured all they wanted; but each tiny increment took them a small step further into the complex structure that was the University of Cambridge.

All the while that Thena and her colleagues were lobbying government and manoeuvring within Cambridge, they were also having to cope with their own students' growing restiveness and impatience. The experience and knowledge of war had extended young women's expectations of what they might do, what they might achieve – and they wanted it to happen straightaway. The young men, those who had been too young to fight and those returning from war, often displayed a frantic hedonism. Maisie Anderson, daughter of the Master of Caius, wrote of the young naval officers among the latter group, 'they were sent to College with their contemporaries, in order that the scars left by a burden beyond their years should heal and that they should grow young and irresponsible again. Their conversation . . . was a strange mixture of gay flirtation and grim reminiscence.' Maisie, and every Newnham student of that generation, remembered those years as the years of dance mania. Everyone danced as frenetically and frequently as possible, not simply at grand affairs like May Balls but also at the weekly meetings of the Quinquaginta, the Vingt-et-un and the University Dance Club, to name but three of the ballroom-dancing clubs of the day. Only men were members; but they could invite partners from the women's colleges – and the women students were allowed out to dance once a week.[12]

Dancing was perhaps the most obvious and energetic manifestation of the hunger for a 'normal' social life, the urge to make up for lost time, lost youth, to forget. But there were many others: debating and choral societies, dramatic productions, picnics on the river, etc. etc., and all of these collided with the rigid and elaborate chaperonage rules operated by both Newnham and Girton. The diarist Frances Partridge, who had come up to Newnham in 1918 as Frances Marshall, described the situation:

In October 1918 the propriety of the women's colleges and the virtue of their inmates were protected by a system of regulations as prehistoric as the walls topped with broken glass which used to enclose great estates. And, of course, for four years there had been few marauders. But in my very first term the War ended and young men flooded back, many of whom had been in the forces and were anxious to make up for lost time, and more interested in dancing and taking girls out than in swotting for their degrees.

Frances coped initially with the rule about not visiting a male undergraduate in his rooms or being visited by him without the presence of a married lady, by inventing 'an imaginary duenna called Mrs Kenyon, whose services I called on quite often'. She remembered the students' irritation at this and comparable restrictions eventually exploding at a meeting between Fellows and students, after which the rules were significantly relaxed. This was probably the great meeting of March 1919, at which it was agreed that a sister might go to a brother's rooms without a chaperone; the term 'visitor' in invitations to debates and concerts should be construed as including both men and women and if dancing followed they should be allowed to remain; with tutorial permission students might have unchaperoned parties in their rooms, provided more than one hostess was present; students might go to public meetings, lectures, concerts and have tea in a teashop, but not on the river, without a chaperone.[13]

The relaxations of March 1919 did not, however, put an end to debate: chaperonage and the associated restrictions were a continuing area of friction and skirmishing between students and Fellows in Newnham. The Fellows did their best to contain it by setting up a special joint committee of junior and senior members to discuss this and any other matters the students wished to air – one of the earliest manifestations of the involvement of students in College government.[14] And inch by inch, concessions were made. In May 1920, for example, the river rules were relaxed as follows:

Parties, without chaperones, may with the leave of the Tutor, go on the river in punts or boats, but not in canoes. Such parties may only take place before dinner (8 p.m. on Sundays) and more than one student must be present, except that a student may go alone with her brother or her fiancé. No such parties may include more than one punt or boat, and no parties may take place on Thursdays [Cambridge's early closing day].

In July 1923 it was agreed that the theatre rules would be modified from the following autumn: henceforward students might go to the theatre with men friends provided that more than one student was present and the parties were of a reasonable size. Tutor's leave should be sought, with the names of those in the party listed in writing, at least twenty-four hours before the expedition.[15]

It sounds positively fantastical to the contemporary reader: how on earth did those concerned remember what they couldn't or could do? No wonder breaking, evading, circumventing and questioning the rules became a major sport for the students. Besides those who invented chaperones like the mythical Mrs Kenyon, there were the two students who persuaded their mother to rent a house in Grange Road, where they held frequent parties, out of the reach of the college authorities. Audrey Richards, who came up in 1918 and was to become a distinguished anthropologist, remembered challenging Thena on the theatre rules, which at that point required a chaperone in some part of the theatre, asking what help it would be in case of affront to have a chaperone sitting in the stalls when the students could only afford gallery or pit seats. They also clashed swords over a play produced by the Newnham students, A. A. Milne's *Belinda*, in which the male parts were taken by women, and Thena

decreed that only brothers or fiancés could attend because it was not suitable for any other men to see women in men's clothes! As President of the Dramatic Society, I put up a notice saying that no tickets would be issued to men who were not brothers or fiancés, and gave the reason. Miss Clough who saw that I was writing with my tongue in my cheek summoned me to one of her disciplinary breakfasts, when one was invited at eight o'clock to a very superb breakfast, served by a maid, in the Principal's flat. After breakfast she boomed her disapproval.[16]

The combination of reproof with a luxurious breakfast sounds characteristic of Thena. And more generally the women senior members knew how irksome the students found the web of restrictions and had some sympathy for them. Pernel Strachey had teased Frances Marshall by enquiring warmly after the fictitious Mrs Kenyon.[17] It was surely with tongue in cheek that Thena, as Principal, commented to the joint committee in November 1921 'on the growing practice of using Ground Floor Windows as entrances and exits. She pointed out that the practice badly damaged the flower-beds beneath the windows, and injured the brickwork of the window sill, which was soft. She urged that students should be discouraged from using Ground Floor Windows as thoroughfares.'[18]

Yet the women senior members were between a rock and hard place. The students of Newnham – and Girton – were perceived as 'ladies' and the outside world expected them to be subject to the same restrictions as gently brought up young women at home. As Audrey Richards acknowledged, 'Newnham did not invent the chaperon rules. One's own parents had very much the same ideas and behaved in the same way.'[19] At least as exigent as the students' parents and considerably closer at hand, eager to pounce on every suspected indelicacy, impropriety and misdemeanour, were those who resented the women's entire presence in Cambridge and their aspiration to join the University. In 1912 the poet and Latinist A. E. Housman, coming from University College, London to Trinity as a professorial fellow, had declined election to the Newnham Council in the following terms: 'I am an enemy: not indeed to the existence of Newnham or of colleges for women, but to their existence in the neighbourhood of ancient and monastic Universities, and to the rivalry of young men and maidens in study and examinations.'[20] When in the spring of 1919 the Newnham Council was preparing to concede significant relaxation in the rules of chaperonage, Katharine Stephen was instructed to consult not only with the Mistress of Girton but also with the Tutors of St John's, Caius, King's, Emmanuel, Christ's and Magdalene before the decisions were confirmed.[21] Throughout the negotiations with the University and the deliberations of the Royal Commission the senior members of Newnham were in a constant state of anxiety lest some scandal, real or manufactured, would add to their difficulties – and not without reason. In December 1920 two very influential Cambridge figures, both Fellows of Trinity, the lawyer H. A. Hollond and the physiologist Edgar Adrian, later Lord Adrian, had published a fly-sheet restating the argument of Cardinal Newman, almost three-quarters of a century before, in his *The Idea of a University*: that in higher education, priority should be attached not to what you learned but how you learned it. Cambridge, they argued, was less about curriculum than about socialisation, about the free and open intellectual and social intercourse with peers which the collegiate university nourished; and this, they declared emphatically, could not take place in a mixed society. They wanted their academic world to be as the world of Kenneth Grahame's *Wind in the Willows*, 'clean of the clash of sex'.[22] Trapped in the web of chaperonage, it was impossible for the women even to engage with such arguments, while every allegation of inappropriate behaviour, pounced on and inflated by the popular press through 1920 and 1921, appeared to lend credence to them.[23] The women students chafed at the restrictions and impatiently guyed the attitudes of their elders. The women senior members were all too conscious of the continuing fragility of their position.

Endless rather demeaning skirmishing with the students about discipline and propriety, the work on the Royal Commission and the long-drawn-out struggle within the University all took their toll of Thena. Since smoking, even in one's own room, was against the rules in Newnham until the end of the War – a rule fully supported by the students' parents – she had rented a small garden nearby, to which she could retreat for a quiet cigarette.[24] Burley Hill, with its surrounding landscape and woods, as ever provided repose and refreshment in the vacations. In the summer of 1922 Thena managed a good spell bird-watching, mostly bitterns, sleeping out in a sleeping-bag in a hide. Then Edith Sharpley, who, since retirement in 1920, had been living in a cottage near Burley, haled her off to France for a complete change of scene and some good food.[25] However, by the beginning of 1923 it was already clear that little more could be expected from Government or from the University of Cambridge: the modest gains, so hardly won, must be consolidated, but the next big 'push' was some way off. Thena, at the age of sixty-two, could reasonably feel that preparing this was a matter for the new generation. She had been through battles of this kind twice, in 1896–7 and in 1920–1: in these recent bruising encounters the younger senior members had seen for themselves the nature of the opposition and the work and tactics needed to make any headway at all. That experience would enable them to prepare for the next time, for a next time there would surely be, but under a fresh general. And younger people might feel less weary, containing the impatience of the stroppy young. There were personal reasons too for feeling that the time really had come to leave Newnham. Thena very much hoped that Kitty would come up to Newnham in due course and thought it better for both of them if she were no longer Principal if and when that happened. So on 26 January 1923 she announced to the Governing Body her intention to retire from the Principalship at the end of the following September, and they in turn recognised the finality of this decision.[26]

After the shambles of the election in 1920, the Governing Body had held an extended inquest into process and even considered changing the very new Statutes.[27] Sensibly, they had come to the conclusion that they could work perfectly well within these, provided they had some clear procedural rules, and the real work, including any caballing, went on outside the formal Governing Body meetings. This time they decided to advertise and put arrangements in the hands of a committee, headed by Thena. Advertisement produced some unreal candidates, but also two, the philosopher Frances Melville and the medieval historian Ada Levett, whose names had been canvassed last time. There is a hint that an informal meeting of Fellows was held at the beginning of March; but by the time of the Governing Body meeting for election on 15 March, only one name was formally proposed and seconded, that of Pernel Strachey, who was unanimously elected.[28] It was all very smooth: no last-minute coup by the Praetorian Guard, the seamless succession of one known to all, student 1895–9, College Lecturer in French since 1905, Tutor in charge of Peile Hall since 1910, and Newnham secretary of the joint committee with Girton through the recent troubles. She was also the first Principal of the College to have been at secondary school and then gone on to read for a full Tripos, following what was now the normal pattern among the students and increasingly among the Fellows, a trajectory which offers another measure of the transformation in women's education which the College's creation and growth represented.

Thena was delighted by Pernel's election. They were so different in background, temperament and style, yet their friendship was a deep and enduring one, reinforced by Thena's warm friendship also with Pernel's sister, Pippa. Thena had watched and was confident in Pernel's exercise of both intellectual and administrative judgement. Crucially, too, the same things made them laugh. Some students, like Frances Marshall, found Pernel aloof, although she pictured her brilliantly:

A shy, faintly amused giraffe, [who] advances into the room with her arms folded round her tall, slender body, while her small intelligent face – tilted back (as if in reluctance) on her long neck – is almost obscured by the large round lenses of her spectacles, brilliant with reflected light. From this face emerged a small, precise voice which manifested the peculiar dynamics of her family in miniature.[29]

Entirely distinctive, yet not quite stately; however, younger as well as older Fellows appreciated the sharp mind, quizzical detachment and mordant sense of humour, which undoubtedly helped Pernel maintain her composure in all manner of situations. A little of its flavour is conveyed in a letter to her brother, Lytton, a few weeks after becoming Principal. On 21 November 1923 she wrote:

The young are really most preposterous. This morning a rather pink undergraduate called Mr Rice, called upon me and said he was the Editor of the *Granta* and wished to have an article on me by you for the Xmas number, 750 words by December 1st. So here I am sending on the request, though I don't quite know why. I am to figure alongside of the Senior Proctor as 'One in Authority'. I gathered that it was intended to mark a *rapprochement* with the University. Well, well. I think I shall ask Virginia [Woolf] if you refuse. D'you think her style would look well in the *Granta*?[30]

The deed done and the succession assured, Thena began to make some modest travel plans. Kitty had left St Felix early because of anxiety about her eyesight. However a spell in Italy, learning Italian and looking at pictures, appeared to deal with this; and she then went on to Paris to improve her French and absorb as much culture as possible. Thena decided to spend part of the summer vacation in Paris too, visiting Jane Harrison, who had at last retired there, then sight-seeing with Kitty and returning to Burley with her.[31]

At the College Council meeting on 3 March 1923, the formal resolution of thanks to Thena had been moved by Hannah Floretta Cohen, one of the external members, an Associate and an old student, who had seen for herself over a long period the development of Thena's pivotal role among the various communities that made up the College. The words she chose reflected this:

Miss Clough has been associated with Newnham College since 1884 and has had a large share in building up and perpetuating its traditions. She took up the Principalship at a most difficult time and with generous disregard of personal convenience. She has won the allegiance and affection of the whole College, and has guided its affairs with a rare combination of firmness, tolerance and wisdom.[32]

Old students arranged to have Thena's portrait painted in 1924, by William Nicholson, and presented the finished picture to the College. It is a sombre oil in blacks, whites and greys, as she gazes into the middle distance. Far more attractive is the pencil drawing, commissioned by another group of old students from William Rothenstein in 1927: the expression is sober and the strength of the face apparent, but that image makes it easier to visualise the individual who also knew when to turn a blind eye, who was capable of the tongue-in-cheek comment, and who could command a whole room when she chose. Perhaps the bleakness of the 1924 portrait hints at the bleakness of which the private person was capable, and the bleakness of the prospect for the institution immediately following the defeat of 1921. Jane Harrison had hoped that Nicholson would manage 'to preserve some of your most badger-like characteristics'.[33] Instead he conveys a slightly pinched look, with an overtone almost of bitterness, which seem out of place. Because Thena had low expectations of what life could offer, she faced its setbacks with equanimity; and she was exceptionally well-practised at concealing private feelings, whatever they were, behind a calm public face. The years during and immediately following the War were difficult ones for Newnham. She contributed not only administrative and political skills but also a stoic dignity and an absolute refusal to lose sight of the long-term goals of the institution she had helped to create. Leadership in bad times demands even more than leadership in good times.

17 Thena Clough in 1928, drawing by William Rothenstein

CHAPTER II

Retirement

Thena lived to a great age, dying in 1960 just over a month short of her ninety-ninth birthday. Whatever her hopes for tranquillity and much bird-watching, the period of her retirement had its share of dramas, not only the great public drama of the Second World War but also private excitements and upheavals as well.

Watching Kitty grow up was one of the great pleasures of the 1920s for Thena. The eye-strain which had caused such anxiety during Kitty's last year at school had receded during the year she spent in Italy and France, and in the autumn of 1923, on Pernel Strachey's advice, she was sent off to school just outside Lausanne, where it was thought she would learn both a purer and a more grammatical French, refining the idioms she had acquired in Paris. From Switzerland she did the Newnham entrance examination, Pernel – as well she might – graciously waiving the need for an oral examination; and Kitty was accepted to come up to Newnham in the autumn of 1924, to read French and Italian.[1] She did very well in Part I, at the end of two years, gaining a first class; but in Part II things went less well and she convinced herself she had failed. Thena mixed soothing and bracing words:

I'm very sorry to gather you've been disenjoying yourself so much. It's very bad luck – Well it generally isn't nearly so bad as one thinks. But even if you haven't done as you shd which is no doubt quite like enough – it is only vexatious not serious at all. I am quite sure and so is Aunt Pernel that you haven't come anywhere near failing, quite, quite impossible. I'm so sorry my dear – you will begin to get hold of the unmatteringness of it really, however tiresome.[2]

And indeed, Kitty hadn't failed, simply fallen to a 2(ii). It was – and is – not uncommon for those who romp through the linguistic tests of Part I Modern Languages, to find the primarily literary work of Part II much tougher. When she had picked herself up, Kitty decided to do a post-graduate course in Librarianship at University College, London, which

she considered much harder work than Cambridge. Once Kitty was qualified, Thena took a hand in finding her a job. Sarah Marshall, who had
come up to Newnham in 1876 from Mrs Fleming's School in Ambleside – the successor to Annie's school at Eller How – had married Harry
Toynbee. Thena was a friend of the family as Annie had been: Jocelyn,
one of Sarah's two daughters, had been a Newnham student between 1916
and 1920 and, in process of becoming a distinguished archaeologist of the
classical world, returned to Newnham in 1927 as Director of Studies in
Classics. When Sarah's son Arnold was at school at Winchester, he and his
mother used to come to stay at Burley Hill. By 1929 Arnold was Director
of the Royal Institute of International Affairs at Chatham House in London and Thena asked whether there might be an opening for Kitty. She
was duly interviewed and offered a post which was partly in the library,
partly assisting with research and writing for the annual *Survey of International Affairs*. Thena was delighted: 'Oh I say, my dear Kits, how glo-
rious and wonderful!' and Uncle Arthur promptly began to calculate her
salary.[3]

More was riding on this than simple family pleasure at her success. Kitty
had a small allowance from her father, who in the early 1920s had returned
to fruit farming in California; and she also benefited under the trust Blanche
Mary Shore Clough had set up for her mother, Lily.[4] With her Chatham
House salary as well she could now be entirely self-supporting. This was
both comfort and relief to Thena and Arthur; for the Clough estate was
facing serious financial problems. Arthur had conducted himself as squire
of Burley in a manner more suited to the early nineteenth than to the early
twentieth century. He invested substantially and generously in the village's
infrastructure. He built cottages in Garden Road and Burley Street and in
1907 donated land for the building of the parish hall. During the war the
village welcomed Belgian refugees; and at its end Arthur launched a factory
making handsome and solid wooden toys, in which he made a point of
employing ex-servicemen.[5] Such open-handedness proved much harder to
sustain in the face of wartime price rises and post-war slump than it had in
the Edwardian period, although, drawing heavily on the advice of his cousin
Tommy Coltman, a solicitor, he did his best to diversify and spread risk.
Thena had taken her share of her mother's estate principally in the form
of the house, Burley Hill, and its land; and in March 1922 she mobilised
some of the capital they represented by taking out a mortgage with Barclays Bank. This was repaid a year later but the house and estate were
promptly remortgaged with the Midland Bank, who presumably offered
better terms.[6]

This injection of capital provided only a temporary respite. In January 1927, Thena, recovering from 'flu, wrote to Kitty:

The financial question is very much under discussion. I have been wondering whether it would be right to propose your lending us your fortune for 3 mths – It seems that there is rather a specially difficult period because there are large sums due from the building societies to finance the cottage building and they have promised the money but between the delays due to board meetings & solicitors' proceedings the process of paying is desperately slow & meanwhile large sums in wages have to be paid. I was going to propose that you should invest the money in Government loan the $3\frac{1}{2}$% loan which is selling at 75. This according to my calculations would bring in something over $4\frac{1}{2}$%. You would get interest on the loan of course so it would I hope be quite right and fair. I'll ask Uncle Tommy to make quite sure I'm not exploiting you & if he approves I know you'll be glad to help in this preposterous game which for my part I think rather stirring & interesting than anything else.

She went on to ask whether Kitty could easily lay hands on the bank's deposit note for her 'fortune', all of £530, and to explain what kind of letter would need to be written to them; then concluded, 'I didn't give you your term's cheque. I think I'll write & ask Aunt Pernel if I may delay that a little. It's all very preposterous – but we are not really bankrupt as I understand the village thinks.'[7]

As another short-term expedient, Thena took in a paying guest, Halford Vaughan, a connexion of the Stephens and Fishers. However a much bolder plan was being formed: it was to sell Burley Hill, enabling the mortgage to be paid off and perhaps some further capital raised, and to move to share Castle Top with Arthur and Eleanor, thereby significantly reducing the running expenses of both households. Eleanor began on some interior rearrangement at Castle Top, to create a more or less self-contained portion of the house for Thena, and reduced her own household staff to two, 'a cook general and small house parlour maid'; and Thena began to show parties of possible purchasers over Burley Hill. Eventually, at the beginning of February 1928 Burley Hill was sold to Sir Cecil Lindsay Budd for £11,700. Budd also bought additional land from Arthur, a separate sale of household effects was held, and Thena, with her own cook general and maid, Annie and Emma, moved into Castle Top. She described the final stages of the house clearing and move to Kitty: 'It was such a business really clearing every last object out of the house.' The household effects for sale were laid outside and some of them got rained on; but 'we think we didn't do so badly. The sale made £333' and the remainder would go to auction rooms in Salisbury. Phoenix, the dog, was puzzled by the change of home; but 'she's got her sofa in the maids' room and that consoles her.' As for the other migrants, 'I brought Annie & Emma over with the two canaries in the car & the canaries don't mind at all . . . Annie has been a tremendous trump & toiled away with the greatest competence & never grumped at all. Now of course she is rather depressed – with a new, not so convenient kitchen & all the rest of it, but I hope she will get used to it.'[8] Arthur too was depressed by the upheaval and the loss, and his health began to go downhill from this point. Thena, at least to Kitty, was more matter-of-fact and robust about the situation; although she may have reflected wryly on her lofty refusal to take more than half her allotted salary as Principal of Newnham from 1920 to 1923. Nevertheless she had enough energy left over to engage simultaneously in vigorous and extended combat with the Forestry Commission about felling and planting strategies in Burley and its vicinity. Following this, she found herself in the thick of negotiations with the Electricity Board and all other interested parties in the area over the siting of pylons and cables.[9]

Sadly for them all, the sale of Burley Hill was not the last upheaval they had to face. Arthur was also heavily mortgaged to the Midland Bank; and as the economic situation continued to deteriorate nationally, he came under increasing pressure. The bank was prepared to hold its hand as long as possible; but the solicitors to the local branch in Ringwood, with whose firm he had long had a difficult relationship, advised foreclosure. In September 1933 Arthur petitioned for bankruptcy, almost a hundred years after his Clough grandfather had been in similar straits.[10] There the melancholy symmetry ends, however. By the 1930s the legal regulation of bankruptcy had been transformed; and while Arthur, Eleanor and Thena had to reduce their living standards, they were never as close to penury as the Cloughs had been in Liverpool during the 1840s. Major steps towards liquidating the debt were taken with an auction sale of contents in January 1934, followed by the sale of Castle Top itself, at Easter time that year, to the Mackworth Praed family, although Arthur's discharge from bankruptcy was not finally completed until the beginning of 1938.[11] However Eleanor's resources had all along been protected by her marriage settlement, and these were augmented on her father's death in 1934. They included a house at Mid-Winterslow, in Wiltshire, near Salisbury, to which Arthur and Eleanor retreated, after a spell spent recuperating in North Wales, at Portmeirion, at the kind invitation of the architect Clough Williams Ellis, a distant cousin.[12]

Thena's position was a more vulnerable one. She and Arthur had inherited jointly on the death of their mother; and apart from the devising of

Burley Hill to her at the beginning of 1905, no other formal steps had been taken to separate their shares of the estate. At least one account relating to Burley investments remained in their joint names and creditors had claims against her as well as against him.[13] Thena's letters to Kitty over this period suggest that the bankruptcy was altogether a greater upheaval than the sale of Burley Hill. They are scrappy, news of family and friends interspersed with much financial detail and instructions, not all of which are very clear. The very real anxieties and sense of distintegration, not so easy to withstand in one's seventies, warred with her iron determination to protect Kitty and her interests. She devoted much energy to ensuring, successfully, that Kitty's own capital and possessions were protected. She also prevailed upon Kitty to go ahead that winter with a long-planned trip to the United States, to see her father and to meet for the first time her elder half-sister, Frances.[14]

Thena's own friends rallied to her support magnificently. The question of where immediately she was to live was resolved by an invitation from Gwen Burton to share her London flat at 22 Gerald Road SW1. Gwen is one of Thena's friends about whom we know least. After study at the Royal College of Music, she had come up to Newnham in 1916, at the age of twenty-six, to read Economics. Long after, one of her contemporaries described her as 'an ethereal pre-Raphaelite presence'. Thena had been Gwen's tutor, sustained her when she fell ill and, discovering that she and her sister lived near Burley, enjoyed bird-watching with her in the New Forest. After graduation and her sister's untimely death, Gwen built up a business in London, in Ebury Street, as an antique dealer, specialising in old glass.[15] Meanwhile Harry Stephen and his wife Barbara, who had recently moved from London to Hale, near Fordingbridge, not far from Burley, worked to ensure that resources were in place and secure to enable Thena to find a new base in her beloved New Forest when she was ready. Despite Thena's protests, a group of friends subscribed £250 which Harry and Pernel Strachey held in trust, to ensure that no creditors could lay claim to it. By the end of April 1935 they had found a house which she liked, Folly Hill in Hale Purlieu, not far from the Stephens. It is a much smaller house than either Burley Hill or Castle Top, but with a handsome garden, magnificently situated, and views across the Forest reminiscent of those she had enjoyed at Embley so long before. In August 1935 Pernel, on a visit to Folly Hill, wrote happily to her sister Pippa, 'The house is very nice and it is most pleasant to see so many of the old favourites out and about once more. Lears on the walls, Bewicks in the shelves, tables, chairs and carpets all fitting in most marvellously.'[16] And by the end of May 1935 Thena herself had felt sufficiently secure to make her will. Everything was left to Kitty, including Folly Hill, as the terms of the trust allowed her to do. If Kitty predeceased her, then the house would go to Pernel, or, in the event of her earlier death, to Gwen.[17]

Through the 1920s and 1930s, well before Gwen provided her with a firm base, Thena had been spending time in London, often staying in one of the two adjacent Stephen households at Rosary Gardens in Kensington. Sadly, Katharine had died in 1924; but Thena – and Kitty – were equally close to Harry and Barbara, who then lived next door.[18] Having stood in for Pippa Strachey during her illness in 1916, Thena continued to help out at the London and National Society for Women's Service, as the London Society for Women's Suffrage had now become, which Pippa continued to serve as Secretary. The Society now worked to increase the numbers of women in higher education and in the professions.[19] Often Thena's diplomatic and political skills were called upon; but on occasion she could be positively irresponsible. Both facets were captured in a long, characteristically chatty, letter from Pippa to Pernel in July 1937. 'I had intended first', wrote Pippa,

to answer a business letter from Lady Snowden which ends 'I am gradually getting back my balance. Lovingly yours, dear friend.'

What is one to do in such a world? The only thing I can think of is to ask Thena to draft an appropriate reply!

This reminds me that I have today forged yr signature to a letter to the Princess Royal. I didn't read it as Thena had already altered it to her liking.

Yet earlier in the same letter Pippa had also given a graphic account of 'a most awkward experience' at the offices they shared with various other women's organisations in Marsham Street:

After a late Cttee we went down to a meal & found an enormous party of about 60 suffragettes celebrating Mrs Pankhurst's birthday. We sank into a corner table with our backs turned and just came in for the speeches. Most painful & Thena behaved abominably in making comic interjections in a deep bass voice which resounded through the room (or seemed to to me). Christabel made a quite incredible tub thumping oration full of God & Christ & victory through weakness – Jesus on his Cross, Emmiline [sic] in her prison (but not Christabel) in a professional canting voice & with a large feathered hat on her head. It went on & on, only interrupted by a peevish interjection that she couldn't speak if people talked behind her. I took this to be an allusion to Thena but it wasn't really. She (Thena) didn't catch the remark & immediately afterwards pushed back her chair with a scraping noise & left the room with an expression of extreme contempt on her countenance long before this extraordinary speech dried up.[20]

Plainly Thena now felt she was a private person and need no longer curb the
expression of her own very strong opinions, while Pippa was torn between
agreement with the sentiments and the demands of decorum and coexis-
tence. Yet Thena remained a public figure to the extent that she continued
to play a part in the affairs of Newnham. Under the Statutes of 1917 she had
been elected to the Governing Body in 1924, immediately following her
retirement, and served until 1944, with stints on the Council as well. She
was regularly in Cambridge several times each year and was there, hovering
anxiously, during the process of electing Pernel's successor as Principal, in
1941, trying not to meddle – and be seen to meddle – too much, while desperately concerned that the College should make a good choice.[21] There
is no sign that Pernel felt threatened by her predecessor's presence, any
more than Katharine Stephen had felt threatened by Nora Sidgwick's continuing involvement. Thena and Pernel continued to exchange visits and
corresponded comfortably and regularly. Their letters read as if Thena had
joined the Strachey family circle of correspondents. Pernel described a visit
to Cambridge by Gandhi, secure in the knowledge that Thena shared her
sceptical approach to the Indian leader and his teaching. When Thena and
Arthur agreed to make available Matthew Arnold's letters to their father for
an edition by H. F. Lowry, Pernel shared their irritation that while Clough
had carefully kept all Arnold's letters, Arnold had destroyed all Clough's
letters to him. There was the added bonus for Pernel that Thena understood
exactly some of the absurdities of life in Cambridge in this period. She could
sympathise with the problems of finding grand lecturers for memorial lectures, with anxieties lest the machinery for showing their slides broke down
and with the chores of organising dinner parties for them.[22] In December
1934 Pernel was taken ill with peritonitis and rushed off to the Evelyn
Nursing Home in Cambridge. Thena, who represented Newnham on the
Nursing Home's Board of Directors, hastened to visit. Pippa wrote to Pernel
on 17 December, 'Thena has given a charming account of you in the midst
of your flowery cage . . . [She] seems to have ascertained that it will be quite
OK for me to be at Newnham for Christmas.'[23] Pernel's involvement in the
rescue package which enabled the purchase of Folly Hill grew naturally out
of a friendship which had deepened and matured over nearly forty years
and both of them were grown up enough not to let it constrain or inhibit
that friendship.

A sense of the importance of this friendship prompts more general reflection on the role and nature of friendship with other women for Thena and
for her generation. It is difficult now in a post-Freudian age to recapture
the richness and complexity of same-sex friendships, friendships between

men as well as friendships between women, in the nineteenth century, so conditioned are we by a post-1920 model which attributes a powerful sexual charge to all intimacies. Friendship tends now to be a much more constrained and impoverished notion and condition than it was for our nineteenth-century forebears, especially for women, whose lives and actions were circumscribed by that period's exaltation of the domestic sphere and women's place in it.[24] It seems both linear and crude to interpret powerful female friendships in the period up to the First World War as proto-lesbian, especially when the protagonists used the language of romantic love.[25] The terms of the public discourse do change in the immediate post-war period, when sapphism became positively *chic* in some circles in Paris and Rad-clyffe Hall's 1928 novel of lesbian love, *The Well of Loneliness* was banned in England. Language which had been common currency in the 1890s and much earlier was subsequently seen as sending very different signals and either eschewed altogether or used much more selectively, with a new eye to both context and audience. Yet actual relationships, as so often, were much less tidy, more complex and could evolve over time. Some did have a powerful erotic charge and found physical expression, as in the case of Katharine Harris Bradley, who attended Newnham for a term in 1874 and subsequently settled with Emma Cooper, her niece and partner, in Florence, where they composed lengthy verse dramas together under the pseudonym 'Michael Field'. This was exceptional, however. If other relationships had an erotic strand, particularly when they originated in schoolgirl or student 'crushes', it found expression more often in warm embraces and the language of affection. Subsequently it might wither and die as the friends grew up and apart or fell out; or it might become overlaid, entangled with other bonds of shared experience, interest and family, all of which co-existed with other relationships and friendships, hetero- as well as homo-social. Generalisations on these lines, however unwieldy, are closer to the nuanced and complex realities of the lives of nineteenth- and early twentieth-century women than the black/white dichotomies of hetero- and homo-sexuality.[26]

Thena's vocabulary for the ties of love and friendship had been first shaped in the 1880s and 1890s; but she had long understood that they came in many and often complementary forms. She was well aware that within the family network relationships could be complex and highly charged. The unsparing self-analysis of the early black books records her bond with her brother, her distance from her mother and the growth of love for her aunt almost in spite of herself. At Christmas 1933 Kitty Duff was overwhelmed by her first meeting with her elder half-sister, Frances, in California and almost frightened by the emotion. Thena's response, meant to reassure, was a penetrating one: 'I think I understand about Frances – I've been in love myself & I'm not sure that you ever have before. Your father is tremendously pleased that you fit each other so well.'[27]

Beyond the family circle, Thena knew that she herself had a talent for friendship and came close to despising herself for it. She was able to describe with almost clinical detachment her crush on an unnamed fellow-student in the 1880s. As a Vice-Principal, she was aware she could make an emotional impact on students both individually and in the group: she recognised that this was a situation in which personality and authority could both be brought into play and reinforce each other. This very awareness may have protected her from misusing such power – unlike Jane Harrison, who tended to have favourites. Pernel Strachey and Gwen Burton were both Thena's tutorial pupils; but the friendships flowered after each had graduated and Pernel initially found Thena positively intimidating. In one of the sets of loose sheets of self-examination, which served sometimes as black book substitutes, undated but probably from the inter-war years, Thena mused on her friendship with an unnamed woman, perhaps Gwen. 'I was attracted, stimulated, stung by the spirit of pursuit – stirred too by something like sympathy as well as attraction.' Now 'there is too little of me left for my own use – too little freedom of mind. I want to live somewhat intermittently with a friend.' A little later she reproached herself, as so often, for over-analysis: 'Really one torments oneself to death. Why can I not realize & accept that I have a friend without clawing up my inside & asking am I quite sure I would like to live with her always. Is it not enough that I am thankful, very thankful for a delightful companion on my way through this difficult life.'[28]

In the inter-war years, as in the 1880s and 1890s, Thena kept such musings entirely to herself, realising always that to share them might be to frighten the friend or friends. She was never possessive or exclusive in her friendships: and none of her many friends displayed the kind of possessiveness towards her which Hope Mirrlees, the companion of Jane Harrison's last years, displayed, behaving at times as if Jane was her exclusive property and jealously keeping others away.

Thena's friends had combined forces over the package which bought Folly Hill and they combined again to celebrate her eightieth birthday on 5 August 1941, despite the exigencies of wartime. Sixteen of them, with Kitty, arranged a surprise weekend in Cambridge, with a party, and despatched a box of gifts and a crate of wine to Folly Hill, along with a cheque which was to be spent on taking taxis. Thena was wholly taken aback, but very, very pleased, writing to Kitty, 'why are you and all the others so munificent?

Ought it not all to go to the Red X – or such? I can't feel that living till 80 can deserve such rewards.'[29]

At the outbreak of war on 3 September 1939, Thena was at Folly Hill, grappling with the provision of blackout curtains and waiting for the promised – or threatened – evacuees. She wrote to Kitty: 'Draper [her current cook-housekeeper] and I have been very busy wrestling with the darkness problem as it is impossible to get the curtains I ordered a fortnight ago. We have ingeniously hung a plaid (which my father brought from Scotland probably 100 years ago) across the bow.' The struggle was still going on ten days later, when Gwen Burton had joined them for the weekend: 'Gwen sits sewing linings to curtains endlessly. She has rather high standards. Draper and I were inclined to be content with safety pins.' Some of the surrounding communities had already received their evacuees by 3 September; and Harry Stephen, as Assistant Evacuation Officer, was at full stretch, 'dealing with problems of babies with the wrong food & mothers with fits & children with heads [headlice]. One theory of the non-appearing ones (supplied by Blandford) is that they are being detained at the [Poor Law] Union at Fordingbridge to be cleaned. I don't mention this to Draper.' Ten days later there were still no evacuees but Thena was now also housing Nellie, the maid, and her little daughter. Meanwhile Draper had abandoned her plan to go and nurse – 'she was outraged at being told to go to the Fordingbridge Public Assistance place which she said was full of riff-raff & dirty persons' – so Thena still had what she recognised as the luxury of a full complement of resident help in the house.[30]

The blackout curtains were eventually completed but the issues of evacuees and of domestic help were to recur. Nellie's daughter had been found a secure home in the Convent in Salisbury and there was some discussion of Nellie going to work for Gwen in London. By the beginning of October Thena had recognised that at the age of seventy-eight, she and Draper, whose health and temperament were both uncertain, were unlikely to be able to cope with two child evacuees and had negotiated a deal with Harry Stephen whereby she would house an adult and child instead. In the summer of 1940 she provided accommodation for one of Harry's sisters, Rosamond, for a long spell; but the first actual evacuees to be housed came in the autumn of 1940, to be followed in January 1941 by 'a poor hardly treated little lady with 2 birds & a thousand packages'.[31] By this time Draper, to Thena's considerable relief, had departed and been replaced by the much more energetic and good-tempered Rhoda. Then in the spring of 1942 Rhoda was called up and Thena briefly contemplated letting or closing up the house, warned, however, that if she did so, the Army might requisition it. By the summer some help was at hand in the person of a local daily, Mrs Muspratt; and she continued to work for Thena until her husband was demobbed in November 1945, when Thena managed to find a Miss Matthews to take her place. The steady dwindling of help meant that Thena had to learn to cook, not so easy when food rationing made it near-impossible to abandon one's disasters and start again. There is extra resonance in Thena's report to Kitty in February 1942 that Pernel, who was staying for a week, 'has been most diligent & efficient in blacking out & cooking the supper'. Nevertheless, perhaps because of his age, Thena seems to have succeeded in hanging on to her part-time gardener, Blandford, throughout; and together they planted fruit trees and vegetables among the flowers.[32]

Such trials and tribulations were of course shared with the vast majority of the middle-class population in Britain; and living in the countryside with a large garden meant that the worst rigours of rationing could be alleviated with local produce and barter. At one stage, when there were reports of a national milk shortage, Thena reassured Kitty that locally supplies were holding up: 'I don't know if we are breaking the law. I rather think we must be.'[33] More generally, although eighty in 1941, she tried not to let the increasingly arduous process of daily living elbow all other considerations out of the way. Her interest in politics remained as strong as ever and at the outbreak of war she had acquired a radio, to which she was an avid listener. Its periodic breakdown caused at least as much irritation as the problems with domestic help; and Thena's letters to Kitty, which are the principal source for her life in these years, are peppered with comments on this and on the news. She applauded the inclusion of the Labour Party in the coalition government formed in May 1940, remarking shrewdly, 'It seems to be everything to have the Trades Unions brought in'; and she approved of Churchill's broadcasts at the end of May and the beginning of June: he 'left us no illusions'. She continued a supporter of Churchill, although recognising that the general election of 1945 was about more than his war record. She wrote to Kitty,

I'm depressed you voted Liberal. I think it so important Winston should come in though I don't think he's done his speeches well & the whole business has been disgusting & of course Beaverbrook is a bad lot but comparatively unimportant. Mrs Muspratt says all the soldiers are voting Labour because of the mismanagement after the last War . . . We have been voting for Crosthwaite Eyre. He may not be important but he's sound about the Forest.[34]

Kitty's own war was inevitably of particular concern to Thena. At the outbreak of war the Royal Institute of International Affairs became a satellite of the Foreign Office and its staff and papers were initially sent off from Chatham House to a secret location – except that on the vans conveying the papers was written 'Salter, Oxford'. They were housed in Balliol College, Oxford, where Kitty became part of the Latin American research section and settled down to learn Portuguese, finding lodgings close by at 98 Holywell, in the house Jocelyn Toynbee shared with her sister Margaret. Once she had discovered where the 'secret' destination was, Thena was particularly exercised by two matters: the frugality of Margaret Toynbee's housekeeping and the Foreign Office's sharp practice in commandeering the Chatham House staff, yet treating them as unestablished and paying them a pittance. Knowing the Toynbee family as well as she did, Thena presumably had some grounds for her concern about the housekeeping; but she derived comfort from the fact that her old friend Lucy Silcox, Kitty's former headmistress at St Felix, had retired to a house on Boar's Hill, just outside Oxford, and could be relied on for compensatory meals. Issues of salary and status were more intractable but had already attracted publicity; and Thena, spending a week at Newnham with Pernel in December 1939, reported with some glee that, 'the High Table at NC burst into flames over the salary list in the Times & fell upon Jocelyn & abused Arnold & refused to listen when she said it wasn't his fault'. The situation was eventually regularised when the Foreign Office acknowledged the need for a research department, which for the duration the Chatham House staff became; and in 1943 they were all moved back to London, although the price of this, as Thena was disconcerted to discover, was that letters exchanged with Kitty were now censored and consequently travelled much more slowly.[35]

As all of this shows, Thena was determined to remain active, mobile and engaged throughout the war years, although this became more and more difficult. Gwen remained London-based, driving for St George's Hospital throughout the war. However she and Thena's other friends were at one in considering London during the Blitz no place for her. Pippa Strachey wrote in considerable perturbation to Pernel in September 1940,

Gwen Burton & I are a good deal disturbed by the apparition of Thena on the scene because deafness & slowness of movement are not at all helpful in present circs when getting about is really difficult – One can't tell from one minute to the next how the busses [sic] or the trains will be running . . . the only method is to make up one's mind rapidly & be nippy in getting in & out . . . It may also be useful to recognize the sounds of airplanes & swishes(?) so as to prepare for flight & none of this regime is at all suited to Thena.[36]

On this occasion Thena was persuaded to go to Cambridge. Yet in May of the following year, Hester Duff, one of Kitty's Duff cousins, reported meeting her on a bus in London, 'looking so well & rather pretty!' – not a term often used to describe the solid and four-square figure of Thena, usually clad in somewhat mannish tweeds.[37]

Gradually it became harder for Thena to get about. When she had first retired, she had acquired a small car, which she tended to drive around the New Forest too fast. At the outbreak of war, faced with petrol rationing, she attempted to learn to ride a bicycle; but it was not a skill easily mastered at the age of seventy-eight, especially as the bike seems to have had a cross-bar. Barbara Stephen, who was colluding with Pernel in 1942–3 to prepare a draft obituary of Thena for *The Times* 'bank' of such notices, reported that Thena 'keeps pretty well, I think, though of course at a low level', the main problem being the deafness.[38] However at some time after that, either late in 1943 or early in 1944, Thena had a bad car accident, which damaged one of her eyes and definitively put paid to further driving.[39] Over these years she had been sorting family papers; by this stage she had reached the black books, which she was rereading, debating with herself whether to destroy them: 'Why shouldn't I leave Kitty to think I'm much nicer than I am?' The accident, the consequent loss of mobility and difficulties with reading all depressed her profoundly, as well they might; and late in 1944, in a savage note added at the very beginning of her first black book, she wrote, 'I'm no good for anything now.' On a loose sheet, inserted in the fifth of the notebooks, she wrote, 'I am only a not very competent looker-on – but I do not feel it natural that really good minds should fade & fall & cease to count. I can't be content that they should be so dependent on bodies. I don't feel the same discontent with death.'[40]

In making these last comments Thena may have been thinking as much about what was happening to her contemporaries as to herself. Edith Sharpley had moved back from Hampshire to Lincolnshire, to be closer to her family, and in 1940 her health began to fail. Thena travelled to see her one last time: subsequently she took enormous pains over the obituary notice for the Newnham *Roll Letter*.[41] In May 1943 Thena's brother Arthur died, after a long spell in which his mind intermittently wandered and, as reported by Eleanor, he did not want to see anyone at all. Eleanor had summoned Thena, however, shortly before he died; and Thena wrote sadly to Kitty, 'Well, there it is, the great thing is that he hasn't any pain & he likes his dr [doctor] & nurse & as he sleeps a great deal I hope Eleanor is not worn out.' It was as though the farewells and grieving had begun once he retreated into seclusion.[42] Mary Paley Marshall died in March 1944 and Thena and Pernel combined forces to prepare the obituary notice for the Newnham *Roll Letter*.[43] In March 1945 Barbara Stephen died, followed by Harry in November of the same year. On Harry's death, Thena and Kitty did what they could to help his sister Dorothy in sorting out adequate care for James, Harry and Barbara's mentally disturbed only son.[44] It was a melancholy list, which could only lengthen, and the correspondence surviving from these years grows increasingly sombre. Only occasionally are there matters to celebrate or laugh about. In October 1945 Thena was delighted to read in *The Times* of the election of Patrick Duff, Hester's brother and another of Kitty's multitude of Duff cousins, to the Regius Professorship of Roman Law in Cambridge and hastened to write a warm note of congratulations, with greetings to all the family. In July 1946, she was exulting in the Government's near-defeat on the Pensions Bill in the House of Lords, and scribbling a note to Kitty in the train, she added, 'Aunt Pernel [who had not been well] has now been told she is to go to an island – so she is busy looking for one. The dr [doctor] suggested IoW but we all shriek at the idea.'[45]

Some time during 1947 'dependence on the body' finally overwhelmed Thena herself. What happened is not clear: those who could have related the details are now themselves dead. However in the course of that year Thena moved to a private nursing home in Putney, at 95 Howard's Lane, not far away from Kitty in Deodar Road. There she remained until her death on 14 June 1960. No letters from her written later than 1946 have been found. Between 1947 and 1950 Folly Hill was sold; and the decisions to deposit a major portion of the family papers in the Bodleian Library, at Balliol College, Oxford and at Newnham in the early 1950s were all effectively taken by Kitty. Thena's death certificate recorded the causes of death as pneumonia, arteriosclerosis and recurrent cerebral haemorrhages.[46] Perhaps the first stroke, and one sufficiently disabling to make it impossible for her to continue to live on her own, came in 1947. In December 1947 the Senate of the University of Cambridge at last carried a Grace admitting women to full membership of the University and in 1948 women began to matriculate and to take degrees in the same way as men. It is a particular sadness that Thena, who had borne so much of the burden and heat of the day, could not be at Newnham to share in the celebration of the eventual victory: one can only hope there was quiet rejoicing in Putney.

Conclusion

The two women whose lives and work form the central thread of this study were very different personalities. Anne Jemima Clough – Annie – had an impetuousness, a human sympathy, a directness and spontaneity which at times she herself regretted but which enabled her to make contact with every sort of person: what you saw was what you got. With this went a buoyant optimism, not unlike her father's: however difficult the situation, she would see ways of making something positive out of it; and she retained to the end of her life an inexhaustible interest in the life around her. Margaret Verrall, who had come up to Newnham in 1875 and stayed on to teach Classics, set down her sense of the person she had known for sixteen years, in her diary at the end of April 1892, not long after Annie's death:

the secret of the charm of a talk with Miss Clough was that to the experience and tolerance of age she added the interest in life and appreciation of things new which one expects in the young only. If I had a new scheme in hand, or a new idea to develop, there was no one on whose interest I could count on whose advice I could depend on as on hers. There was nothing I could not talk of to her, and no subject that her few words did not make clearer or more interesting. She understood without one's having to clothe one's thoughts in words, and she explained without making phrases. I know of no one else who can do that, and so many things are exaggerated or altered by the medium of language that the loss of one like her is immense – especially, perhaps to someone who like me feels that language conceals as much as it reveals.

Another point that made Miss Clough's talks so valuable and so dear was that one felt that her interest and kindliness, though individual were not personal – if I may so express it. She cared about you, because you were you, and not because you were a relation or a student or had any claim . . .

I think she taught me one of the lessons I most value – the desirability of frankness about oneself with younger people who have no right to it. It is impossible to me ever to forget how, when I first came to Newnham, she told me frankly one evening that her difficulty all through life had been her quick temper. She had been with someone else in my presence, and in the evening she told me this. I can't describe the effect it had on me that a woman of her years and position should say this quite simply to a girl not eighteen, and a girl whom she considered such a child that she took me to the station and put me in charge of Professor Seeley(!) when I went home. It gave me a sense of self-respect never to be lost, and has made me realize once for all the dignity that is in every human being.[1]

Margaret Verrall also became a staunch friend and supporter of Blanche Athena Clough: first she taught her and later urged her on when she was uncertain whether to accept a Vice-Principalship at Newnham.[2] Thena, however, was very different from her aunt. The public persona was assured and composed: she seemed a woman of few words, yet with a talent for drawing out those around her. As Elsie Butler had put it, 'no-one ever talked so well unless she was there'.[3] Her skills as administrator and negotiator were exceptional. Long after her death Kitty Duff still felt the loss of Thena's diplomatic skills: 'as we say about her now, if only she could tell me what to say in that letter. If only we could consult her about this.'[4] Yet buried far underneath this calm exterior was someone who suffered from periods of black depression, who was prone to judge herself by the harshest standards, putting the worst construction possible on her own motives and actions, whose sense of self-worth was at best fragile and at worst non-existent. The family resemblances between the depressive tendencies and capacity for self-doubt experienced by Thena, her brother Arthur, and their father, are strong. Biographers of the poet have made much of his early separation from family and home. How much more must his children have suffered from never knowing their father at all. Arthur, who was two years old when his father died, may have had a dim memory. Thena never even saw her father and the emotional distance between her and her mother surely added to a sense of distance, if not of alienation, from the image of the poet which Blanche Mary Shore Clough worked to create, through the memoir and the editing of posthumously published poems, in the decade following his death.

As Thena grew older, she learned to manage and contain her moods, writing in her black books or on any scraps of paper that came to hand; learning also that while at times solitude was necessary, to surrender to the mood completely was simply to allow it to feed on itself. As she put it with her customary brutality, 'unless I am kept busy fussing about practical details my mind well occupied with trivialities I become aware that I have no mind & no soul, no tastes no knowledge no appreciation'.[5] Yet she had a considerable talent for friendship; and the warmth and solidity of her relationships especially with Katharine, Harry and Barbara Stephen and with Pernel and Pippa Strachey reflect positively on them all. Thena came also slowly to realise that not everyone had either her understanding of other people or the resultant capacity to persuade them to act and/or to work together: this was a considerable skill, which the infant institution which was Newnham needed. It was a realisation which surfaced properly some time during the decade 1900–10, the decade which began with her journey round the world with Philippa, and during which she became sole mistress of Burley Hill. This was also the period in which Thena became responsible for Kitty, a responsibility and a relationship which brought her great happiness. Kitty's earliest memories of Thena were of great walks together in the New Forest and being read to, first Macaulay's *Lays of Ancient Rome* and then Kipling.[6] It is an agreeable picture of them both. In becoming effectively Kitty's parent, Thena brought to her life an emotional centre, an emotional grounding, which complemented her friendships and surely took the edge off the worst of the self-doubt.

This complex creature, with hidden depths and insecurities, seems poles apart from her spontaneous, transparent, all-of-a-piece aunt. Yet aunt and niece were very close to each other and the bonds and common threads which run through their lives, their friendships and the networks of which they were part are far more powerful and significant than any differences of temperament. At the personal level, Thena warmed to Annie's directness: she knew exactly where she was with her. They laughed at the same things, absurd situations, the foibles of other people, their own predicaments. Annie would have cherished her brother's last child, however spiky her character: as it turned out, the relationship was a rewarding one for both of them. For all her spontaneity and directness, Annie also knew when to keep silent and never pried into Thena's fluctuations of mood: hindsight had shown her what difficulties her brother had laboured under and she respected his daughter's privacy as, much earlier and understanding much less, she had done her best to respect his. Nor did Annie expect devotion as her due. As Thena put it in the autumn of 1891, 'she just laughed as she always did when things were getting nearly sentimental'.[7]

Annie's life offered Thena a way to finding her father which need not involve her mother, both in conversations during Annie's lifetime and in the preparation of the *Memoir* after her death. Work on the *Memoir* also gave Thena an exceptional understanding of the cause to which Annie had committed her life, and into whose service Thena herself was being drawn, that of education for women. Their contributions were distinctive and complementary. Annie could dream dreams, with her plans for networks of intellectually ambitious girls' schools, the schemes for outreach into local communities which would provide the model for University Extension, and the crown, what she always would persist in calling 'the Higher Education' for women. Yet she was at the same time so down-to-earth, so humble and modest, that she was prepared to start on a much less ambitious scale – Eller How, the North of England Council, Newnham Hall – and see what could be grown and where it might lead. The humility and modesty – their roots far back in the experience of being Arthur's younger sister, without any formal schooling and in awe of University men – meant, too, that she happily worked with others, one of the workhorses, with Henry and Nora Sidgwick, of the extraordinary committee of liberal intellectuals which started and ran Newnham in its early years. Her motherly and homely style, and her hands-on experience of running her own small school, combined with her warm interest in everyone around her to give Newnham an initial informal domesticity, which must have disarmed some of those who were deeply suspicious of the new colleges for women. Few, if any, of those who poked fun at her sometimes muddled sentences, or her talent for beginning an argument in the middle, can have known of the range of her own reading, of the rigorous programme of lonely study she prepared for herself in the early 1840s, and of the tenacity with which she pursued her wish to teach.

As Newnham grew bigger, it began to need more formal structures; and if it was to endure and adapt to new demands and situations, it needed an organisational framework which did not depend upon a handful of exceptional individuals. This was where Thena made a major contribution. She was not a visionary – and she was sceptical about some of Jane Harrison's wilder notions: but she had a considerable talent for making others' visions happen, tackling practical problems, whether drains, building plans or muddled drafting, and negotiating with a multiplicity of interested parties, domestic staff, academics, students, old students and the grandees of the Senate and the Royal Commission. With all of this went an enduring engagement with and concern for all the people involved, less immediately obvious than Annie's but no less deep or real. She took time to write for the Newnham *Roll Letter* of 1940 a long affectionate tribute to Fred Blows, the retiring Head Gardener, who had first come to the College in 1888 as the gardener's boy, and who had been her stout henchman and collaborator in the creation of one of Cambridge's great gardens. She described how, when after 1894 students were at last allowed to ride bicycles in Cambridge, Fred and Katharine Stephen used to test the cyclists' prowess in the Newnham grounds, before they were let loose on the public highway; and she confessed that three of the pigs kept during the first World War had been christened Henry, Mildred [Nora Sidgwick's middle name] and Anne.[8]

The making of Newnham leads directly into the changing experience of middle-class women in nineteenth- and twentieth-century Britain. Virginia Woolf's feminist essay *A Room of One's Own* (1929), picking up and developing a point Annie had made as early as 1875, about the importance of physical space and a modicum of financial support to the development of women's minds, had originated in after-dinner talks at Newnham and Girton. In 1931 Virginia gave a talk to the London and National Society for Women's Service, which eventually became a companion essay, *Three Guineas* (1938), in which she made what she saw as the linked cases for contributing to anti-war policies, women's higher education and women's professional employment: it is a meditation on citizenship as contemporaries construed it, and the continuing restrictions on women's access to this. Pippa Strachey wrote to Pernel, 'I have ordered a copy to be sent to Thena . . . because she in reality receives two out of the 3 gs!'[9] A study of the Cloughs and their circle is an exploration of the slow emergence of middle-class women from the private domestic sphere to which the dominant ideology of the first half of the nineteenth century had confined them. Even then, practice had been in tension with ideology: teaching was one of the few things a lady could do without losing status and Annie took advantage of this. Yet the response of both her parents to even slight improvements in the family fortunes was to propose that she give it up. Thena's relationship with her mother was not a warm one: yet she faced no objections to her 'so-called career', although the status of a Cambridge women's college was rather higher than that of a private adventure school in Liverpool. By the time of the third generation, Kitty's generation, it was taken for granted that she should have a solid formal education and continue on to Newnham, if she proved able enough.[10] As it turned out, this was the passport to employment which secured her financial independence.

The family's financial vicissitudes show how fragile the economy and status of middle-class life often was and dramatise the ways in which the expansion of professional occupations provided a lifeline. In 1859, Anthony Trollope had defined a profession as 'a calling by which a gentleman not born to the inheritance of a gentleman's allowance of good things might ingeniously obtain the same by some exercise of his abilities'. This was essentially what Arthur Hugh Clough had had to do, in the face of James' last bankruptcy; and Annie did what she could to follow suit. Thena and her brother were sustained initially by the money of their mother's family; but eventually 'some exercise of their abilities' provided important support for both Thena and Kitty. Studies of the rise of the professionals in this period have concentrated on the men who followed Trollope's prescription.

The Cloughs, their family, friends and students, show 'ladies' beginning to do likewise.

The making of Newnham, irreverently symbolised by those three grandly named pigs, also shows the 'lights of liberalism' at work on what would prove to be one of their most successful and enduring projects, reforming and secularising higher education, and enlarging access to it. It fed and was fed by a developing rhetoric of service to the larger society. Annie's life had been one of service, to family, to her pupils and to her students, as she had always wished it to be. Thena was always more ambivalent about the concept and its authority; yet her practice was not so very different. Having experienced life as a Newnham student, she spent the remainder of her own working life helping to support and develop the structures of the institution. After retirement, she contributed her experience and skills to the London and National Society for Women's Service. Annie's notions of service and the duties owed to family and fellow human beings were rooted in her Anglican upbringing. Although her subsequent experience bred in her a settled opposition to sectarian rivalries and a conviction that education, learning and research did not need formal religious affiliation as a prop, she retained enough of her original faith to wish for a Christian burial. Having either lost her faith, or realised that she had no faith, very early, Thena remained consistent and untroubled by her unbelief. Musing on paper probably quite late in her life, she asked herself, 'Do I believe in the Xtian religion? Vigorously not.' She thought it 'a kind of fairy story' that the salvation of the planet should depend upon believing the New Testament. Nor did she 'understand what is meant by God'. At the same time, 'I cannot help believing that some things are good – that there is such a thing as Goodness or good – that I must choose it & forward it as much as I can.'[11] It is possible that the ease with which she acknowledged her lack of faith was a positive element in her complex inheritance from her father: he had already made the journey for her. Certainly the distinction she drew between God and Goodness was not unlike the one he drew between Christian dogma and the moral code associated with it. And she forwarded those things she considered good with all her considerable vigour. Although in one of the bouts of fierce self-criticism in her Newnham days she had described 'what acts as a conscience for me [as] the fear of disapprobation & perhaps also of receiving money under false pretences',[12] Thena's record of service suggests that, despite the black depressions and the self-doubt, much more powerful factors were at work. At Newnham's Memorial Meeting for Thena in October 1960, Gwen Burton recalled one of Thena's favourite quotations from Wordsworth's *The Excursion*:

> We live by admiration, hope and love,
> And even as these are well and wisely fixed,
> In dignity of being we ascend.[13]

Thena did not believe in God but she most certainly believed in people, and worked, as her aunt had done, to help them realise their potential. For the successive generations of liberal activists and professionals to which Annie, Arthur, Henry, Thena and Pernel belonged, unbelievers as well as believers, the call of duty was fully as peremptory and as absolute as George Eliot had acknowledged it to be.

Notes

ABBREVIATIONS USED IN THE NOTES

Place of publication is London, unless otherwise stated. When a book is cited only a few times in the references, the full details are given in the first citation; thereafter author's surname and an abbreviated title are given. Likewise, when a manuscript source is cited only a few times, full finding details are given in the first citation.

AHC (Bal)	*A. H. Clough Papers*, Balliol College, Oxford
AHC (Bod)	*A. H. Clough Papers*, Bodleian Library, Oxford
AJC	*A. J. Clough Papers*, Newnham College, Cambridge. This collection includes *Notebooks 1–12*, twelve soft-covered notebooks which Anne Jemima Clough used for recollections, notes and more conventional diary entries.
BC	*Bonham Carter Papers*, Hampshire County Record Office, Winchester
Biswas	R. K. Biswas, *Arthur Hugh Clough. Towards a Reconsideration*, Oxford, 1972
Chorley	Katharine Chorley, *Arthur Hugh Clough. The Uncommitted Mind*, Oxford, 1962
CSHB	*The Cambridge Social History of Britain 1750–1950*, ed. F. M. L. Thompson, 3 vols., Cambridge, 1990
CSS	*Clough – Shore Smith Papers*, British Library Additional Mss. This collection includes B. A. Clough's five 'black books', 72830A–E, containing reflections, notes and more conventional diary entries.
Dawson	*Dawson Papers*, West Yorkshire Archives Service, Leeds
Gayer, Rostow and Schwarz	Arthur D. Gayer, W. W. Rostow and Anna Jacobson Schwartz, *The Growth and Fluctuation of the British Economy 1790–1850*, 2 vols., Oxford, 1953
L&R	*Letters and Remains of Arthur Hugh Clough*, privately printed, 1865
Memoir	B. A. Clough, *Memoir of Anne J. Clough*, 1897
MT	Rita McWilliams Tullberg, *Women at Cambridge*, 2nd edition, Cambridge, 1998

Mulhauser   *Correspondence of Arthur Hugh Clough*, ed. F. Mulhauser,
                     2 vols., Oxford, 1957
NA   *A Newnham Anthology*, ed. Ann Phillips, Cambridge, 1979
NCA   Archives of Newnham College, Cambridge
NCCL   *Newnham College Club Letters*, Cambridge, privately
                     printed; the annual letters of the Old Students' Club. From
                     1918, following the grant of the Charter and Statutes, these
                     became the annual *Newnham College Roll Letters*.
ODNB   *Oxford Dictionary of National Biography*, Oxford, 2004
Oxford Diaries   *The Oxford Diaries of A. H. Clough*, ed. Anthony Kenny,
                     Oxford, 1990
Poems   *The Poems of Arthur Hugh Clough*, ed. F. L. Mulhauser, 2nd
                     edition, Oxford, 1974
PP   Parliamentary Papers
PRFD   Principal Registry of the Family Division, High Holborn,
                     London
PRO   Public Record Office, Kew
Register   *Newnham College Register 1871–1971*, 3 vols., privately
                     printed, Cambridge, 1979
SCHS   Manuscript Collections of the South Carolina Historical
                     Society, Charleston, South Carolina
SJCA   Archives of St John's College, Cambridge. Transcriptions of
                     all the correspondence and papers relating to Newnham's
                     site and buildings are also available in NCA, by kind
                     permission of the Master, Fellows and Scholars of St John's
                     College.
SM   A[rthur] S[idgwick] and E[leanor] M[ildred] Sidgwick,
                     Henry Sidgwick. A Memoir, 1906
Strachey   *Strachey Papers*, British Library Additional Mss
Stubbs/Duff   NCA, transcript of conversation between Joan Stubbs and
                     Kitty Duff, 6 January 1977
TCA   Archives of Trinity College, Cambridge
WL   Manuscript Collections of The Women's Library, London
                     Metropolitan University

1 CHILDHOOD AND CHARLESTON

1. Federal Census figures quoted in Michael O'Brien and David Moltke Hansen
eds., *Intellectual Life in Antebellum Charleston* (Knoxville, 1986), p. 382,
fn. 26. Walter J. Fraser, *Charleston* (Columbia, SC, 1989), p. 194. Fraser offers
an accessible one-volume introduction to the history of Charleston. For a fuller
account of intellectual and cultural life in these years, see O'Brien and Moltke
Hansen eds., *Intellectual Life*, and Michael O'Brien, *A Character of Hugh Legaré*
(Knoxville, 1985). A more detailed account of the economic and institutional
structure is to be found in W. H. Pease and Jane Pease, *The Web of Progress*.

Private Values and Public Style in Boston and Charleston (New York, 1985). On the physical environment, see Albert Simons and Samuel Lapham eds., *The Early Architecture of Charleston* (Columbia, SC, 1970, 2nd edition); Kenneth Severens, *Charleston. Antebellum Architecture and Civic Destiny* (Knoxville, 1988); Jonathan H. Poston, *The Buildings of Charleston* (Columbia, SC, 1997).

2. *L&R*, p. 7.

3. A. H. Dodd, 'The Beginnings of Banking in North Wales', *Economica* 6 (1926), p. 22. For the Clough genealogy, see *L&R*, pp. 1–3.

4. Joel Mokyr, 'Technological Change' in *The Economic History of Britain since 1700*, ed. Roderick Floud and Donald McCloskey (Cambridge, 1994, 2nd edition), 3 vols., I, p. 18. But see also Gayer, Rostow and Schwartz, I, chs. i and ii; and Julian Hoppit, *Risk and Failure in English Business 1700–1800* (Cambridge, 1987), pp. 75–81. For the importance of Liverpool, see M. M. Edwards, *The Growth of the British Cotton Trade 1780–1815* (Manchester, 1967), pp. 110–11.

5. Dodd, 'Beginnings of Banking', pp. 27–8.

6. Underlinings in the originals of letters and notebooks are reproduced; however, italics are used in quotations taken from the Mulhauser edition of A. H. Clough's correspondence.

7. *Dawson*, DW 822 J. B. Clough to John Perfect [his brother-in-law] 6 January 1819, his emphasis.

8. Anne Clough to A. H. Clough 1 March 1853, Mulhauser II, 341. *Dawson*, DW 815 Mosley pedigree, compiled 15 May 1821, in which Anne Perfect is recorded as 'm. Charles [*sic*] Clough of Liverpool'; Mosley was the maiden name of Catherine Maria Perfect; another Mosley cousin also married a Crowder. See the Perfect family tree on p. xii. For the emergence of such private banks see L. S. Pressnell, *Country Banking in the Industrial Revolution* (Oxford, 1956), esp. ch. 3; the material in the *Dawson Papers* would make a fascinating case-study.

   The question of J. B. Clough's partners is a confused one. In 1853 his widow described him as having been in partnership with Wilkes and J. H. Clough to 1810; however *Gore's Liverpool Directories* for 1807, 1810 and 1811 show Wilkes and Clough as trading separately from James Henry Clough (1807, 1810) and John Henry Clough (1810, 1811). In 1814 and 1816 James Butler Clough is recorded as trading on his own; 1816–17 sees the first appearance of Clough, Crowder & Co., who reappear in the *Directories* of 1818, 1819, 1821, 1823 and 1825. Then in the bankruptcy proceedings of 1825–6 (see below, n. 14) Henry Perfect is cited along with Clough and Crowder; but this is the only mention of him. Neither J. B. Clough nor Thomas Crowder appears in the *Directory* for 1827; Thomas Crowder reappears as trading on his own in the *Directories* from 1829; and J. B. Clough is to be found, likewise apparently trading on his own, from 1837. I am indebted to Christine Hill for gathering the entries from *Gore's Directories*.

9. Anne Clough to A. H. Clough 1 March 1853, Mulhauser II, 341.

10. *AJC Notebook 1*, f. 2. Notebook 1 is labelled 'AJC Recollections from 1822 till June 1836' and deals with life in Charleston. Textual comparison shows it to be an early or even the first version of the account in pp. 3–9 of *L&R*; see chapter 4

below for a discussion of the composition of this. In *L&R*, p. 3, this has become, 'The first distinct remembrance I have of my brother [Arthur] is of his going with me in a carriage to the vessel which was to take us to America. This must have been in the winter of 1822–3, when he was not quite four years old.'

Unless otherwise indicated, the narrative that follows is based on *Notebook 1*. Only direct quotations from this are referenced. The folio numbers given were added by me to the xerox copy from which I worked, the original being frail. In these quotations I have supplied minimal punctuation, since there is virtually none in the original, but have made no other changes, retaining the original spellings, ampersands and liberal use of capitals and dashes.

11. *L&R*, p. 3.
12. *Ibid.* James Butler Clough's journal for part of the summer of 1823 can be found in *AHC (Bal)* 287, ff. 1–64.
13. Anne Clough to A. H. Clough 1 March 1853, Mulhauser II, 341. On the general crisis, see Gayer, Rostow and Schwarz I, ch. iv, esp. pp. 171–4 and 204–5.
14. West Sussex County Record Office, *Clough Mss*. 10, Declaration of bankruptcy. On the 1825 Act and the confused and complex state of the law, see Ian P. H. Duffy, *Bankruptcy and Insolvency in London during the Industrial Revolution* (1985), esp. pp. 24–5. *Dawson*, DW 822 Thomas Crowder to John Perfect 21 July 1826.
15. A. H. Clough to A. J. Clough 28 May 1833, Mulhauser I, 4.
16. *L&R*, p. 5.
17. *Ibid.*, p. 9.
18. US Federal Census 1830, CHAR 041 CHARLEST, CLOUGH, JAMES BUTTER [*sic*].
19. *AJC Notebook 1*, f. 7.
20. *L&R*, p. 5.
21. *AJC Notebook 1*, f. 22.
22. Gillian Sutherland, 'Education' in *CSHB* III, pp. 132–7.
23. *L&R*, p. 8.
24. *AJC Notebook 1*, f. 10. The European travels, which were repeated during each of J. B. Clough's subsequent spells based in England, may well have had business objectives. It was not uncommon for merchants trading in raw cotton and other goods from the Americas to deal also in finished cotton goods and cotton yarn from Lancashire, which they shipped to Europe, through Hamburg. The finished goods often went south to Frankfurt and Augsburg, while the cotton yarn found a ready market in Switzerland. See Hoppit, *Risk and Failure*, pp. 156–60.
25. *L&R*, p. 8.
26. *AJC Notebook 1*, f. 22.
27. *Ibid.*, ff. 16–17.
28. *Ibid.*, f. 13.
29. Fraser, *Charleston*, p. 189. He scared the recently arrived British consul, William Ogilby, who had visited him the day before the fever declared itself; see SCHS 34/414, Diary of William Ogilby, entries for 8 and 9 September 1830.

30. *AJC Notebook 1*, f. 18.
31. *Ibid.*, f. 25.
32. *Ibid.*, ff. 29, 31.
33. *Ibid.*, f. 44; SCHS 30–04 LANCE.
34. A. H. Clough to A. J. Clough 30 December 1835 and 23 January 1836, Mulhauser 1, 20.
35. *AJC Notebook 1*, f. 33.
36. *Ibid.*, f. 40.
37. A. H. Clough to A. J. Clough 28 April 1834, Mulhauser 1, 6.
38. *AJC Notebook 1*, f. 27.
39. *Ibid.*, f. 38.
40. *Ibid.*, ff. 36–7.
41. *Ibid.*, f. 38. Presumably this preacher was William Barnwell – see Pease and Pease, *Web of Progress*, p. 132.
42. *AJC Notebook 1*, f. 43.
43. *Ibid.*, f. 30.
44. *Ibid.*, ff. 67–8.
45. George C. Rogers Jr., *Charleston in the Age of the Pinckneys* (Columbia, SC, 1969), pp. 147–8.
46. *AJC Notebook 1*, f. 43.
47. This has to be a ruthless over-simplification of a complex and prolonged conflict. See William W. Freehling, *Prelude to Civil War. The Nullification Controversy in South Carolina 1816–1836* (New York, 1965; Oxford paperback edition, 1992) and Richard E. Ellis, *The Union at Risk. Jacksonian Democracy, States' Rights and the Nullification Crisis* (New York, 1987).
48. Pease and Pease, *Web of Progress*, pp. 77–89, 161; see also Fraser, *Charleston*, pp. 199–203.
49. *AJC Notebook 1*, f. 64.
50. The legislation forbidding blacks to read or write was carried in South Carolina in 1835; see Janet Duitsman Cornelius, *"When I Can Read My Title Clear". Literacy, Slavery and Religion in the Antebellum South* (Columbia, SC, 1991), pp. 37–58. The position of manumitted slaves was more complex – and even more difficult – than Annie understood. In 1820 the South Carolina legislature had forbidden manumission except by special acts of the legislature and also forbidden the entry of free blacks into the state. In 1822 to this was added legislation requiring all free blacks who left the state to do so permanently. See Michael P. Johnson and James L. Roark, *Black Masters. A Free Family of Color in the Old South* (New York, 1984), pp. 36, 43.
51. *AJC Notebook 1*, f. 43.
52. *Ibid.*, f. 31.
53. *L&R*, pp. 8, 11; *Memoir*, p. 8.
54. *AJC Notebook 1*, f. 41.
55. SCHS 0107.00, *Clough Letters*, J. B. Clough to A. J. Clough 7 September 1833.
56. A. H. Clough to A. J. Clough 4? 11? September 1834, Mulhauser 1, 7.
57. A. H. Clough to A. J. Clough 8 October 1833, Mulhauser 1, 5.

58. See pp. 46–8 of Tim Barringer, 'The Course of Empires: Landscape and Identity in America and Britain 1820–1880' in Andrew Wilton and Tim Barringer, *American Sublime. Landscape Painting in the United States 1820–1880* (2002), pp. 38–65.

59. *AHC (Bod)*, Ms. Eng. lett. c. 189, f. 40. This is simply an itinerary. Presumably there were also several long descriptive letters, now lost. However, the account in *AJC Notebook 1* is of a piece with the rest and there is no sign that it, any more than any other section of this manuscript, is based on a contemporary record. The fragmentary entries in *Notebooks 11* and *12* seem closer to a contemporary record.

60. *AJC Notebook 1*, ff. 54, 55.

61. *Ibid.*, ff. 57–8, 59.

62. *AJC Notebook 4*, p. 44 and *Notebook 5*, p. 73. (*Notebooks 1* and *2* are foliated; *Notebooks 4, 5, 6* and *10* are paginated.)

63. *AJC Notebook 1*, ff. 61–2.

64. Maria Lance teased her about Atkinson's 'tender recollections of you' in a fragment of a letter from 1836 or 1837 – SCHS 0107.00, *Clough Letters*; see also *CSS*, 72824A, f. 6, MRL(B?) to A. J. Clough 26 April 1837. For what little else is known of Atkinson, see below, chapter 2. For R.D., see *AJC Notebook 4*, p. 9 (7 June 1840) and *Notebook 5*, pp. 3–4 (20 February 1841) and 17 (April 1841).

65. Fraser, *Charleston*, p. 211.

66. This account of the economic situation is drawn primarily from Pease and Pease, *Web of Progress*, esp. pp. 49–60; but see also Severens, *Charleston*, pp. 64, 78–81.

67. *AJC Notebook 1*, f. 65.

68. *Ibid.*, f. 73.

2 'A LAND . . . WITH STRONG FOES BESET'

1. *AJC Notebook 1*, ff. 73–4; A. H. Clough to J. N. Simpkinson 16 July 1836, Mulhauser I, 30.

2. P. J. Waller, *Democracy and Sectarianism. A Political and Social History of Liverpool 1868–1939* (Liverpool, 1981), p. 1. The account of Liverpool which follows is indebted to Waller's chapter 1. The speed with which the city's streets and buildings changed is a minor theme in Herman Melville's novel *Redburn*, published in 1849 but based on his own voyage to Liverpool from New York at the end of the 1830s. See also Quentin Hughes, *Seaport. Architecture and Townscape in Liverpool* (1964) and Joseph Sharples, *Liverpool* (2004).

3. *The Centenary Edition of the Works of Nathaniel Hawthorne*, ed. William Charvat, Roy Harvey Pearce, Claude M. Simpson and Thomas Woodson, Ohio State University Center for Textual Studies: vol. xxi (1997), *The English Notebooks 1853–56*, pp. 13 (9 August 1853) and 8 (8 August 1853). I am indebted to Susan Manning for drawing my attention to the writings of Hawthorne and Melville about nineteenth-century Liverpool.

4. *Charleston City Directories* 1837–8 (C. Atkinson, merchant, 116 King St) and 1840–1 (C. Atkinson, firm of J. B. Clough & co, 67 Church St); SCHS, *Clough Papers*, Charles Clough to A. J. Clough 11 May ?1837.

5. *Ibid.*, J. B. Clough to A. J. Clough 7 September 1833; *AJC Notebook 1*, f. 74.

6. See Leonore Davidoff and Catherine Hall, *Family Fortunes. Men and Women of the English Middle Class 1780–1850* (1987), esp. chs. 3 and 8; John Tosh, *A Man's Place. Masculinity and the Middle-Class Home in Victorian England* (1999), esp. ch. 2; Amanda Vickery ed., *Women, Privilege and Power. British Politics 1750 to the Present* (Stanford, 2001), p. 4.

7. Hawthorne, *English Notebooks 1853–56*, pp. 4 and 13 (4 and 9 August 1853); Hawthorne, *Letters 1853–56, Centenary Edition* vol. XVII (1987), no. 663 Hawthorne to W. B. Pike 13 September 1853; no. 692 same to same 6 January 1854; no. 848 Hawthorne to W. D. Ticknor 1 February 1856.

8. *AJC Notebook 1*, f. 75.

9. Annie's letters seem not to have survived. Maria's, with copious salt-water stains and usually horribly crossed, can be found in SCHS, *Clough Letters*, undated fragment ?1837, M. R. Lance to A. J. Clough 7 October 1837, M. R. L. Bacot to A. J. Clough 8 June 1842; and in *CSS*, 72824A, ff. 1–41. The first letter in this latter group, in which Maria reports her engagement, is surely out of sequence and wrongly dated to 1835.

10. *AJC Notebook 1*, f. 75.

11. *ODNB*, Mary and Rebecca Franklin; cf. also *ibid.*, Maria, Frances and Katherine Byerley, who kept the school called Avonbank in Warwickshire, attended by Mrs Gaskell.

12. *AJC Notebook 5*, pp. 1–2 *et seq*. For the range of her reading and study, see *Notebooks 4* and *5 passim*. The Greek is not always easy to spot because she often records it simply with a rather slapdash Greek letter. The conversation with Margaret Clough took place in July 1840 – *Notebook 4*, p. 29. *Notebooks 4* and *5* are the first diaries of the conventional type, in which she wrote on both sides of the sheets. The originals are frail and she was sometimes careless about dating entries. Where there are dates they are recorded, but I also numbered the pages of the xerox copies from which I worked, for greater ease of reference.

13. A. H. Clough to A. J. Clough 16 November 1840, Mulhauser 1, 73. 'Murray' was probably Lindley Murray's *English Grammar*, written for a girls' school, which went into multiple editions in the late eighteenth and early nineteenth centuries – see Ian Michael, *The Teaching of English from the Sixteenth Century to 1870* (Cambridge, 1987), p. 523.

14. See Christina de Bellaigue, 'The Development of Teaching as a Profession for Women before 1870', *The Historical Journal* 44, 4 (2001), pp. 963–88, esp. p. 966.

15. *AJC Notebook 3*, ff. 1–6; *Notebook 1*, f. 76. Thena states that she also eventually took a class of the older girls at home – *Memoir*, p. 17. I can find no mention of this in *Notebooks 4* and *5*. Teaching at home seems only to begin when Annie starts taking paying pupils in the spring of 1842.

16. *AJC Notebook 3*, ff. 8–18.

17. Hawthorne, *English Notebooks 1853–56*, pp. 18–19 (20 August 1853); see also pp. 24–6 (24 and 25 August 1853).
18. *AJC Notebook 3*, ff. 1–3, 24–6; *Notebook 1*, f. 76; *Notebook 5*, pp. 3 (20 February 1841) and 5 (1 March 1841). For district visiting, see F. K. Prochaska, *Women and Philanthropy in Nineteenth Century England* (Oxford, 1980), ch. iv, 'In the Homes of the Poor'.
19. *AJC Notebook 4*, p. 7 (10 May 1840); also the opening paragraphs, p. 1 (3 May 1840). See also *Oxford Diaries*; on the Evangelical sense of the need always to keep account and the role of the journal in this, see H. C. G. Matthew, *Gladstone 1809–1898* (Oxford, 1997), p. 7 and Anne Stott, *Hannah More. The First Victorian* (Oxford, 2003), pp. 152–3.
20. *AJC Notebook 4*, p. 69 (22 November 1840).
21. See above chapter 1, n. 64.
22. *AJC Notebook 4*, p. 83 (10 January 1841); *Notebooks 4* and *5 passim*.
23. *AJC Notebook 4*, p. 19 (?24 June 1840). Cf. also her revulsion at the tone of a Protestant meeting in the autumn of 1841 – 'such things are not likely to encourage a Christian spirit of kindness & Charity' – *Notebook 5*, p. 45 (5 October 1841).
24. *AJC Notebook 4*, pp. 36 (9 August 1840), 40 (1 September 1840) and 42–3 (12 September 1840). Cf. also *Notebook 5*, p. 14 (3 April 1841).
25. See for example *AJC Notebook 5*, pp. 31–2 (20 June 1841), 34–5 (10 July 1841) and 48 (11 October 1841).
26. *AJC Notebook 4*, pp. 87–9 (21 January 1841); see also *Notebook 5*, p. 15 (3 April 1841), 'I have been scratching a little poetry on the Israelites' passage of the Red sea. The subject Arthur gave me.' Is the fragment on the back of a sheet of Arthur's birthday letter in 1841 – *AHC (Bod)* MS. Eng. Lett. d. 175 – also one of Annie's rhymes?
27. *AJC Notebook 4*, p. 97 (12 February 1841); A. H. Clough to Charles Clough 7 February 1841, Mulhauser 1, 74.
28. *AJC Notebook 5*, p. 28 (6 June 1841); A. H. Clough to A. J. Clough 6 June 1841 and 13 June 1841, Mulhauser 1, 79 and 80.
29. Gayer, Rostow and Schwarz 1, ch. v, esp. pp. 242–4.
30. *Dawson*, DW 920.
31. *AJC Notebook 5*, pp. 40–1 (? August 1841).
32. A. H. Clough to J. P. Gell 11 September 1841, Mulhauser 1, 83; *Oxford Diaries*, p. xlvi.
33. *AJC Notebook 5*, pp. 33–4, 42 (10 and 22 August 1841) and 47 (11 October 1841). Annie was made very cross by Atkinson's behaviour to her father.
34. Annie describes Charles' job as being with a Mr Gair; *ibid.*, p. 52. By the end of 1843 James Clough was addressing letters to him c/o Baring Brothers in Liverpool; SCHS, *Clough Letters*, J. B. Clough to Charles Clough 8 December 1843.
35. *AJC Notebook 5*, pp. 55, 58 (5 and 12 December 1841).
36. See the correspondence between members of the Crowder family and W. M. Perfect for 1841–2 in *Dawson*, DW 920, and Annie's oblique comment, 'I fear

there has [*sic*] been some wrong feelings about the Crowders rather a jealousy of their superior advantage in commencing & of the great help they have had'; *AJC Notebook 5*, pp. 49–50 (24 October 1841). However, although there was no formal partnership, Atkinson was helping the Crowders in their dealings with American creditors; see *Dawson*, DW 920 Thomas Crowder to W. M. Perfect 11 July 1842.

37. *AJC Notebook 5*, p. 44 (5 October 1841); J. B. Clough to A. H. Clough 9 February 1842, Mulhauser 1, 85.

38. *AJC Notebook 5*, pp. 42 (22 August 1841) and 44 (5 October 1841). Annie's Crowder aunt and cousins were also thinking about 'trying their hands at keeping School'; *Dawson*, DW 920 Thomas Crowder Junior to W. M. Perfect 6 September 1841.

39. *AJC Notebook 5*, p. 44 (5 October 1841). They moved to Pembroke Gardens, Brownlow Street in late November, *ibid.*, p. 51 (22 November 1841). For the move from Hope Street, see *Notebook 1*, f. 77.

40. *AJC Notebook 5*, p. 52 (22 November 1841). What Annie actually wrote was, 'invites me to come to stay with her to learn French & see Mlle Brioland's plans in her school'. This is puzzling, since she had begun to learn French with her mother and then with the visiting master in Charleston (see chapter 1 above) and her earlier reading (see *Notebook 4*) had included Lamartine. I have therefore construed it as meaning learning to *teach* French rather than learning the language itself.

41. *AJC Notebook 5*, pp. 52 (28 November 1841) and 55 (5 December 1841). See also p. 59 (26 December 1841).

42. *Ibid.*, pp. 53 (28 November 1841) and 56–8 (5 and 12 December 1841).

43. *Ibid.*, pp. 59 and 61 (26 December 1841); p. 63 (20 January 1842).

44. *Ibid.*, pp. 64–5. He came at Easter time; the journal entry seems to belong to late June 1842. Cf. also Dr Thomas Arnold to A. H. Clough 2 April 1842 and Alfred B. Clough to Edward Hawkins, Provost of Oriel, 2 April 1842, Mulhauser 1, 86 and 87.

45. *Oxford Diaries*, pp. xlviii–li; A. P. Stanley to A. H. Clough June 1842, Mulhauser 1, 89. Annie wrote, 'Dr Arnold dies. Arthur comes home for one day & appears in great distress'; *AJC Notebook 5*, p. 65, her emphasis.

46. *Ibid.*, pp. 73–4. The page begins 27 July [1842]; but the sequence of events recorded suggests that George actually left in early September.

47. SCHS, *Clough Letters*, M. R. L. Bacot to A. J. Clough 8 June 1842. Interestingly, she goes on to talk about the problems other friends who run schools in Charleston are having and about the consequences of the slump in trade more generally.

48. *AJC Notebook 5*, pp. 65–71, 73, 79, 80.

49. J. B. Clough to A. H. Clough 9 February 1842, Mulhauser 1, 85.

50. *AJC Notebook 5*, p. 78.

51. SCHS, *Clough Letters*, J. B. Clough to A. J. Clough 7 March 1843. Cf. also *AJC Notebook 5*, pp. 81 and 84.

52. *Ibid.*, pp. 91, 92, 95, 97, 102.

53. *Ibid.*, pp. 103–4; SCHS, *Clough Letters*, J. B. Clough to A. J. Clough 1 December 1843. George's gravestone remains in St Michael's Churchyard. For James' arrival first in Boston, see *AJC Notebook 2*, f. 13.

54. SCHS, *Clough Letters*, J. B. Clough to A. J. Clough 31 December 1843, J. B. Clough to A. J. Clough 19 February 1844 and J. B. Clough to Anne Clough 24 May 1844. See also *ibid.*, J. B. Clough to A. J. Clough 14 April 1844 and *AJC Notebook 6*, p. 2 (February 1844). It is not wholly clear where Mrs Ross was based. *Notebooks 4* and *5* and the SCHS *Clough Letters* show that there were Rosses and Ogilbys both sides of the Atlantic, as there were Calders and Wotherspoons.

55. SCHS, *Clough Letters*, J. B. Clough to A. J. Clough 1 May 1844. As this letter shows, certainly Mrs Ross and possibly Lady Ross were then *en route* from Charleston to Liverpool.

56. A. H. Clough to Anne Clough 6 September 1844 and A. H. Clough to J. P. Gell 24 November 1844; Mulhauser 1, 100 and 107; *AJC Notebook 2*, ff. 15 and 16; *Notebook 7*.

57. I am indebted to the Hill family for finding the grave and transcribing the inscription.

58. See *AJC Notebook 7*.

59. *Memoir*, p. 21; *Poems*, pp. 308–10.

60. *CSS*, 72824A, ff. 57–8 Maria Lance to Anne Clough 14 November 1844 and SCHS, *Clough Letters*, same to same 13 March 1845. By this time Mrs Lance was also keeping a school to aid the family fortunes.

61. A. H. Clough to T. Burbidge 31 December 1844 and 1 January 1845, Mulhauser 1, 108.

62. A. H. Clough to A. J. Clough 14 November 1844, Mulhauser 1, 105; A. H. Clough to B. M. S. Smith 18 and 21 March 1853 and same to same 21 April 1853, Mulhauser 11, 347 and 358; *AJC Notebook 2*, f. 17.

63. A. H. Clough to A. J. Clough 21 February 1845, Mulhauser 1, 111.

64. *AJC Notebook 6*, pp. 33–53 (June–July 1845).

65. A. H. Clough to T. Burbidge 31 December 1844 and 1 January 1845, Mulhauser 1, 108; *AJC Notebook 6*, pp. 23–5 (April–May 1845).

66. *Ibid.*, pp. 61 and 63 (June–July 1845); Charles appears to have left Mr Wotherspoon's employ on 1 May, *ibid.*, p. 28.

67. *Ibid.*, p. 62 (July 1845).

68. *Ibid.*, pp. 54–60 (July 1845); also pp. 68 (September 1845) and 78 (January 1846). The *Life of the Rev. Joseph Blanco White*, ed. John Hamilton Thom, a mixture of autobiography, letters and diary extracts, was published in three volumes in 1845.

69. A. H. Clough to A. J. Clough 9 November 1845, Mulhauser 1, 119; see also same to same 17 February 1846, Mulhauser 1, 131.

70. A. H. Clough to T. Burbidge 19 January 1846, Mulhauser 1, 130; for the wedding, which took place in North Wales, see *AJC Notebook 6*, pp. 80–3.

71. The journey from England to Como is described in *AJC Notebook 9* and the time with Charles and Margaret in *Notebook 8*.

3 Confirming a vocation

1. *AJC Notebook 6*, p. 33 (June 1845); *Notebook 9*, pp. 46 and 48–9. Cf. also *Notebook 6*, pp. 88–9 (April 1846).
2. A. H. Clough to A. J. Clough 9 August 1846, Mulhauser I, 134. Archibald Alison's *History of Europe* had gone into its sixth edition in 1844.
3. *AJC Notebook 6*, pp. 95–6 (March 1847, rehearsing the events of the preceding nine months).
4. An account of the difficulties over the engagement occupies pp. 1–11 of *AJC Notebook 10*, written up at the end of May 1847; but it is never clear exactly what were the grounds of objection to Migault or why he was so hostile to Augusta's parents.
5. *AJC Notebook 6*, pp. 15–17 (13 April 1845), 20 (20 April 1845), 72, 74 (October 1845), and 94–101, 103, 106 (March 1847, rehearsing the events of the preceding nine months); summarised in *Memoir*, pp. 62–3.
6. *AJC Notebook 10*, p. 12; pp. 12–30 describe the visit and all the walking and exploration in loving detail.
7. See above, p. 38.
8. On Arnold's objectives, see David Newsome, *Godliness and Good Learning. Four Studies on a Victorian Ideal* (1961), I, pp. 28–91, 'The Ideal'.
9. See above, p. 28. This account of the Tractarians and Ward has to be ruthlessly brief and crude. For a fuller account, see Anthony Kenny's excellent introductory essay to *Oxford Diaries* and P. B. Nockles, '"Lost causes and . . . impossible loyalties": The Oxford Movement and the University', chapter 7 of *The History of the University of Oxford*, vol. VI: *Nineteenth-Century Oxford*, Part 1, ed. M. G. Brock and M. C. Curthoys (Oxford, 1997). The period is covered also in Chorley and in Biswas, but Kenny's grasp of the theology, the politics of the University and the college dynamics is superior.
10. A. H. Clough to A. J. Clough 4–23 May 1847, Mulhauser I, 149. See also the undated fragment A. H. Clough to Margaret Clough, Mulhauser I, 268.
11. *Oxford Diaries*, pp. lvi, lviii–lix; correspondence printed in Mulhauser I, 136–8, 158–65, direct quotation from 165, Hawkins to A. H. Clough 24 January 1848.
12. *AJC Notebook 10*, pp. 35–6 (entry on 27 October 1847, recording events of the autumn and specifically since Charles' and Margaret's return on 10 September). The 'good deal of fuss & trouble' to which she cryptically refers, just before writing as she does, no doubt describes the reception by their mother and Charles and Margaret of the news of Arthur's intentions.
13. *Memoir*, pp. 67–8; Gayer, Rostow and Schwarz, I, ch. vi, pp. 304–6, 329–40; A. H. Clough writes to Tom Arnold from 51 Vine St, 16 July 1848, Mulhauser I, 181.
14. *AJC Notebook 6*, p. 107 (April 1847); *CSS*, 72830B, f. 51.
15. A. H. Clough to A. J. Clough 26 July 1847, Mulhauser I, 151; *AJC Notebook 6*, p. 103 (March 1847, rehearsing the events of the preceding nine months); A. H. Clough to A. J. Clough before 27 November 1848, Mulhauser I, 191. The absence of any entries for 1848 in *Notebook 10* is a source of frustration.

16. British and Foreign Schools Society Archives Centre, Borough Road Normal School Applications and Testimonials – Women, 1848–1850: A. J. Clough to Henry Dunn 2 December 1848; A. H. Clough's formal endorsement 1 December 1848; testimonial from J. Jones, Rural Dean and Incumbent of St Andrew's, Liverpool 27 November 1848; testimonial from J. D. Morell HMI 11 December 1848, enclosed in a further short note from A. J. Clough to Henry Dunn, 22 December 1848. I owe these references to Christina de Bellaigue. For Morell, see Nancy Ball, *Her Majesty's Inspectorate 1839–49* (Birmingham, 1963).

17. de Bellaigue, 'Teaching as a Profession for Women', pp. 970–1.

18. *AJC Notebook 10*, pp. 41–4, 47, 49.

19. *Ibid.*, pp. 50–4; *CSS*, 72830C, f. 10.

20. *AJC Notebook 10*, pp. 41–2 (an account of the London visit begun on 18 March 1849), 31–2 (11 July 1847) and pp. 55–9, direct quotation from p. 56 (25 March and 1 April 1849).

21. *Ibid.*, p. 57.

22. Biswas, ch. vii; the principal primary source is A. H. Clough's own correspondence and this, reproduced in Mulhauser I, gives a vivid account of his French and Italian journeys; and of his appointment to University Hall. The poems and their publishing history can be found in *Poems*.

23. *AJC Notebook 10*, pp. 64–5.

24. A. H. Clough to Anne Clough 2 April 1850, Mulhauser I, 252. For an earlier exchange about a move, see A. H. Clough to A. J. Clough 22 March 1846, Mulhauser I, 132; it was also discussed during the European journey later that year – see above, p. 39.

25. See e.g. her summary of what she thought she had learnt in London, *AJC Notebook 10*, pp. 68–9.

26. *Memoir*, p. 77; *Register*, I, p. 55.

27. *AJC Notebook 6*, p. 106 (April 1847); *Notebook 10*, p. 35 (October 1847).

28. *The Poems of Arthur Hugh Clough, with a Memoir by Charles Eliot Norton* (Boston, 1862), pp. xxiv–xxv.

29. Derek Hudson, *Munby. Man of Two Worlds* (1972), p. 20; Anthony Trollope, *The Eustace Diamonds* (first published 1873), ch. xxiv.

30. Quoted in Biswas, p. 321.

31. *Poems*, pp. 616–17; J. C. Shairp to A. H. Clough November 1849 (two letters), Mulhauser I, 235 and 237; H. F. Lowry ed., *The Letters of Matthew Arnold to Arthur Hugh Clough* (1932), 43, Matt Arnold to A. H. Clough 21 March 1853.

32. A. H. Clough to R. Martineau 18 February 1851, same to same 12 December 1851, Mulhauser I, 247 and 259.

33. For fuller discussion, see the essays by Richard Johnson and Gillian Sutherland in *Studies in the Growth of Nineteenth Century Government*, ed. Sutherland (1972).

34. See Biswas, pp. 417–56 and Mulhauser II, 298–398. For the Smiths, see Pam Hirsch, *Barbara Leigh Smith Bodichon. Feminist, Artist and Rebel* (1998), ch. 1, and below, pp. 60–2.

35. *AJC Notebook 2*, f. 35, 'the old and the new in his life were as yet unmixed & he was uncomfortable but uncomplaining & true. His home saw but little of him after the settlement at University Hall. Circumstances were floating him away.' An embarrassed letter from Arthur to Annie, about 'some little separation between us', Mulhauser I, 139, marked Wednesday, 18 November and tentatively dated to 1846, seems more likely to belong to 1852 or 1853, even though 18 November was respectively Thursday and Friday in those years, since it refers to a visit to Ambleside by 'her whom I hope someday to be your sister'. For the stroke, see *Memoir*, p. 78.

36. *Letters of Charles Eliot Norton, with Biographical Comment*, ed. Sara Norton and M. A. DeWolfe Howe, 2 vols., (1913) I, p. 148, C. E. Norton to A. H. Clough 21 September 1856.

37. University of London Library, Parents' National Education Union Archives, Ms 808, Charlotte Mason, 'Recollections of Miss Clough and her Connexion with the PNEU'. Harriet Martineau's primary purpose in 1848 was to help the local artisans and farm workers. But two substantial houses were built as well as cottages and presumably Eller How was one of these. See Harriet Martineau, *Autobiography*, 2 vols. (3rd edition, 1877), II, pp. 306–8. In Liverpool they had been paying £34 a year to rent – see A. H. Clough to Anne Clough 2 April 1850, cited above n. 24. For Harriet Martineau in the Lakes, see Barbara Todd, *Harriet Martineau at Ambleside* (Carlisle, 2002), which also reprints Harriet Martineau's 'A Year at Ambleside'.

38. *Memoir*, p. 96.

39. *Ibid.*, p. 99.

40. PRFD, Will of Anne Clough, made and witnessed 25 August 1852, proved 19 July 1860.

41. Martineau, *Autobiography*, II, pp. 305–6; WL, 9/ ALC, vol. 7, AL/2147–AL/2149 Microfiche Box no. 3, Harriet Martineau to A. J. Clough Tuesday? 1855, same to same Tuesday morning? 1855 and same to same 18 May 1861.

42. *Memoir*, p. 87.

43. I am indebted to the present owners, Mr and Mrs J. Philbrook, for allowing me to see the interior of the house.

44. *Memoir*, pp. 87, 89. PRORG9/3963/9, 1861 Census, Ambleside, Eller Rigg, Eller How School. I owe this reference to Christina de Bellaigue.

45. *Memoir*, p. 87; John Sutherland, *Mrs Humphry Ward. Eminent Victorian, Pre-eminent Edwardian* (Oxford, 1990), p. 15; Bernard Bergonzi, *A Victorian Wanderer. The Life of Thomas Arnold the Younger* (Oxford, 2003), p. 101.

46. Sutherland, *Mrs Humphrey Ward*, pp. 14–16; CSS, 72830B, f. 76.

47. *Memoir*, p. 92; British and Foreign School Society Archives Centre, BFSS814: Home and Colonial School Society Reports, *Quarterly Paper*, January 1861. I owe this latter reference to Christina de Bellaigue.

48. *Memoir*, p. 93.

49. *The Cornhill Magazine*, new ser. 48 (June 1920), pp. 674–84, T. C. Down, 'Schooldays with Miss Clough', pp. 677, 680.

50. *Memoir*, p. 91.

51. *Ibid.*, pp. 89, 97–8; PRO PROB11/2262, Will of William Perfect of Pontefract, proved 3 December 1857.
52. *CSS*, 72830B, ff. 78–80; PRFD, Will of Anne Clough, made and witnessed 25 August 1852, proved 19 July 1860.

4 FAMILY DUTY

1. A. H. Clough to C. E. Norton 13 July 1860, Mulhauser II, 533.
2. PRO, RG9/3963/9, 1861 Census, Ambleside, Eller Rigg, Eller How School. It is unclear precisely when Jane Wilkinson came; the *Home and Colonial School Quarterly Paper*, January 1861 records the appointment of Selina Healey, British and Foreign School Society Archives Centre, BFSS814, Home and Colonial School Society Reports. I am indebted to Christina de Bellaigue for these references.
3. See Cecil Woodham Smith, *Florence Nightingale 1825–1910* (1950), pp. 1, 13. Peter Nightingale's will, dated 1 September 1803, can be found in the PRO, 11/1399 RC3004. I am indebted to Professor Lynn McDonald for this reference.
4. Woodham Smith, *Nightingale*, pp. 306, 330; cf. *BC*, 94M72/F538, pt ii, undated fragment 'Wednesday', Joanna Bonham Carter to Alice Bonham Carter.
5. A. H. Clough to C. E. Norton 22 December 1859, Mulhauser II, 529.
6. A. H. Clough to C. E. Norton 15 February 1861, Mulhauser II, 540. Charles Darwin was sent there in 1849 and again in 1850; Adrian Desmond and James Moore, *Darwin* (1991), ch. 24, 'My Water Doctor'.
7. *BC*, 94M74/F563 B. M. S. Clough to Alice Bonham Carter, 'Monday': 'Pollock [the doctor] . . . says we must keep him at <u>some</u> sea for months & months possibly two years.'
8. Colin Ford, *Julia Margaret Cameron. Nineteenth Century Photographer of Genius* (2003), pp. 28–33; Henrietta Garnett, *Anny. A Life of Anne Thackeray Ritchie* (2004), pp. 19–20, 33, 54–5.
9. B. M. S. Clough to Miss Norton 10 March 1861, Mulhauser II, 541; *AJC*, B. M. S. Clough's Record of 1861, 23 February to 26 March. This Record is the source for the paragraphs that follow, covering the period to the end of November 1861, unless otherwise indicated.
10. Ford, *Cameron*, pp. 35–9.
11. A. H. Clough to C. E. Norton 27 April 1855, Mulhauser II, 437.
12. B. M. S. Clough to A. H. Clough 7 July 1861, same to same 20 July 1861, A. H. Clough to B. M. S. Clough 23 July 1861, B. M. S. Clough to A. H. Clough 26 July 1861, A. H. Clough to the Secretary, Education Department 28 July 1861, Mulhauser II, 545, 550, 552, 553 and 554.
13. B. M. S. Clough and Mary Shore Smith to A. H. Clough 1, 4 and 5 August 1861, A. H. Clough to B. M. S. Clough 8 August 1861, Mulhauser II, 556 and 558.
14. A. H. Clough to B. M. S. Clough 23 August 1861, same to same 26 August 1861, same to same 31 August 1861, same to same 7 September 1861, B. M. S.

Clough to A. H. Clough 10 September 1861, Mulhauser II, 561, 562, 563, 566, 567.

15. British Institute, Florence, Harold Acton Library, c/091 HOR, ms *Diary of Susan Horner*, 10 October 1861.
16. *Ibid.*, 20 October 1861.
17. *Ibid.*, 1 November 1861.
18. *Ibid.*, 10 November 1861.
19. B. M. S. Clough to C. E. Norton 15 January 1862 (mis-dated 61), Mulhauser II, 573.
20. See *CSS*, 72826, ff. 138, 139.
21. *Horner Diary*, 15 November 1861; also 18, 27, 30 November and 8 December.
22. *AJC*, A. J. Clough to Lucy Cumming 17 November 1861.
23. Possibly the letter 'to a friend', now lost, from which B. A. Clough quotes in the *Memoir*, p. 100, was the version sent. For Lucy Cumming, who married William Smith, see George S. Merriam ed., *The Story of William and Lucy Smith* (1889).
24. *Horner Diary*, 10, 12, 13 December 1861.
25. *Ibid.*, 23 December 1861.
26. *Memoir*, pp. 100–1; *AJC*, A. J. Clough to B. M. S. Clough n.d. but, from the content, between January and April 1862.
27. *Memoir*, pp. 94–5.
28. *Ibid.*, pp. 101–2.
29. They left the house unchanged but, buying extra land, embarked on schemes verging on the megalomaniac in the garden; see Clara Boyle, *A Servant of the Empire* (1937), pp. 6–7.
30. *AJC*, fragment A. J. Clough to B. M. S. Clough n.d. but, from its content, probably March 1862.
31. *Ibid.*, Memorial from the residents of Ambleside, 16 April 1862.
32. See prefaces to the first and second editions of *Poems* (Oxford, 1951 and 1974). Both are reprinted in the second edition and detailed page references are to that; the negotiations with Norton are recounted on p. xiv.
33. *CSS*, 72826, ff. 55–6, B. M. S. Clough to A. J. Clough n.d. and f. 58, B. M. S. Clough to A. J. Clough n.d. The absence of a date on these letters and one other belonging to the same sequence – ff. 51–3, B. M. S. Clough to A. J. Clough – is a nuisance. Almost certainly they date from the period January–April 1862, before Annie moved south. Their contents suggest that the appropriate chronological order might be f. 58, ff. 51–3 and ff. 55–6; but BMSC was not orderly in her approach to the issues. Some portion of Jowett's side of the correspondence can be found in *AHC (Bal)*, 292, Benjamin Jowett to B. M. S. Clough, November 1861, 25 February, 31 March and 13 May 1862. For the drama of Froude's departure from Oxford, see J. A. Froude to A. H. Clough 28 February 1849, Mulhauser I, 212.
34. *CSS*, 72826, ff. 55–6, B. M. S. Clough to A. J. Clough n.d.
35. B. M. S. Smith to A. H. Clough, 4 March 1853, quoted in fn. 1 to A. H. Clough to B. M. S. Smith 24 March 1853, Mulhauser II, 349; *Poems*, p. xv.

36. *Ibid.*; for the dithering, see *CSS*, 72826, ff. 51–3, B. M. S. Clough to A. J. Clough n.d.
37. *AHC (Bal)*, 292, Benjamin Jowett to B. M. S. Clough 31 March 1862 and 13 May 1862. On the question of whether both parts of *Easter Day* were written at the same time, see *Poems*, pp. 674–5.
38. *CSS*, 72826, ff. 55–6, B. M. S. Clough to A. J. Clough n.d.
39. B. M. S. Clough to C. E. Norton 15 January 1861[62], Mulhauser II, 573; Lowry ed., *Letters of Arnold to Clough*, p. vi.
40. *CSS*, 72826, ff. 58, B. M. S. Clough to A. J. Clough n.d.
41. *AJC Notebook 10*, p. 66; Mulhauser II, 312, 322, 339, 346, 359, 366, 395; *AJC*, A. J. Clough to B. M. S. Clough n.d. but by content between January and April 1862.
42. *CSS*, 72826, ff. 51–3, B. M. S. Clough to A. J. Clough n.d.; *AHC (Bal)*, 292, Benjamin Jowett to B. M. S. Clough 25 Feburary 1862. I have been unable to identify Fisher.
43. *AHC (Bod)*, MS. Eng. Lett. e. 84, ff. 35–7, B. M. S. Clough to Henry Sidgwick 19 September 1869.
44. *Poems*, p. 653.
45. Version 1 of the text headed '1837' is *AJC Notebook 2*, which has thirty-eight leaves. Another, slightly longer version – forty-four leaves – is in *AHC (Bal)*, 2, with amendments and annotations in Blanche's hand and, in fragments A–C, yet more versions of particular sections, showing more reworking. I surmise that the Newnham text preceded the Balliol texts, because it is as much about the whole family's experiences as about Arthur. If this is correct, together the drafts show how Blanche prepared and reworked material initially provided by her sister-in-law, sharpening the focus upon Arthur, in preparing the memoir.
46. *Poems*, p. 653. Both Chorley and Biswas discuss Blanche's editorial efforts; however, the most incisive introduction is that of Anthony Kenny, in *God and Two Poets. Arthur Hugh Clough and Gerard Manley Hopkins* (1988), esp. pp. 143–6. The publishing history of Clough's poetry has generated a minor scholarly industry – see R. M. Gollin, Walter E. Houghton and Michael Timko, *Arthur Hugh Clough. A Descriptive Catalogue* (New York Public Library, n.d. [1967]).
47. *Memoir*, pp. 104, 106; *CSS*, 72830B, f. 52.
48. *CSS*, 72830C, f. 10.
49. *Memoir*, pp. 105–6; *BC*, 94M72/F570 Journal of Elinor Bonham Carter, 1863.
50. Biswas, p. 419.
51. *Memoir*, p. 106.
52. For a fuller account, see Hirsch, *Barbara Leigh Smith Bodichon*, chs. 11 and 12.
53. For Avonbank, see Jenny Uglow, *Elizabeth Gaskell. A Habit of Stories* (1993), pp. 34–9; for the domestic model more generally, see Christina de Bellaigue, '"Les murs de la pension". The School Community in French and English Boarding Schools for Girls, 1810–1867', *Paedagogica Historica* 40, 1&2 (April 2004), pp. 107–21. For class stratification and funding, see Sutherland, 'Education' in *CSHB* III.

54. Quoted in Lawrence·Goldman, *Science, Reform, and Politics in Victorian Britain. The Social Science Association 1857–1886* (Cambridge, 2002), p. 1.
55. *Ibid.*, p. 120; *AJC*, A. J. Clough to Emily Davies 28 July 1864.
56. Gillian Sutherland, 'Secondary Education' in *Government and Society in Nineteenth-Century Britain. Commentaries on British Parliamentary Papers: Education*, ed. Sutherland (Dublin, 1977), pp. 138–9.
57. *Ibid.*, p. 145; Goldman, *Social Science Association*, p. 240; PP 1867–8, XXVIII–II, *Report of the Schools Inquiry Commission*, vol. II, Miscellaneous Papers, pp. 192–4.
58. *Ibid.*, pp. 84–7; *Macmillan's Magazine* 14 (1866), pp. 435–9.
59. *CSS*, 72824A, ff. 79–90. This, headed 'Scene at Dolhyfryd', is not in Annie's writing but is signed and dated 'August 1887' by her. It was presumably prepared for and/or dictated to George S. Merriam, biographer of the Smiths.
60. The new institutional initiatives are summarised in Sutherland, *CSHB* III, pp. 148–9. In *Feminists and Bureaucrats. A Study in the Development of Girls' Education in the Nineteenth Century* (Cambridge, 1980) Sheila Fletcher showed the importance of the legislation which followed the Schools Inquiry Commission in this process.
61. Margaret J. Tuke, *A History of Bedford College for Women 1849–1937* (1939), chs. i–vii.
62. Gillian Sutherland, 'The Plainest Principles of Justice: The University of London and the Higher Education of Women' in *The University of London and the World of Learning 1836–1986*, ed. F. M. L. Thompson (1990). The best account of Emily Davies' strategy and tactics remains that of Barbara Stephen in *Emily Davies and Girton College* (1927), ch. vi. Janet Browne, *Charles Darwin. Voyaging* (1995), p. 91.
63. PP 1867–8, XXVIII–I, *Report of the Schools Inquiry Commission*, ch. 6, p. 569 and XXVIII–IV, *Report of the Schools Inquiry Commission, Minutes of Evidence*, qq. 17,823–17,861; *CSS*, 72824A, ff. 79–90, f. 86. For the Oxford thinking and activity, see Lawrence Goldman, *Dons and Workers. Oxford and Adult Education since 1850* (Oxford, 1995), pp. 11–31.
64. The account of the formation of the North of England Council which follows is based, except where otherwise indicated, on Annie's own account, written in 1873, *AJC*, 'A History of the North of England Council', and on the *Memoir*, pp. 116–46.
65. See Judith R. Walkowitz, *Prostitution and Victorian Society. Women, Class and the State* (Cambridge, 1980), esp. ch. 6.
66. *CSS*, 72830C, f.10.
67. Bodleian Library, Oxford, *Bryce Papers*, 159, ff. 167–8, A. J. Clough to James Bryce ?Spring 1867, ff. 189–92, same to same 4 November 1867, ff. 204–5, same to same 13 November 1867; see also ff. 201–2, Josephine Butler to James Bryce 12 November [1867].
68. *AJC*, pamphlet, 'Suggestions for the Training and Examination of Governesses'.

69. *AJC*, A. J. Clough to B. M. S. Clough n.d., but, from the content, mid-1868. For Emily Davies' efforts to intimidate Annie, see *ibid.*, Emily Davies to A. J. Clough 29 April 1868, same to same 1 May 1868, and same to same 2 May 1868. For the organisational efforts, see Stephen, *Emily Davies and Girton College*, ch. xii.

70. *AHC (Bod)*, MS. Eng. Lett. e. 84, ff. 24–5, Henry Sidgwick to B. M. S. Clough 26 July 1869; ff. 47–8 Henry Sidgwick to A. J. Clough 23 October 1869; and f. 49 same to same 30 October 1869; NCA, Letterbook, Rev. T. Markby to A. J. Clough 21 July 1869.

71. *AJC*, A. J. Clough to Emily Davies 28 July 1864.

72. *AHC (Bal)*, 292, Benjamin Jowett to B. M. S. Clough 4 August 1868. For Sidgwick's engagement with Arthur's poetry and through this with Blanche, see below, pp. 84–7.

73. *BC*, 94M72/F570 Journal of Elinor Bonham Carter, entries 1869 and 1870.

5 THE BEGINNINGS OF NEWNHAM

1. *SM*, p. 70. He quotes and misquotes from Clough's poetry on a number of occasions – *ibid.*, pp. 98–9, 246, 279, and below, n. 5. See also Ross Harrison ed., *Henry Sidgwick* (Oxford, 2001, for the British Academy, *Proceedings of the British Academy* 109) and Bart Schultz, *Henry Sidgwick: Eye of the Universe. An Intellectual Biography* (Cambridge, 2004).

2. *AHC (Bod)*, Ms. Eng. Lett. e. 84, ff. 1–2, Henry Sidgwick to B. M. S. Clough 27 April 1866. A typewritten copy is in TCA, Sidgwick Papers, Add. Ms. c. 105, 24.

3. See letters quoted in chapters iii and iv of *SM* and originals in *AHC (Bod)*, MS. Eng. Lett. e. 84. The direct quotation comes from *ibid.*, ff. 30–1, Henry Sidgwick to B. M. S. Clough 6 August 1869.

4. For Jowett's correspondence with BMSC, see *AHC (Bal)* 292. For Jowett's relationship with Florence Nightingale, see Geoffrey Faber, *Jowett. A Portrait with Background* (1957), pp. 306–13 and Woodham Smith, *Nightingale*, pp. 350–2. Both J. C. Shairp and Matt Arnold had reacted against *Amours de Voyage*, when shown it in draft, see above, p. 52.

5. *SM*, pp. 214 and 227. The 'Gordian Knot' is a reference to Clough's lines,

> To finger idly some old Gordian knot
> And with much toil attain to half-believe.

6. *SM*, pp. 200–1; original in *AHC (Bod)* MS. Eng. Lett. e. 84, ff. 27–8, Henry Sidgwick to B. M. S. Clough 31 July 1869.

7. This is brilliantly explored in Janet Browne, *Charles Darwin. The Power of Place* (2002); see also W. E. Houghton, *The Victorian Frame of Mind, 1830–1870* (1957).

8. A. J. Engel, *From Clergyman to Don. The Rise of the Academic Profession in Nineteenth-Century Oxford* (Oxford, 1983), esp. chs. i–iii.

9. *SM*, pp. 188–9.

10. Above, pp. 81–2; *SM*, p. 198.
11. *CSS*, 72830C, f. 23; see also Christopher Harvie, *The Lights of Liberalism. University Liberals and the Challenge of Democracy 1860–1886* (1976).
12. NCA, vol. *Records of Newnham College 1869–80*, Lecture prospectus 1869. On the Fawcetts, see Lawrence Goldman ed., *The Blind Victorian. Henry Fawcett and British Liberalism* (Cambridge, 1989) and David Rubinstein, *A Different World for Women. The Life of Millicent Garrett Fawcett* (Hassocks, 1991). On the Garretts, see Elizabeth Crawford, *Enterprising Women. The Garretts and their Circle* (2002).
13. NCA, box file 'History of the College', ms for AJC's talk, September 1875.
14. *MT*, chs. 2, 3 and 4.
15. *CSS*, 72830B, ff. 23–4; NCA, box file 'History of the College', J. S. Mill to Henry Sidgwick 14 March 1870. This and the other donations and gifts that followed are listed in the *Newnham College Record of Benefactors, made in the Jubilee Year of the College, 1921* (Cambridge, privately printed, 1921).
16. *Memoir*, pp. 193–4.
17. *Ibid.*, p. 145; *SM*, pp. 244, 246; NCA, Letterbook, Henry Sidgwick to A. J. Clough 18 March 1871, Henry Sidgwick to A. J. Clough 25 ?April ?May 1871.
18. NCA, vol. *Records of Newnham College 1869–80*, prospectus, *Lectures for Women*, June 1871.
19. Unless otherwise indicated, information about students is taken from the *Register*. These first five were vividly characterised by Mary Paley Marshall in her memoir, *What I Remember* (Cambridge, 1947), pp. 10–14.
20. *AHC (Bod)*, MS. Eng. Lett. e. 84, Henry Sidgwick to B. M. S. Clough 25 May 1872. Part of this is quoted in *SM*, p. 265. See also *CSS*, 72830C, ff. 26, 48 and 63.
21. *SM*, p. 268, Henry Sidgwick to Oscar Browning May 1872.
22. *CSS*, 72824A, ff. 123–7, Edith Creak to B. M. S. Clough 29 January 1893.
23. NCA, vol. *Records of Newnham College 1871–81*, prospectus for Merton Hall, October 1872.
24. NCA, General Committee Minutes (henceforward Gen. Cttee Min.), 11 March 1886.
25. NCA, Minutes Council Newnham Hall Company, 12 June 1877. For accusations of godlessness, see NCA, Gen. Cttee Min., 30 April 1884.
26. NCA, vol. *Records of Newnham College 1869–80*, notice of the first AGM, 17 November 1873.
27. *Ibid.*, Report of the committee of the Association for the Higher Education of Women, 2 November 1878. For patterns of teaching and learning in nineteenth-century Cambridge, see Jonathan Smith and Christopher Stray eds., *Teaching and Learning in Nineteenth-Century Cambridge* (Woodbridge/Cambridge University Library, 2001) in general, and my essay in that collection, 'Girton for Ladies, Newnham for Governesses' in particular.
28. See Harvie, *Lights of Liberalism*, pp. 204–9, and Goldman, *Dons and Workers*, pp. 13–16. For the local associations see *Memoir*, pp. 131–43.
29. Fletcher, *Feminists and Bureaucrats*, pp. 114–18.

30. NCA, Minutes of the Association for the Higher Education of Women 1873–80 (hereafter Min. AHEW).

31. NCA, vol. *Newnham Hall*, minutes of the meetings of the Council, of the Building Committee and of the shareholders of the Newnham Hall Company, 1874–80 (hereafter *Newnham Hall*), entries for 1874 and 1875.

32. *Ibid.*, 27 March, 27 April, 2 June, 22 June and 6 July 1874; SJCA, SB21/cb/N/11.1–60. I am indebted to Phyllis Hetzel for drawing my attention to these papers.

33. *AHC (Bod)*, MS. Eng. Lett. e. 84, Henry Sidgwick to B. M. S. Clough 19 March 1873; *SM*, p. 279.

34. NCA, copies in box file, *History of the College* and vol. *Records of Newnham College 1871–81*; cf. also *Memoir*, pp. 158–60.

35. *SM*, p. 284, Henry Sidgwick to F. W. H. Myers 30 October 1873.

36. NCA, vol. *Records of Newnham College 1871–8*, following leaflet 22 October 1873.

37. NCA, *Newnham Hall*, meetings 2 June and 21 October 1874.

38. *Ibid.*, meeting 6 March 1874; NCA, box file, *History of College*, AJC's ms account, September 1875.

39. *Memoir*, pp. 199–200, 204–5.

40. NCA, box file, *History of College*, AJC's ms account, September 1875. The address, with a personal addendum, is copied out in the hand of whoever delivered it – perhaps, with his Yorkshire connections, J. G. Fitch?

41. *NCCL*, 1884, p. 7.

42. NCA, *Newnham Hall*, Report of the Newnham Hall Co., 1875.

43. Paley Marshall, *What I Remember*, pp. 13–14, 16, 20; NCA, box file, *History of College*, Henry Sidgwick to Mary Paley 28 May [1875].

44. NCA, *Newnham Hall*, Report of the Newnham Hall Co., 1875, minutes of 24 February 1877, Report of the Newnham Hall Co., December 1878; vol. *Records of Newnham College 1869–80*, minutes AHEW standing sub-committee, 3 November 1877.

45. *Ibid.*, Report of Principal to Shareholders, 27 June 1878.

46. *Register*; see also Tanya Novak, 'Women's Education: Connections between America and Cambridge 1874–1914', unpublished dissertation submitted for Part II of the Cambridge Historical Tripos, 1990.

47. NCA, *Newnham Hall*, meetings 21 June 1875, 11 November 1875, 24 February 1877.

48. NCA, vol. *Records of Newnham College 1869–80*, prospectus for Lectures hand-dated 1870–1.

49. *Ibid.*, prospectus announcing the formation of the Association, 1873; NCA, Min. AHEW, 30 May 1874.

50. NCA, box file, *History of the College*, AJC's ms account, September 1875.

51. NCA, *Newnham Hall*, meetings 11 November 1875, 12 June 1877, 1 June 1878.

52. See Gillian Sutherland, 'The Movement for the Higher Education of Women: Its Social and Intellectual Context in England c.1840–1880' in *Politics and Social Change in Modern Britain*, ed. P. J. Waller (Brighton, 1987).

53. *SM*, p. 333, Henry Sidgwick to his mother 2 January 1878.

54. NCA, *Newnham Hall*, meetings 14 April and 18 December 1875, 19 June and 11 December 1876, 24 February 1877, 2 March, 1 June, 26 June, 29 November and 12 December 1878.

55. *Memoir*, pp. 302, 342; recollections of Edith Sharpley 1930, quoted *NA*, pp. 11–12. In the mid-1880s they would house the first students of Hughes Hall; M. V. Hughes, *A London Girl of the 1880s* (Oxford, 1946, 1978 pbk), pp. 94–5.

56. NCA, *Newnham Hall*, meetings November 1878–80 and Min. AHEW, 1879–80.

57. *ODNB*.

58. NCA, Letterbook, Henry Sidgwick to A. J. Clough 30 July [1875]; Helen Fowler, 'Eleanor Mildred Sidgwick 1845–1936' in *Cambridge Women: Twelve Portraits*, ed. Edward Shils and Carmen Blacker (Cambridge, 1996); Janet Oppenheim, 'A Mother's Role, a Daughter's Duty: Lady Blanche Balfour, Eleanor Sidgwick, and Feminist Perspectives', *Journal of British Studies* 34 (April 1995), pp. 196–232 and 'Academic Partners: Henry and Eleanor Sidgwick and the Growth of Newnham College', *The Cambridge Review* (May 1996), pp. 17–23.

59. NCA, Minutes of the meetings of the Council and General Meetings of Newnham College (hereafter Min. Council & GM), 19 November 1881.

60. *Memoir*, pp. 197–8; Paley Marshall, *What I Remember*, p. 20.

61. *Register*.

62. NCA, Min. Council & GM, 22 May 1880.

63. NCA, box file, 'History of the College'.

64. *SM*, p. 359.

65. Paley Marshall, *What I Remember*, p. 16 and plate 5.

66. NCA, Letterbook, Rev. Thomas Paley to *The Times* 21 December 1874, covering note Henry Sidgwick to A. J. Clough n.d.; Examiners' Letters 1874–82.

67. MT, ch. 5.

68. *NA*, pp. 19, 20.

69. Sutherland, 'Movement for the Higher Education of Women', table 4.3, p. 104.

6 ENTER BLANCHE ATHENA CLOUGH

1. *BC*, 94M72/F563.

2. *AHC (Bod)*, MS. Eng. Lett. e. 84, ff. 111–22, four letters from Henry Sidgwick to B. M. S. Clough 1876–8.

3. Woodham Smith, *Nightingale*, p. 517; NCA, Kitty Duff to Joan Stubbs 4 September 1980.

4. The house, now a school, was extensively altered and rebuilt after 1895. I am indebted to the Bursar of Embley Park School for permission to explore the site in 2003.

5. *CSS*, 72829, f. 87, undated.

6. *AHC (Bod)*, MS. Eng. Lett. e. 84, ff. 42–3, Henry Sidgwick to B. A. Clough 1869; *SM*, p. 268, Henry Sidgwick to his mother 25 June 1872; TCA, *Sidgwick*

Papers, Add. Mss c. 97/25 Henry Sidgwick journal letter to J. A. Symonds 17/31 July 1884.

7. NCA, Kitty Duff to Joan Stubbs 4 September 1980.
8. *CSS*, 72830A, ff. 5–7.
9. Mulhauser II, Appendix II, p. 620. Elinor Bonham Carter subsequently attended Rachel Martineau's school also – *BC*, 94M72/F571.
10. *Register*, 1876.
11. Stephen, *Emily Davies and Girton College*, pp. 367–8 (biographical index); Girton College Archives, ED IX/ LSMI – Minute Book 1866–74, /LSM4 – printed list of members May 1869, /LSM7b – printed list of members May 1875; Charles Eyre Pascoe, *Schools for girls and colleges for women. A handbook of female middle class education* (1879), p. 57; *Paton's List of Schools and Tutors* (1911), pp. 668–9. I am indebted to Christina de Bellaigue and Janet Howarth for these references.
12. WL, *J. P. Strachey Papers*, 7/JPS 53B, draft obituary of B. A. Clough prepared by Pernel Strachey and Barbara Stephen in 1942 or 1943.
13. J. A. Venn, *Alumni Cantabrigienses* (Cambridge, 1940–54); W. C. Lubenow, *The Cambridge Apostles 1820–1914* (Cambridge, 1998), Appendix: biographical directory.
14. *CSS*, 72830A, f. 57.
15. *NA*, pp. 24–5.
16. *CSS*, 72830B, f. 53.
17. Victoria Glendinning, *A Supressed Cry. Life and Death of a Quaker Daughter* (1969), p. 68.
18. *Ibid.*, p. 65; *CSS*, 72828, ff. 1–2, Lucy Silcox to B. A. Clough 12 April 1885, 72829, ff. 1–4, Edith Sharpley to B. A. Clough 25 September 1885.
19. *CSS*, 72830A, ff. 11, 13, 15.
20. The five black notebooks are in *CSS*, 72830A–E. The loose sheets are collected in 72829. The title 'black books' was used by Thena herself, in notes inserted at the beginning of 72830A late in 1944 or early in 1945: it is a bleak pun on their covers and the main use to which she put them in trying to contain her bouts of depression. However volumes B, C and D also include some more typical 'journal' entries, records of travel and encounters, in particular relating to the preparation of the *Memoir* of her aunt and her journey round the world 1899–1900.

Some of the entries appear to have been dated as they were written, others subsequently. Volumes A and E record major rereadings in 1910 and again in 1944; there may have been others. In addition a number of the entries include lengthy retrospects: for example, in A, which formally begins in July 1885, there are accounts of earlier episodes and moods; and B, which formally begins in March 1892, contains recollections of Annie's last years of life. Although in the rereading of 1944 Thena assigned the date of mid-1916 to the ending of E, some entries seem to belong to a slightly later period. The dating of the volumes as follows must therefore be treated as approximate: A 1884–92, B 1892–4, C 1894–8, D 1898–1901, E 1901–19. The loose sheets in 72829 are almost all undated, although there are occasional internal clues.

21. See M. Knappen, *Two Elizabethan Puritan Diaries* (London, 1933).
22. *CSS*, 72830A, ff. 21–2 (5 February 1886).
23. *NA*, p. 11.
24. *CSS*, 72829, ff.1–4, Edith Sharpley to B. A. Clough 25 September 1885.
25. *AJC*, A. J. Clough to Maria Bacot 20 April; from the content of this and what is clearly a subsequent letter, A. J. Clough to Maria Bacot 29 February 1884, the probable year is 1883. A. J. Clough to B. A. Clough Thursday – dated in another hand 'October '85'; A. J. Clough to B. A. Clough Monday – dated in another hand 1887; cf. also A. J. Clough to B. A. Clough 28 December – dated in another hand 1886.
26. Glendinning, *A Suppressed Cry*, p. 65. Lionel Tennyson was the poet's second son; Anne Thackeray Ritchie was the daughter of W. M. Thackeray and herself a writer, see Garnett, *Anny*.
27. *NA*, p. 29; *NCCL*, 1886, p. 11 and 1888, p. 9. *CSS*, 72828, f. 4, fragment of a letter from Margaret Verrall to B. A. Clough 14 April 1886; Rubinstein, *Different World for Women*, ch. 10.
28. *CSS*, 72829, ff. 1–4, Edith Sharpley to B. A. Clough 25 September 1885; f. 7, fragment of a letter from Edith Sharpley to B. A. Clough, dated by BAC to September 1886.
29. NCA, Gen. Cttee Min., 5 May 1886 and 5 October 1887; Min. Council & GM, 17 November 1888.
30. *CSS*, 72830B, f. 7, cf. also f. 2; B, ff. 24–5.
31. TCA, Sidgwick Papers, Add. Ms. c. 97/25, f. 42, Henry Sidgwick to J. A. Symonds (journal letter) entry for 11 May 1885.
32. *Ibid.*, f. 68, Henry Sidgwick to J. A. Symonds (journal letters) 21 November 1885, f. 90, 15–17 May 1886 and f. 136, 11 June 1888, copy of the notes on the opening provided for *The Banner* by Henry and Nora Sidgwick; NCA, Min. Council & GM, 7 November 1885, 21 November 1885, 13 February, 15 May and 6 November 1886, 19 November and 10 December 1887; *CSS*, 72824A, ff. 91–6.
33. NCA, box file, 'History of the College', G. W. Prothero to A. J. Clough 11 November 1887, same to same 17 November 1887 and same to same 24 November 1887; Min. Council & GM, 19 November and 10 December 1887.
34. *Ibid.*, 28 April and 7 November 1891; box files 12 and 15, Land 1879–1913 and Building 1874–1910; SJCA, SB21/CB/N/11, 200–316.
35. *NA*, pp. 25–30.
36. Biographical data is drawn from the *Register* unless otherwise indicated.
37. See Sutherland, 'Movement for Higher Education of Women', pp. 93–105.
38. NCA, Minutes of Council, Education Committee, General Committee, Library Committee, Examinations Committee 1889–93; *NCCL*, 1881–90.
39. NCA, Gen. Cttee Min., 18 October 1888.
40. NCA, Newnham Club Minutes, AGM 19 January 1889 and AGM 16 January 1890; 1895–1908.
41. *NA*, p. 30.
42. *CSS*, 72830B, ff. 4–5; 72830A, f. 69.

43. NCA, Min. Council & GM, 16 November 1889, 15 February 1890, 16 May 1891.
44. *CSS*, 72830B, f. 26.
45. *Ibid.*, ff. 6–8. See also Hermione Lee, *Virginia Woolf* (1996), pp. 64–5.
46. *CSS*, 72830B, ff. 11–12; cf. 72830A, ff. 76, 78–9.
47. *CSS*, 72830B, f.10.
48. MT, ch. 6.
49. Stephen Siklos, *Philippa Fawcett and the Mathematical Tripos* (Cambridge, privately printed, 1990).
50. *AJC*, A. J. Clough to Ellen Crofts Darwin 11 October 1890; *CSS*, 72830B, f. 13.
51. *Ibid.*, f. 26.
52. Pauline Adams, *Somerville for Women. An Oxford College 1879–93* (Oxford, 1996), pp. 10, 16.
53. *Memoir*, pp. 322–3; Grace King, *Memories of a Southern Woman of Letters* (New York, 1932), pp. 110–12. I owe this latter reference to Michael O'Brien.
54. *AJC*, copies of the original letters and papers held in the University of Sydney Women's College Archives.
55. *CSS*, 72830B, f. 40.
56. *CSS*, 72824A, ff. 97–102, Alfred Marshall to A. J. Clough 27 January 1889; *AJC*, A. J. Clough to Alfred Marshall 28 January 1889 (draft).
57. *Ibid.*, A. J. Clough to Mary Paley Marshall 12 March 1891.
58. *CSS*, 72830B, ff. 16–17, 28–9.
59. *Ibid.*, ff. 27, 35.
60. *Ibid.*, ff. 18–21.
61. *Ibid.*, ff. 30, 19.
62. *Ibid.*, ff. 40, 37.
63. *Ibid.*, ff. 30–2; *Memoir*, pp. 339–43.
64. NCA, Min. Council & GM, 12 March 1892.

7 'AN OUGHT WHICH HAS TO BE RECKONED WITH'

1. *CSS*, 72830B, f. 2, see also ff. 3, 45; ff. 46–7.
2. PRFD, Will of A. J. Clough, signed 24 August 1891, proved 8 August 1892.
3. NCA, envelope re AJC memorial.
4. *CSS*, 72830B, f. 22; ff. 48–9; f. 50.
5. *CSS*, 72824A, esp. ff. 147–64, notes by Ellen Crofts Darwin, and ff. 165–70 typescript notes from Margaret Verrall; 72830B and C.
6. *CSS*, 72830B, f. 65; f. 69; see also ff. 51, 70–1, 83.
7. *Ibid.*, f. 66; f. 53; see also 72830C, f. 70.
8. *Ibid.*, ff. 48–50, 54, 70; see also 72830B, f. 58; 72830C, f. 71; 72830B, f. 66.
9. A. O. J. Cockshut, *Truth to Life. The Art of Biography in the Nineteenth Century* (1974), p. 148 and *passim*.
10. *SM*, p. 204; *CSS*, 72824A, ff. 175–6, Frank Darwin to B. A. Clough 8 April 1897; ff. 189–90, Anna Bateson to B. A. Clough 28 November 1897 and f. 195, Herbert Bell to B. A. Clough 15 December 1897. Bell's archive is held in The Armitt Museum, Ambleside. Girton College Archives, GCPP Bodichon 11/28,

B. A. Clough to Anne Leigh Smith 30 January (1898). I am indebted to Pam Hirsch for this reference.

11. Compare the frontispiece of the first edition, 1897, with that of the second, 1903. On the Clough eyes, see Thomas Arnold, 'Arthur Hugh Clough: A Sketch', *The Nineteenth Century* 42 (January 1898), pp. 105–16, at p. 105, T. C. Down, 'Schooldays with Miss Clough', *The Cornhill Magazine* (June 1920), p. 680 and Clara Rackham, 'In Memoriam Miss B. A. Clough', *NCCL*, 1961.

12. *CSS*, 72830C, f. 71; ff. 30, 56; ff. 2–5.

13. TCA, *Babington Smith Papers*, esp. HBS 13/27, A. H. Clough to H. Babington Smith 7 November 1887.

14. NCA, Kitty Duff to Joan Stubbs 16 December 1985.

15. Private collection, F. Nightingale to B. M. S. Clough 7 January 1893.

16. TCA, *Babington Smith Papers*, HBS 11/9 diary entry for 9 February 1893; see also entry for 25 February 1893; Lubenow, *Cambridge Apostles*, p. 76.

17. *CSS*, 72828, ff. 37–41, Arthur and Eleanor Clough to B. A. Clough Monday – dated 1894 by envelope; TCA, *Babington Smith Papers*, HBS 70/93 Arthur Clough to Henry Babington Smith 19 November 1894?; HBS 70/94 Arthur Clough to Henry Babington Smith 26–7 February 1895?; HBS 70/95 Arthur Clough to Henry Babington Smith 1895?; F. Hardcastle, *Records of Burley. Aspects of a New Forest Village*, 2nd edition 1987, Spalding, Lincs, p. 180. Information about the cost of the land is taken from records in the possession of Mrs Carolyn Brebbia, the present owner of Burley Hill.

18. TCA, *Babington Smith Papers*, HBS 5/67 Arthur Clough to Henry Babington Smith 24 May 1898; HBS 70/103 same to same 10 August 1898; HBS 70/104 same to same 3 November ?1898; HBS 70/105 same to same 6 December 1898. Further information on Castle Top and Arthur Clough as architect, builder and landlord was provided by Mr Philip Mackworth Praed and Miss Dionis McNair of Burley, in conversation in 1998.

19. *CSS*, 72829, f. 118. Cf. also e.g. 72830B, f. 66.

20. NCA, Min. Council & GM, 4 November 1893.

21. *CSS*, 72830C, unnumbered leaf between ff. 3 and 4, f. 4; ff. 11–12.

22. SJCA, SB21/cb/NII, 11.350–11.359; *SM*, p. 525.

23. NCA, Min. Council & GM, 16 November 1895, 21 November 1896; *CSS*, 72830C, ff. 71–2, NCA, Min. Council & GM, 3 August 1896; *CSS*, 72828, ff. 43–5, Margaret Verrall to B. A. Clough 22 November 1895; 72830A, f. 56, entry 13 July 1887.

24. MT, ch. 8, is the source for what follows, unless otherwise indicated.

25. *NCCL*, 1894, pp. 18–22.

26. NCA, Mins. Council & GM, 15 February 1896; see also 20 November 1897.

27. NCA, box file printed material 1895–7, letter to the Syndicate signed by B. A. Clough and Katharine Jex-Blake 3 November 1896.

28. Gordon Johnson ed., *University Politics. F. M. Cornford's Cambridge and his Advice to the Young Academic Politician* (Cambridge, 1994), p. 105.

29. NCA, box file printed material 1895–7, Memorandum from B. A. Clough and Katharine Jex-Blake 28 April 1897.

30. NCA, box file printed material 1895–7, Clarice M. Wilson to Principal 13 February 1951.

8 Regrouping

1. NCA, Education Cttee Min., 9 and 18 August 1897.
2. NCA, Min. Council & GM, 6 November 1897.
3. B. M. Herbertson, *The Pfeiffer Bequest and the Education of Women. A Centenary Review* (Cambridge, privately printed, 1993).
4. NCA, Min. Council & GM, 9 May 1896; for Henry and Elizabeth Yates Thompson, see Elizabeth Robins, *Portrait of a Lady* (printed, for private circulation, by the Hogarth Press, 1941; reprinted, for private circulation, with an afterword by Jean Gooder, by Newnham College, Cambridge, 2002).
5. NCA, Min. Council & GM, 12 May 1906.
6. *Ibid.*, 21 November 1903, 13 February and 5 November 1904, 12 May 1906.
7. *Ibid.*, 17 November 1894, 21 November 1896 and 13 February 1897.
8. *Ibid.*, 18 February and 13 May 1899, 24 May 1900.
9. *CSS*, 72824A ff. 128–37, Alice Gardner to B. A. Clough 8 September 1896.
10. NCA, Min. Council & GM, 6 November 1897; Mary Lago, *Christiana Herringham and the Edwardian Art Scene* (1996).
11. NCA, Min. Council & GM, 12 February 1898; Annabel Robinson, *The Life and Work of Jane Ellen Harrison* (Oxford, 2002), chs. 3, 4 and 5.
12. NCA, Min. Council & GM, 1 November and 15 November 1902, 11 February 1905; Research Fellowship Cttee Min., 8 and 12 November 1902, loosely inserted letter Christiana Herringham to Nora Sidgwick 21 December 1904.
13. *Ibid.*; *Register*; Engel, *Clergyman to Don*, pp. 264–72.
14. NCA, Min. Council & GM, 2 and 16 November 1907.
15. Engel, *Clergyman to Don*, esp. pp. 273–85; Phyllis Deane, *The Life and Times of J. Neville Keynes* (Aldershot, 2001), esp. ch. iii.
16. NCA, Min. staff meetings 1907–12; Min. Council & GM, 17 November 1906, 9 February 1907, 16 May 1908, 23 January and 15 May 1909, 12 February 1910, 13 May 1911.
17. *CSS*, 72830D, ff. 1–3; 72830C, ff. 89–91.
18. NCA, Min. Council & GM, 13 May 1899; *CSS*, 72830D, f. 11.
19. *Ibid.*, f. 12.
20. *CSS*, 72830D; 72826, ff. 72–128; NCA, ms *Travel Diary of Philippa Fawcett 1899–1900*, 2 vols. The account of their journey which follows is based on these three sources; only direct quotations and other sources are separately footnoted.
21. TCA, *Babington Smith Papers*, HBS 70/106 Arthur Clough to Henry Babington Smith 22 October 1899; 70/107 Arthur Clough to Henry Babington Smith, n.d. but 1899.
22. *CSS*, 72830D, ff. 36–8.
23. NCA, *Fawcett Diary I*, 30 January 1900.
24. NCA, *Fawcett Diary II*, 11 March 1900; *ibid.* 13 June 1900.

25. *CSS*, 72826, ff. 110–13, B. A. Clough to B. M. S. Clough 13 March 1900, f. 112.
26. *CSS*, 72830D, f. 42.
27. *CSS*, 72826, f. 124, B. A. Clough to B. M. S. Clough 1 May 1900.
28. NCA, *Fawcett Diary II*, 13 May 1900; for such codes, see David Kahn, *The Codebreakers. The Story of Secret Writing* (2nd edition, New York, 1996), pp. 836–53. I am indebted to Chris Stray for this reference.
29. *CSS*, 72830D, ff. 46–50.
30. *CSS*, 72828, ff. 69–70, P. G. Fawcett to B. A. Clough 18 March [1902].
31. Cf. *CSS*, 72824A, ff. 173–4.
32. *BC*, 94M72/F972, Sibella Bonham Carter to Maurice Bonham Carter 24 May and 1 June 1901; PRFD, declaration of intestacy for Florence Anne Mary Clough, 8 July 1901.
33. *CSS*, 72830E, f. 55; the letters themselves are reprinted in Mulhauser II.
34. Stubbs/ Duff.
35. PRFD, Will of Blanche Mary Shore Clough, died 7 May 1904, probate granted 3 June 1904.
36. *CSS*, 72830E, ff. 21–8.
37. CSS, 72828, ff. 53–6, Harry Stephen to B. A. Clough 17 May 1900, ff. 64–8, Harry Stephen to B. A. Clough 28 July 1901.
38. Barbara Caine, *Bombay to Bloomsbury. A Biography of the Strachey Family* (Oxford, 2005).
39. *Strachey*, 60725, ff. 202–3, J. P. Strachey to Lady Strachey 14 August 1902; 60726, f. 22, J. P. Strachey to Lytton Strachey 26 September 1903; *CSS*, 72828, ff. 81–2, J. P. Strachey to B. A. Clough 27 July 1907.
40. *CSS*, 72830E, ff. 42–3.
41. NCA, Min. Council & GM, 4 November 1899, 10 May 1902, 21 November 1903, 13 February and 14 May 1904, 23 January, 13 February and 13 March 1909.
42. *CSS*, 72830E, ff. 34–8.
43. Claire Breay, 'Women and the Classical Tripos 1869–1914' in *Classics in Nineteenth- and Twentieth-Century Cambridge. Curriculum, Culture and Community*, ed. Christopher Stray (Cambridge, 1999), pp. 61–2.
44. E. M. Butler, *Paper Boats. An Autobiography* (1949), pp. 39–40.
45. NCA, Min. Council & GM, 4 June 1910.
46. *CSS*, 72830E, ff. 38–42; 72829, ff. 74–81; 72830C, ff. 89–90; NCA, Min. Council & GM, 17 November 1900; 11 June 1910.

9 WAR AND ITS CONSEQUENCES

1. *NA*, p. 122; personal information – conversations with E. E. H. Welsford, who was an undergraduate 1911–15 and became a Research Fellow in 1918.
2. Above, pp. 122, 128; Lee, *Virginia Woolf*, pp. 63, 102; B. A. Clough, 'Katharine Stephen', *NCCL* 1925, pp. 12–28.
3. Above, pp. 145–7.
4. *CSS*, 72829, f. 84, undated fragment.

5. NCA, Min. Council & GM, 2 November 1907, 11 June 1910 and 4 November 1911.
6. NCA, box file, 'Charter and Statutes', B. A. Clough to G. L. Elles 18 December 1911. The detail of the process can be tracked in this file, in the Minutes of the Council and of the NC Old Students' Club 1910–14.
7. Stubbs/Duff; *CSS*, 72827, f. 1, B. A. Clough to L. K. Duff 4 July 1915.
8. *NA*, p. 67; Miranda Seymour, *Ottoline Morrell. Life on the Grand Scale* (first published 1992, paperback 2nd edition 1998), p. 213.
9. *NCCL* 1914, p. 5. 'Mays' were important intercollegiate examinations before the Tripos proper.
10. NCA, Gen. Cttee Min., 20 October 1915; Vera Brittain, *Testament of Youth* (1933), ch. iv, 'Learning versus Life'; *Register*.
11. *Ibid.*; *NCCL* 1915, pp. 57–60, 1916, pp. 25–40. See Margot Lawrence, *Shadow of Swords. A Biography of Elsie Inglis* (1971), ch. 9 *et seq.*; Leah Leneman, *In the Service of Life. The Story of Dr Elsie Inglis and the Scottish Women's Hospitals* (Edinburgh, 1994); Eileen Crofton, *The Women of Royaumont. A Scottish Women's Hospital on the Western Front* (East Lothian, 1997); Audrey Fawcett Cahill ed., *Between the Lines. Letters and Diaries from Elsie Inglis's Russian Unit* (Durham, 1999); Butler, *Paper Boats*, pp. 63–76.
12. NCA, Min. Council & GM, 15 May 1915 and 13 May 1916; R*egister*.
13. *Strachey*, 60728, ff. 82–101.
14. WL, 9/ALC, vol. 2, AL/1631, Microfiche Box no. 2, B. A. Clough to Miss M. M. Longley 29 June 1916 and 9/ALC, vol. 1, AL/1141, Microfiche Box no. 2, B. A. Clough to Pippa Strachey 8 March 1917; NCA, Min. Council & GM, 4 November 1916; *CSS*, 72830E, ff. 31–2; Caine, *Bombay to Bloomsbury*, p. 314.
15. NCA, Minutes of Council 17 November 1917, 26 January 1918.
16. NCA, Minutes of House Committee 1914–22 – rationing continued beyond the end of hostilities.
17. *NA*, pp. 107, 113–14.
18. *CSS*, 72830E, f. 45; ff. 50–1.
19. *Ibid.*, f. 45.
20. *CSS*, 72827, ff. 2, 3–4, 7, 8 B. A. Clough to L. K. Duff 25 March ?1917, 15 June 1917, n.d. (?1917) 'Sat'.
21. NCA, box file 'Constitution', BAC's leaflet, draft for the AGM 6 November 1915, printed Petition for Charter and draft Statutes; Min. Council & GM, 6 November and 20 November 1915, 4 November 1916, 2 June 1917; NC Club Min. 15 January 1916; Minutes of the Governing Body of Newnham College (henceforward GB Min.), 2 June 1917.
22. NCA, GB Min., 26 January, 22 May, 25 May and 7 June 1918.
23. NCA, GB Min., 1 August, 31 October and 15 November 1919.
24. NCA, GB Min., 30 and 31 January, 19 February, 5 and 17 March, 1 and 8 May, 4 and 21 June 1920.
25. MT, chs. 9 and 10, the source for the account of the discussion in Cambridge in the paragraphs that follow, unless otherwise indicated.

26. Brian Harrison ed., *The History of the University of Oxford*, vol. VIII: The Twentieth Century (Oxford, 1994), ch. 2, John Prest, 'The Asquith Commission 1919–22', p. 30.

27. Bodleian Library Oxford, *H. A. L. Fisher Papers*, box 63, ff. 254–7, H. H. Asquith to H. A. L. Fisher 29 August 1919, f. 259, G. W. Balfour to H. A. L. Fisher 7 September 1919. Somerville College, Oxford, *Penrose Papers*, box file 'Royal Commission', H. A. L. Fisher to Emily Penrose 20 September 1919.

28. *H. A. L. Fisher Papers*, box 54, ff. 357–8, H. A. L. Fisher to Gilbert Murray 7 September 1919; see also ff. 359–60, same to same 8 September 1919.

29. Bodleian Library Oxford, *H. H. Asquith Papers*, 137, ff. 45–54 6 January 1920, f. 54; 138, ff. 69–95 May 1920, f. 95.

30. University Library, Cambridge, Cam.a.922.4, Appendices to the Report of the Royal Commission 1919–22, pp. 280–2, 289–90, Appendix 12, (ii), 1 & 2, Statements of Needs 23 and 24 July 1920, Appendix 13, (ii)(a), Joint Memorandum 23 July 1920.

31. University Library, Cambridge, Cam.a.922.2 Minutes of Evidence submitted to the Royal Commission 1919–22, box 9, pp. 37–8, 40–1.

32. *H. H. Asquith Papers*, 140, ff. 211–14, Minutes of informal meeting of a sub-set of Commissioners at All Souls College, Oxford 30 September (1920).

33. *Penrose Papers*, box file 'Royal Commission', B. A. Clough and E. Penrose typescript report of sub-committee on the women's colleges.

34. *Ibid.*, Notes of the discussion of the report of the women's sub-committee 21 January 1921; Christopher Brooke, *A History of the University of Cambridge*, vol. IV: *1870–1990* (Cambridge, 1993), ch. 11.

35. NCA, GB Min., 17 and 28 January 1921, Council Min., 29 January 1921.

36. NCA, GB Min., 4 March 1921, Council Min., 5 March 1921.

37. NCA, Council Min., 17 June 1921.

38. NCA, Council Min., 31 July, 13 and 27 November 1920, 5 March, 7 May and 17 June 1921.

39. *NA*, p. 145.

10 Salvage operations

1. Maisie Anderson, 'Time to the Sound of Bells', *The Caian* 1988–9 (Cambridge, privately printed), p. 73; *NA*, p. 137; NCA, Gen. Cttee Min., 2 November 1920.

2. Archives of Gonville and Caius College, Cambridge, ms *Diaries of Maisie Anderson*, 02/03, 20 and 22 October 1921; MT, p. 167.

3. NCA, GB Min. 25 October 1921, Letterbook, 2 letters from undergraduate committee October 1921, cutting from *Westminster Gazette* 2 November 1921.

4. NCA, Council Min. 12 November 1921; Cambridge University Library, Cam.a.922.2 Appendices to the Report of the Royal Commission on Oxford and Cambridge 1919–22, Appendix 13 (ii)(b), pp. 290–1; MT, p. 169.

5. NCA, Council Min. 28 January 1922.

6. NCA, GB Min. 3 March 1922.
7. Report of the Royal Commission on Oxford and Cambridge 1919–22, PP 1922 x paras. 191–9; pp. 254–5 Reservation by Mr Graham; Note by Miss Clough; *Anderson Diaries*, 02/03, 20 October 1921.
8. MT, p. 173.
9. Fletcher, *Feminists and Bureaucrats*, pp. 19–29.
10. *CSS*, 72828, f. 88, M. G. Fawcett to B. A. Clough 20 November [postmarked 1922]; TCA, *J. R. M. Butler Papers*, JRMB c7/9, A. D. McNair to J. R. M. Butler 9 April ?1923; NCA, Council Min., 5 May 1923; MT, pp. 176–7.
11. NCA, Council Min., 1 November and 9 December 1922, GB Min., 4 November 1922; MT, pp. 174–5.
12. Anderson, 'Time to the Sound of Bells', *The Caian* 1989–90, pp. 90–6; NA, pp. 137, 145; Frances Partridge, *Memories* (1981, paperback edn 1982), pp. 62–3.
13. *Ibid.*, pp. 61–2; NCA, Council Min., 15 March 1919.
14. *Ibid.*, 10 May 1919.
15. *Ibid.*, 8 May 1920, 30 July 1923; NCA, Gen. Cttee Min., 1917–23 *passim*.
16. *NA*, pp. 133–4.
17. Partridge, *Memories*, p. 61.
18. *NA*, p. 151.
19. *Ibid.*, p. 134.
20. NCA, Letterbook, A. E. Housman to B. A. Clough 23 October 1912.
21. NCA, Council Min., 15 March and 10 May 1919.
22. Peter Green, *Kenneth Grahame 1859–1932. A Study of His Life, Work and Times* (1959), p. 197. Grahame's own words for the publisher's blurb in 1908.
23. MT, pp. 141–5.
24. NCA, Letterbook, petition of Senior Student to Principal on relaxation of the smoking rules, 24 February 1915; printed questionnaire sent to students' parents 12 March 1915; draft of Principal's reply noting that 160 out of 165 sets of parents had replied, 123 opposed to relaxation of the rules; Council Min. 16 November 1918. On BAC's garden, see *NA*, p. 125 and Jane Brown and Audrey Osborne, '"We shall have very great pleasure": Nineteenth-Century Detached Leisure Gardens in West Cambridge', *Garden History. The Journal of the Garden History Society* 31, 1 (Spring 2003), pp. 97, 102–3.
25. *CSS*, 72827, ff. 9–10, B. A. Clough to L. K. Duff 5/8 July 1922; *NCCL* 1941, obituary notice of Edith Sharpley.
26. NCA, GB Min., 26 January 1923; *CSS*, 72827, ff. 11–12, B. A. Clough to L. K. Duff 1 February 1923.
27. NCA, GB Min., 29 April and 3 June 1921; associated correspondence in box file, GB correspondence 1920–53.
28. NCA, GB Min., 26 January, 27 February, 2 and 15 March 1923.
29. Partridge, *Memories*, p. 60; but see *NA*, p. 149.
30. *Strachey*, 60726, f. 152, J. P. Strachey to Lytton Strachey 21 November 1923.

31. *CSS*, 72827, ff. 11–12, 13, 14, 15–16, 17–18, B. A. Clough to L. K. Duff 1 February, 12 May, 25 May, 17 June, 3 July 1923; Stubbs/Duff.
32. NCA, Council Min., 3 March 1923.
33. Both portraits hang in the College. *CSS*, 72828, ff. 89–91, Jane Harrison to B. A. Clough 1 June 1924.

11 RETIREMENT

1. Stubbs/Duff; *CSS*, 72827, ff. 19–20, 21, 26, B. A. Clough to L. K. Duff 2 February 1924, fragment undated, 14 March 1924.
2. *Ibid.*, f. 195, B. A. Clough to L. K. Duff n.d. [May 1927].
3. Stubbs/Duff; *CSS*, 72827, f. 201, B. A. Clough to L. K. Duff n.d. but surely 1929.
4. *Ibid.*, ff. 19–20, B. A. Clough to L. K. Duff 2 February 1924; PRFD, Will of B. M. S. Clough, died 7 May 1904.
5. Hardcastle, *Records of Burley*, p. 180; information from Miss Dionis McNair and Mr Philip Mackworth Praed in 1998.
6. Mortgage indenture 13 March 1922 and reconveyance 13 March 1923 between B. A. Clough and Barclays Bank; mortgage indenture 15 May 1923 between B. A. Clough and the Midland Bank, in the possession of Mrs Carolyn Brebbia.
7. *CSS*, 72827, ff. 30–1, B. A. Clough to L. K. Duff 14 January 1927.
8. *Ibid.*, ff. 34–5, B. A. Clough to L. K. Duff 22 January 1928; ff.32–3, same to same, 6 February 1927; conveyances (with plans attached) between B. A. Clough and Sir Cecil Lindsay Budd 9 February 1928 and between Arthur Hugh Clough and Sir Cecil Lindsay Budd 10 March 1928, in the possession of Mrs Carolyn Brebbia.
9. *CSS*, 72827 ff. 36 and 37, B. A. Clough to L. K. Duff 8 and 18 December 1928; f. 66, B. A. Clough to L. K. Duff 2 December, addressed from Castle Top, probably belongs here too; NCA, Council Min. 7 May 1921; *CSS*, 72827, ff. 32–3, 34–5, 38, B. A.Clough to L. K. Duff 6 February 1927, 22 January 1928, 20 July 1928/9; Stubbs/Duff.
10. *CSS*, 72827, ff. 47–8, 51–2, B. A. Clough to L. K. Duff 21 and 23 August 1933; *London Gazette*, 1933, p. 6197, no. 3040.
11. Hampshire Record Office, 35M78/E61 Catalogue for auction sale to take place 24 and 25 January 1934; 159M88/255 advertisement for the sale of the house from *Country Life*, 21 April 1934; *London Gazette* 1933, p. 6577, 1935, p. 7482, 1936, p. 2136, 1938, p. 888. I am indebted to Shirley Dex for gathering and transcribing the entries from the *Gazette*.
12. *CSS*, 72827, ff. 63–4, B. A. Clough to L. K. Duff 11 January 1934; PRFD, death certificate of Eleanor Clarens Clough, 25 May 1948, copy of her will made 28 May 1937.
13. *CSS*, 72827, ff. 179, 185, B. A. Clough to L. K. Duff, January, 30 April, with no year dates but since there is a reference in the first letter to the death of Harry Stephen, which took place on 1 November 1945, probably 1946.

14. *Ibid.*, ff. 51–2, 56–8, 59–60, 61–2, 63–4, B. A. Clough to L. K. Duff 23 and 30 August, 14 and 27 December 1933, 11 January 1934.

15. *Register* 1916; *NCCL* 1966, pp. 59–60.

16. *CSS*, 72828, f. 110, Harry Stephen to B. A. Clough 11 May 1934; deed recording the sale of Folly Hill by Mr W. S. Dear to Sir H. L. Stephen and Miss J. P. Strachey, April 1935, in the possession of Mr and Mrs Templeton, the present owners; *Strachey*, 60726, f. 172, J. P. Strachey to Philippa Strachey 27 August 1935.

17. PRFD, copy of will of B. A. Clough, made 31 May 1935, accompanying entry of death 14 June 1960.

18. *CSS*, 72827, ff. 24–5, 28, 32–3, B. A. Clough to L. K. Duff 'Monday in the train' [June/July 1924], 27 August 1926, 6 February 1927.

19. In 1953 this would become the Fawcett Society. See London Society for Women's Suffrage, London Society for Women's Service and London and National Society for Women's Service in Elizabeth Crawford, *The Women's Suffrage Movement. A Reference Guide 1866–1928* (first published 1999, paperback edition 2001).

20. *Strachey*, 60728, ff. 226–7, Philippa Strachey to J. P. Strachey 14 July 1937. Pippa alludes to the fact that Christabel Pankhurst directed the campaign of civil disobedience conducted by the suffragette organisation, the Women's Social and Political Union, from the safety of Paris.

21. *CSS*, 72827, ff. 134, 135, 136 and 137, B. A. Clough to L. K. Duff 4 February, 22 April, 15 May and 18 June 1941.

22. *CSS*, 72828, ff. 102–4, 105–6, 108–9, J. P. Strachey to B. A. Clough 24 August 1930, 1 and 22 November 1931; also *Strachey*, 60726, f. 170, J. P. Strachey to Philippa Strachey 5 May 1935.

23. *Strachey*, 60728, f. 206, Philippa Strachey to J. P. Strachey 17 December 1934; also ff. 205 and 207, same to same 15 and 20 December 1934.

24. Carroll Smith-Rosenberg, 'The Female World of Love and Ritual: Relations between Women in Nineteenth-Century America', *Signs: A Journal of Women in Culture and Society* 1 (1975), pp. 1–29; Nancy Cott, *The Bonds of Womanhood. 'Woman's Sphere' in New England 1780–1835* (New Haven, 1977, 2nd edition 1997); Anne C. Rose, *Transcendentalism as a Social Movement*, 1830–1850 (New Haven and London, 1981), ch. 5, 'Men, Women and Families'. I am indebted to Richard Gooder for this last reference.

25. Lilian Faderman, *Surpassing the Love of Men. Romantic Friendship and Love between Women from the Renaissance to the Present* (1982); Martha Vicinus, *Independent Women. Work and Community for Single Women 1850–1920* (1985), pp. 158–62, 187–210; Elizabeth Edwards, 'Mary Miller Allan: The Complexity of Gender Negotiations for a Woman Principal of a Teacher Training College', in *Practical Visionaries. Women, Education and Social Progress 1790–1830*, ed. Mary Hilton and Pam Hirsch (2000), esp. pp. 157–61.

26. Emma Donoghue, *We Are Michael Field* (Bath, 1998); but cf. Mary Beard, *The Invention of Jane Harrison* (Cambridge, Mass., 2000), esp. pp. 81–4, and

Vineta Colby, *Vernon Lee. A Literary Biography* (Charlottesville, Va., 2003), esp. ch. 10.

27. *CSS*, 72827, ff. 63–4, B. A. Clough to L. K. Duff 11 January 1934.
28. Above, pp. 113–14, 167; CSS, 72830C, ff. 6–8; *Strachey*, 60724, ff. 109–11, J. P. Strachey to Philippa Strachey 21 January 1897; *CSS*, 72829, ff. 119–20, 126.
29. *CSS*, 72827, f. 139, B. A. Clough to L. K. Duff 6 August 1941; also f. 140 same to same 15 August 1941.
30. *Ibid.*, ff. 73–4, 75–6, B. A. Clough to L. K. Duff 3 and 13 September 1939.
31. *Ibid.*, ff. 78, 80, 110, 126, 131–2, 133, B. A. Clough to L. K. Duff 24 September and 4 October 1939, 7 July 1940 and 31 October [1940], 8 and 23 January 1941.
32. *Ibid.*, f. 147, B. A. Clough to L. K. Duff 15 February 1942 (direct quotation); ff. 84–5, 88, 148, 149, 150, 152, 153, 154, 188, same to same 15 October and 24 November 1939, 28 February 1942, 'Sunday' [March 1942], 22 May 1942, 9 June [1942], 27 June 1942, 'Monday night' [June 1942], 14 November [1945].
33. *Ibid.*, 72827, f. 199, B. A. Clough to L. K. Duff, undated fragment.
34. *Ibid.*, direct quotations from ff. 105, 107, 176, B. A. Clough to L. K. Duff 25 May and 4 June 1940, n.d. [summer 1945]; also ff. 73–4, 88, 103, 109, 110, 175, B. A. Clough to L. K. Duff 3 September, 24 November 1939, 11 May, 23 June, 7 July 1940, 6 May [1945].
35. *Ibid.*, ff. 89–90, B. A. Clough to L. K. Duff 5 December 1939 (direct quotation); also ff. 73–4, 75–6, 77, 88, 98, 164, B. A. Clough to L. K. Duff 3, 13, 17 September, 24 November 1939, 6 April 1940, 8 June 1944. Stubbs/Duff.
36. *Strachey*, 60728, ff.250–1, Philippa Strachey to J. P. Strachey 15 September 1940.
37. Hester Duff to the author 6 March 2000, quoting from her letter to her mother, Laura Duff, of 4 May 1941; author's interview with Belinda Norman-Butler, one of Thena's god-children, 31 August 2000.
38. WL, *Papers of J. P. Strachey*, 7/JPS/B, box no. 53, Barbara Stephen to J. P. Strachey 30 August 1942 or 1943.
39. M. G. Burton, *NCCL*, 1961, pp. 38–9; *CSS*, 72827, ff. 78, 86, 203, B. A. Clough to L. K. Duff 24 September, 16 October 1939, n.d.
40. *CSS*, 72830A, f. 1; 72830E; cf. 72827, f. 105, B. A. Clough to L. K. Duff 25 May 1940.
41. *Ibid.*, ff. 99, 100–1, 130, 131–2, B. A. Clough to L. K. Duff 10 and 16 April, 29 December 1940, 8 January 1941, *NCCL*, 1941, pp. 28–38.
42. CSS, 72827, f. 158, B. A. Clough to L. K. Duff 13 May 1943; PRFD, death certificate of Arthur Hugh Clough, died 21 May 1943.
43. *NCCL*, 1945, pp. 40–5.
44. *CSS*, 72827, ff. 187, 189, 188, B. A. Clough to L. K. Duff 25 October, 7 and 14 November 1945.
45. B. A. Clough to Patrick Duff 13 October 1945, letter in the author's possession; *CSS*, 72827, f. 186, B. A. Clough to L. K. Duff 3 July [1946].
46. *NCCL Address Lists 1948–60*; *The Post Office London Directories 1948–60* show that 95, 97 and subsequently 99 Howard's Lane all formed part of Miss Barber's Private Nursing Home; information from the owners of Folly Hill

in 2003; PRFD, death certificate of Blanche Athena Clough, died 14 June 1960.

CONCLUSION

1. Ms *Diary of Margaret Verrall, née Merrifield*, 28 April 1892, in private hands.
2. Above, pp. 113, 115, 137–8.
3. Above, p. 158.
4. Stubbs/Duff.
5. *CSS*, 72829, f. 102 n.d., but from the deterioration of the handwriting, late in her life.
6. Stubbs/Duff.
7. Above, p. 128.
8. *NCCL*, 1940, pp. 34–41; Jane Brown, *The Making of the Gardens* (Cambridge, privately printed for Newnham College, 1988).
9. *Strachey*, 60728, f. 231 n.d. [1938]; Morag Shiach, editor's introduction to Virginia Woolf, *Three Guineas* (Oxford paperback 1992), pp. xviii–xix.
10. Stubbs/Duff.
11. *CSS*, 72829, ff. 97–102 n.d. but an earlier sheet – f. 89 – muses on people's assumptions that the old should wish to be merely spectators – she didn't wish that at all.
12. *Ibid.*, ff. 82–3 n.d. except 10 February, but preceded by an attempt to describe what she feels like during term.
13. *NCCL*, 1961, p. 39.

Index